CHARTERS OF THE VICARS CHORAL OF YORK MINSTER

II

THE YORKSHIRE
ARCHAEOLOGICAL SOCIETY
FOUNDED 1863 INCORPORATED 1893

RECORD SERIES
VOLUME CLVI
FOR THE YEAR 2002

CHARTERS OF THE VICARS CHORAL OF YORK MINSTER:

II

COUNTY OF YORKSHIRE AND APPROPRIATED CHURCHES TO 1538

EDITED BY

NIGEL J. TRINGHAM

YORKSHIRE ARCHAEOLOGICAL SOCIETY

THE BOYDELL PRESS

2002

First published 2002

A publication of the Yorkshire Archaeological Society
in association with The Boydell Press
an imprint of Boydell & Brewer Ltd
PO Box 9, Woodbridge, Suffolk IP12 3DF, UK
and of Boydell & Brewer Inc.
PO Box 41026, Rochester, NY 14604-4126, USA
website: www.boydell.co.uk

ISBN 0 902122 92 4

A catalogue record for this book is available
from the British Library

This publication is printed on acid-free paper

Typeset by Joshua Associates Ltd, Oxford
Printed in Great Britain by
St Edmundsbury Press Ltd, Bury St Edmunds, Suffolk

Contents

Preface

This book is a companion to the volume of medieval charters relating to the property of the vicars choral of York Minster in the city of York, edited by the present editor and published by the Society in 1993 (volume cxlviii). Most of the present documents are part of the vicars' archive kept in York Minster Library and they are published with the kind permission of the dean and chapter of York. A few charters are published with the kind permission of the dean and chapter of Canterbury and of the principal archivist at the Leeds office of the West Yorkshire Archive Service.

Besides sections on the vicars' acquisition of land and houses in various parts of Yorkshire and on the appropriation of churches, the Introduction also considers the general economic background to the vicars' accumulation of common property. A full review of their finances, however, would require consideration of income from stipends and pensions, and must be reserved for a more wide-ranging study of the vicars' life, both at work in the Minster and domestically in their common hall, the Bedern.

The completion of this book was greatly helped by the grant of sabbatical leave by the University of Keele in the autumn of 2000, and by the simultaneous award by the University of York of a Visiting Fellowship at the Borthwick Institute of Historical Research. The expense of publishing this volume was assisted by the continuing help of the Elisabeth Exwood Memorial Trust for the work of the Record Series. The York Minster archivist then in office (Mrs. Louise Hampson) and her staff are thanked for their help, as are my luncheon companions at the King's Manor for their interest and encouragement. As with the previous edition, the presentation of this volume owes much to the careful reading of my former Victoria County History colleague at Stafford, Douglas Johnson, and the map of Yorkshire was drawn by Andrew Lawrence of the University of Keele.

Manuscript Sources

BORTHWICK INSTITUTE OF HISTORICAL RESEARCH, YORK

C.C. V/C 10	Church Commissioners' deeds and plans
Reg.	Archbishop's registers
9a	William Melton
10	William de la Zouche
11	John Thoresby
12	Alexander Neville
19	John Kempe
20	William Booth
23	Thomas Rotherham

CANTERBURY CATHEDRAL ARCHIVES

DCc/Chartae Antiquae	Dean and chapter deeds

LEEDS DISTRICT ARCHIVES

Vavasour deeds	Deeds of Vavasour family

YORK MINSTER ARCHIVES

Hailstone collection	Misc. deeds

Dean and Chapter Archive

H 1/2	Chapter Act book, 1343–68
H 1/3	Misc. register, 1352–6
L 2/2a	'Domesday Book' (14th-cent. cartulary)
L 2/4	Register of wills
M 2/2c	Misc. register, 13th–15th centuries
M 2/4d	Register of vicars' choral documents and memoranda (early 15th-cent.)

Vicars' Choral Archive

VC 1/1	Statute Book
VC 3/1/1	Cartulary
VC 3/1/2	15th-cent. register of documents *re* appropriation of Huntington and St. Sampson's churches
VC 3/2	Royal grants
VC 3/3	Foundation deeds of obits and chantries
VC 3/4	Documents *re* appropriated churches
VC 3/Vv	Property deeds (Yorkshire)

Abbreviations and Short Titles

BIHR   Borthwick Institute of Historical Research
Cal. Close R.   *Calendar of the Close Rolls* (H.M.S.O.)
Cal. Papal Letters   *Calendar of Papal Letters* (H.M.S.O.)
Cal. Pat. R.   *Calendar of the Patent Rolls* (H.M.S.O.)
CCA   Canterbury Cathedral Archives
Chs. Vicars Choral, i   *Charters of the Vicars Choral of York Minster: City of York and its suburbs to 1546*, ed. Nigel J. Tringham (YASRS cxlviii, 1993)
ER   Yorkshire, East Riding
EYC   *Early Yorkshire Charters*, vols. i–iii, ed. W. Farrer (Edinburgh, 1914–16); iv–xii, ed. C. T. Clay (Wakefield, 1935–65)
Fasti, York   *John le Neve, Fasti Ecclesiae Anglicanae, 1066–1300, VI, York*, compiled by D. E. Greenway (1999)
LDA   Leeds District Archives
mag.   magister (master)
NR   Yorkshire, North Riding
VCH   *Victoria History of the Counties of England*
    City of York   ed. P. M. Tillott (1961)
    Yorks. iii   ed. W. Page (1913)
    Yorks. ER, iv   ed. K. J. Allison (1979)
WR   Yorkshire, West Riding
YASRS   Yorkshire Archaeological Society, Record Series
YMA   York Minster Archives
YMF   *York Minster Fasti*, ed. C. T. Clay, 2 vols. (YASRS cxxiii–iv, 1958–9)

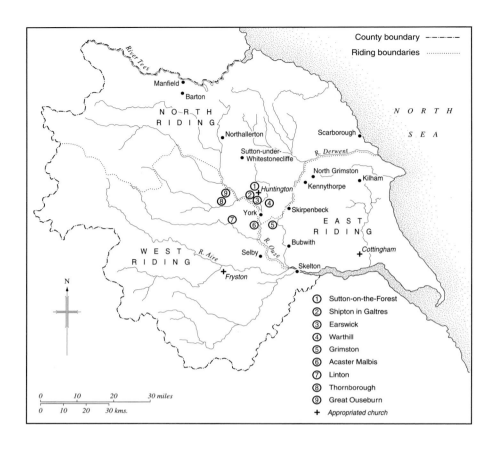

County boundary ----·-----
Riding boundaries ....

① Sutton-on-the-Forest
② Shipton in Galtres
③ Earswick
④ Warthill
⑤ Grimston
⑥ Acaster Malbis
⑦ Linton
⑧ Thornborough
⑨ Great Ouseburn
✛ Appropriated church

Map of Yorkshire showing the principal places where the vicars choral held property and their appropriated churches

Introduction

ACQUISITION OF COMMON PROPERTY

As with the common property which the vicars acquired in the city of York and its suburbs,[1] most of the much smaller amount of land or rent charges granted to them in the Yorkshire countryside was given in the 13th century, and almost invariably for spiritual benefits (Table I). The most considerable benefactors were cathedral dignitaries, either directly or through their executors: William de Laneham, archdeacon of Durham (1240s); Simon de Evesham, archdeacon of the East Riding (1261); and William de Langton, dean of York (1281).[2] An earlier dean of York, Richard de Insula, and leading canons (especially John le Romeyn the elder) may also have promoted the grants of land made in the 1220s: they head the witness lists in the charters.

TABLE I
Grants made to the vicars of land or rent charges in Yorkshire

Date	Grantor	Land or rent charge	Condition	Reference
1220 × 1228	Robert de Marske	arable and toft in Barton (NR)	in free alms; for souls of parents	6–7
1220 × 1228	Oliver de Buscy	arable in Kennythorp (ER)	in free alms	63
1220 × 1228	Agnes dau. of Thorphin de Manfield, widow	arable and tofts in Manfield (NR)	in free alms	67
1220 × 1228	Richard de Scholes, knight	arable in Great Ouseburn (WR)	in free alms	69
earlier 13th century	Richard son of Walter de Grimston	arable and toft and croft in North Grimston (ER)	in free alms; for souls of grantor and parents	27
earlier 13th century	Richard del Kenne	arable and tofts in Thornborough (WR)	in free alms; for souls of grantor and family	130
first half of 13th century	Hugh son of Richard de Northallerton	arable in Northallerton (NR)	in free alms; for souls of ancestors	68
first half of 13th century	Beatrice, Isold, and Sybil, sisters	tofts and crofts in Sutton-on-the-Forest (NR)	in free alms; for souls of family	104–5
1240s	William de Laneham, archdeacon of Durham	carucate in Sutton-under-Whitestonecliff (NR)	in free alms	107 note

[1] *Chs. Vicars Choral*, i, pp. xxiii–xxxix.
[2] The vicars were also granted the collation to a chantry endowed by Dean Langton with land in Kilham (**64**).

Date	Grantor	Land or rent charge	Condition	Reference
1261	Simon de Evesham, archdeacon of East Riding	arable in Bubwith (ER)	for obit	11, 19
later 1260s	executors of James de Cawood, canon of York	arable in Grimston (ER)	for obit	26
later 13th century	Thomas de Drenton	arable in Earswick (NR)	in free alms; for souls of grantor and family	23
later 13th century	Peter de Tadcaster	12d. rent charge in Earswick (NR)		25
later 13th century	Gilbert son of John de Camera	12d. rent charge in Sutton-on-the-Forest (NR)		106
1279	John le Cras, canon of York	arable and tofts and crofts in Warthill (NR)	for obit	133
1281	executors of William de Langton, dean of York	46s. 8d. rent charge in Skirpenbeck (ER)	for obit	98
c. 1290	John son of John Burdon	arable in Skirpenbeck (ER)	in free alms	102
1349	Roger de Neusum, barber of York	messuage in Scarborough (NR)		76
1359	John de Skidbrook	messuages in Shipton in Galtres (NR)		94–5
1368	John de Swathorpe	land in Scarborough (NR)		88
1411	executors of Roger de Weel, of York	meadow in Acaster Malbis (WR)		5
1411	Robert de Haldenby	lease of arable in Clifton (NR)	for 10 years	22
1431	heirs of Robert Huntyngton	lease of garden in Huntington (NR)	for 200 years	58
1439	John de Welwick, of York	arable in Selby (WR)		91
1452	widow of Richard Wandesford, of York	lease of close and arable in Huntington (NR)	for 30 years	59
1497	Thomas Wandesford, of York	arable and tofts and crofts in Huntington (NR)		51

Most of the Yorkshire property granted to the vicars lay within a few miles of York, or along the upper reaches of the River Derwent in the East Riding. Sutton-under-Whitestonecliff and Northallerton, in the North Riding, although further away, lay on or near main roads, as did Barton and Manfield near the boundary with County Durham. Communication with Scarborough on the east coast was also not a matter of inconvenience. Some of the more distant properties, however, had been lost (or relinquished) by the early 14th century (Barton, Manfield, and Northallerton), as had the land closer to York at Sutton-on-the-Forest.

Women do not figure prominently as grantors, although part of the estate in Bubwith which Simon de Evesham gave to the vicars had been held by an heiress who had been obliged to give up her land because of financial difficulties (12, 15–17). Also of interest in the Bubwith collection is the quitclaim made in Evesham's favour by a woman who was born in bastardy and so needed her husband's consent for the transaction (10).

There are a few strays in the archive (66, 137–40), of which the most interesting is the late 12th-century grant of land in Westmorland to a York hospital (137). Three 12th-century charters relating to land in Carlton Miniott held by the Mowbray family have been published elsewhere.[3]

THE APPROPRIATED CHURCHES

Four churches were appropriated to the vicars in order to augment their income, each appropriation taking place at a time of particular difficulty: Fryston, near Pontefract (WR), in 1332, after agricultural depression and Scottish invasions; Huntington, near York, in 1353, after the Black Death; St. Sampson's in York, in 1395, when the continuance of the vicars' common life in the Bedern was under threat; and Nether Wallop, in Hampshire, in 1461, during an economic slump. The appropriation of Cottingham church, near Hull (ER), in 1485, was abortive.

The documentation for the successful appropriations is extensive, especially for Fryston and Huntington, where all the main stages of the process are illustrated: grant of advowson by original donor; royal licences to assign and receive in mortmain; the vicars' petition to the archbishop asking him to appropriate the church; the archbishop's mandate to the official of York to investigate the truth of the petition; articles drawn up by the vicars detailing their economic difficulties; depositions of witnesses questioned on the articles; grant of appropriation and ordination of vicarage by the archbishop; and induction into corporal possession of the church.

Cottingham

Richard III's grant to the vicars of the advowson of Cottingham church and then of a licence to appropriate it in December 1484 occurred shortly after Cottingham manor had fallen into royal hands as a result of the confiscation of the estates of Margaret Beaufort, countess of Richmond and mother of the future Henry VII.[4] Richard visited York in late August 1483,[5] in advance of his son's investiture as prince of Wales on 8 September, and his stay was marked by acts of generosity to the city and an ambitious plan to establish a college for a hundred chantry priests.[6] His attention, perhaps, would have been drawn to the vicars choral during the elaborate service marking his reception in the Minster, and twelve vicars were among the guests invited to a four-hour banquet held to celebrate the prince's investiture in the archbishop's palace.[7]

The vicars' economic difficulties had recently affected their numbers,[8] and

---

[3] VC 3/Vv 21, 21a, and 21b = *Charters of the Honour of Mowbray, 1107–1191*, ed. D. E. Greenway (Records of Social and Economic History, new series I, 1972), nos. 352–4.

[4] *VCH Yorks. ER*, iv. 68. There is no evidence in the vicars' archive to support the statement (ibid. 79) that the Crown had previously granted Cottingham to the vicars in 1379.

[5] For the city's preparations for the visit see *The York House Books, 1461–90*, ed. Lorraine C. Attreed (2 vols., Alan Sutton, 1991), i. 287–8, 291–2; ii. 713.

[6] *VCH City of York*, 62; *A History of York Minster*, ed. G. E. Aylmer and R. Cant (1977), 98.

[7] An account of the Minster service and the investiture is given in YMA, M 2/2c, fo. 70 (from which printed in *Fabric Rolls of York Minster*, ed. J. Raine (Surtees Society, xxxv, 1859), 210–12). The text was also written into the vicars' Statute Book: VC 1/1, p. 48 (ink pagination).

[8] The number of vicars had been declining steadily since the mid 15th century: see below, Economic Background.

according to Archbishop Rotherham the king had determined to restore them to their full complement of 36.[9] It was not until late June 1485, however, that the archbishop authorised the appropriation of Cottingham and ordained a parochial vicarage there (145),[10] and the subsequent events at the battle of Bosworth in August rendered the act ineffective: the new king, Henry VII, restored Cottingham, along with her other estates, to his mother.[11]

Fryston

Henry le Vavasour's grant of the advowson of Fryston church to the vicars in 1331 was made on the condition that the vicars maintained three chantry chaplains for Henry and his wife Constance (two in York Minster and one in the chapel of St. Leonard in the family's castle at Hazlewood, near Pontefract), and also celebrated obits for Henry's father and mother (William and Nichole) during Henry's lifetime and for Henry and Constance after their deaths (146).

The Vavasours had strong connections with the Minster, much of its stone having come from quarries at Thevesdale on the Hazlewood estate. A quarry there had apparently been granted to the Minster in the early 12th century by the Percy family (before they enfeoffed the Vavasours), and in the 1220s Robert le Vavasour granted the Minster a right of way to carry stone from the quarry.[12] In the early 14th century William le Vavasour (Henry's father) had granted stone from other quarries at Thevesdale to several religious houses and notably in 1302 to the Minster for repairs to the precentor's house.[13] Almost certainly William (who died in 1313) and his sons Walter (d. in or before 1315) and Robert (d. 1322)[14] assisted in the provision of stone for the reconstruction of the Minster nave, commenced in 1291, and it would have been another son, Henry (the vicars' benefactor), who controlled the quarries when Archbishop William Melton restarted work *c.* 1330.[15] Melton's task was the completion of the west front, with its great window, and significantly the sculpture over the west door apparently comprised the archbishop in the apex, flanked on the left by a figure representing a member of the Percy family holding a finished ashlar block and on the right by a Vavasour holding a block of rough ashlar, as if straight from the quarry.[16] It seems likely, therefore, that in granting the church of Fryston to

[9] BIHR, Reg. 23/i, fo. 100 (comment by archbishop in his appropriation of Minster prebends to the precentorship and chancellorship in July 1484).

[10] The ordination is interesting for the involvement of Cambridge university as patron of the vicarage, in order to ensure a well-educated parochial vicar. The archbishop, himself a Cambridge graduate and from 1469 chancellor of the university, had strong educational ideals: R. B. Dobson, 'The educational patronage of Archbishop Thomas Rotherham of York', *Northern History*, xxxi (1995), 65–85.

[11] *Rotuli parliamentorum* (Record Commission), vi. 284–5. For the vicars' attempt to revive their claim to Cottingham in 1499–1500, see below, Economic Background.

[12] J. Browne, *The History of the Metropolitan Church of St. Peter, York* (1847), 13, 46–7; *Fabric Rolls of York Minster*, ed. Raine, 147–8.

[13] Browne, *Hist. of Metropolitan Church*, 48–9 (citing deeds then at Hazlewood but no longer surviving in the Vavasour family archive when it was acquired in the later 1960s by what is now West Yorkshire Archive Service, Leeds).

[14] G.E.C. *Complete Peerage*, vi. 234–5.

[15] For the dating of the new west end see T. French and D. O'Connor, *York Minster: A Catalogue of Medieval Stained Glass. Fascicule 1, The West Windows of the Nave* (Corpus Vitrearum Medii Aevi, Great Britain, III; Oxford, 1987), 3.

[16] Browne, *Hist. of Metropolitan Church*, 47, 50 note. The present figures date from the 1802–16 restoration, and they were probably anticipated by Joseph Halfpenny in his plate of the west door published in 1800: J. Halfpenny, *Gothic Ornaments in the Cathedral Church of York* (title page dated 1795, but list of subscribers

the vicars, Henry le Vavasour was ensuring that he and his family were commemorated liturgically in the Minster, as well as in its fabric.

In his 1331 grant Henry agreed to pay the costs of acquiring a royal licence to appropriate the church to the vicars, and that was duly obtained soon afterwards (**147**). It was not until July 1332, however, that the process of effecting the appropriation was started, with a renewed grant of the advowson (**148**) and a petition from the vicars to the archbishop to allow it (**149–51**). The commissary of the official of York held an inquiry into the truth of the petition in late August, and the surviving depositions provide detailed evidence for the vicars' economic difficulties at that time (**154–68**).[17] With the archbishop having approved the appropriation, Vavasour confirmed his initial grant of advowson at York in October 1332, in a quadripartite indenture which involved the archbishop and the dean and chapter besides the vicars and himself (**170**). Two days later the vicars acquired seisin of the advowson, with the contents of the relevant charters being explained to the parishioners at Fryston in English (**172**). The archbishop's authorisation of the appropriation and his ordination of a parochial vicarage followed in February 1332/3 (**174**). Besides land and small tithes, the parochial vicar was also assigned a stipend of £3 13s. 4d., but that was presumably to enable him to fulfil his obligation to find a chaplain to celebrate at Wheldale chapel in Fryston parish.

The vicars choral received no immediate financial benefit from the church because its rector, Roger de Gunnerthwayt, was still living, and it was not until August 1335 that they acquired full possession of the church's revenues, following Gunnerthwayt's resignation (**182–4**). An equal division of the arable and meadow was then made between the vicars choral (as rector) and the parochial vicar (**190**).

Under the terms of the 1331 grant of advowson, Vavasour had agreed to maintain the three chantry chaplains out of his own pocket during the lifetime of the present incumbent (Roger de Gunnerthwayt), and immediately before the grant of seisin in 1332 he duly bound himself to pay the vicars the necessary £10, although only for an initial period of four years (**173**). The bond was renewed in 1335 at a much increased level of security (**179–80**), and again in 1344 by Henry's son (**194**). By the time of the first surviving financial account for Fryston (1350–1), Gunnerthwayt was evidently dead, as no payment to him is recorded. The vicars, however, were burdened with paying the parochial vicar's stipend of £3 13s. 4d.; in addition, the two Minster chantry priests each received 33s. 4d., and there were distributions of 36s. at obits for Henry le Vavasour (who had died in 1342) and his mother Nichole;[18] the third chantry, at Hazlewood, had been established but was then vacant.[19] Nichole was still being prayed for in 1372–3, but by 1376–7 the obit was for Henry's widow Constance.[20] Both Minster chantries were still celebrated in 1531–2 but only one by 1533–4, and the cantarist there last received his full stipend

---

at end of volume dated 1800), plate 80. (The plate is reproduced on the title page of *The Great West Door*, a booklet published by the Dean and Chapter of York to commemorate the unveiling of the restored carvings in 1998.) The figures have been identified as members of the Percy and Vavasour familes by their heraldic arms on shields which supported angels on either side of the central figure in the apex: F. Drake, *Eboracum* (1736), 484. Interestingly, the chapel at Hazlewood has two Vavasour effigies of *c.* 1330 on its south wall, probably for William Vavasour and one of his sons: W. I'Anson, 'The medieval military effigies of Yorkshire', *Yorkshire Archaeological Journal*, xxix (1929), 36–7 and fig. 80.

[17] The evidence is discussed below, Economic Background.
[18] VC 4/2/FF and Hun/1, m. 1, dorse; G.E.C. *Complete Peerage*, vi. 235.
[19] VC 4/2/FF and Hun/1, m. 2, dorse.
[20] VC 4/2FF and Hun/5; VC 6/1/5.

in 1534–5.[21] The Hazlewood chantry survived until its dissolution under the Chantries Act of 1547.[22]

Huntington

The decision to appropriate Huntington church to the vicars had already been made by March 1351 when the king granted Whitby abbey a licence to assign the church's advowson (199). The initial idea, therefore, probably surfaced in 1350 in the immediate aftermath of the Black Death. The abbey's grant to the vicars followed in July 1351 (200) and seisin took place in August, the church building and rectory house being handed over symbolically (203). A petition from the vicars to Archbishop William de la Zouche to have the church appropriated to them led to an inquiry, held in December 1351; and as in the case of Fryston, the witness depositions provide detailed information on the vicars' economic difficulties (204–19).[23] Zouche died in July 1352, but the appropriation was authorised in September 1353 by his successor, John Thoresby (220). It was not until May 1354, however, following the resignation of the incumbent rector, that Thoresby ordained a parochial vicarage, after which the vicars gained possession of the church as rector (223–5).

The initial costs of acquiring the church are recorded in a financial account drawn up by the vicars' warden, Ellis de Walkington, in 1351, probably shortly before the December inquiry.[24] Whitby abbey received £60 for its grant of the advowson, the money being taken from the vicars' common chest. Most probably the money represented in part or in whole a cash gift to the vicars, but the identity of the donor is unknown. The expenses incurred in obtaining the royal mortmain licence amounted to £8 0s. 2d.

Huntington lay in the archdeaconry of Cleveland, and in the early 15th century the archdeacon attempted to make a visitation there but was rebuffed by the vicars: an agreement of December 1415 (226) records what seems to be a stalemate. Contemporary financial accounts provide details of the vicars' costs in the dispute. An account for June 1414 to June 1415 includes payments to a notary, William Driffeld, for drawing up an inhibition (in the house of the rector of St. Martin's, Coney Street, in York), and incidental expenses incurred in a meeting with mag. Thomas Grenewode.[25] Grenewode, who became the archbishop's vicar general in 1416,[26] was again consulted later in 1415, along with mag. John Southwell; the men were treated with lobsters and lamphreys.[27]

The dispute flared up again, probably soon after a new archdeacon was appointed in 1434. When he attempted a visitation he was met with armed resistance and one of his men was killed. As a condition of the settlement imposed by the archbishop in 1438, the vicars had to celebrate the victim's obit for a 7-year period (230).

[21] VC 6/1/21–3. The chantry was void in 1546: *The Certificates of the Commissioners Appointed to Survey the Chantries, Guilds, Hospitals, etc. in the County of York*, ed. W. Page (2 vols., Surtees Society, xci and xcii, 1894–5), i, p. 40.

[22] VC 6/1/27; *Certificates*, ed. Page, ii, pp. 228–9.

[23] Below, Economic Background.

[24] VC 4/2/FF and Hun/1, m. 2, dorse.

[25] VC 4/2/FF and Hun/14.

[26] A. B. Emden, *Biographical Register of the University of Oxford to A.D.1500*, iii. 2179.

[27] VC 4/2/FF and Hun/15.

St. Sampson's, York

The process by which the vicars acquired their third appropriated church, St. Sampson's in York, may have started with Richard II's brief visit to the city in 1392.[28] The king's 1394 grant of advowson and licence to appropriate the church was made in return for the vicars' promise to celebrate an obit for the king and his consort, and to sing an antiphon daily immediately after compline at the altar of St. John the Baptist; the antiphon was first sung a fortnight later on 14 March.[29]

Archbishop Thomas Arundel, however, may also have taken a leading role: his personal interest in the continuance of the vicars' common life (then under threat) is shown by his consecration of a stone altar in the Bedern chapel in August 1393,[30] and by a return visit on 8 December 1394 when he presented the vicars with a silver cup, with cover, of great weight.[31] Both occasions are rare examples of Arundel exercising a pastoral role in his archdiocese.[32]

The appropriation was made specifically to enable the vicars to resume their common life together in the Bedern (241), and one of the king's later letters concerning the application of the church's revenues (250) reveals that five vicars had been forced, presumably for financial reasons, to abandon common residence with their fellows.

During the initial negotiations the vicars were probably led to believe that they would be exempted from the normal requirement (recently enforced by statute) that as rector they should maintain a parochial vicar, following the ordination of a vicarage by the archbishop. That exemption was not included in the licence, but its omission was rectified three days later when the king issued a letter allowing the vicars to appoint a stipendary chaplain to serve the church (242). Archbishop Arundel confirmed the terms of the appropriation a few days later in March 1394 (243), although it was not until March 1395 that commissary finalised the details (246). In the meantime, the vicars appear to have presented a candidate who was duly instituted as rector. The move was probably an interim measure intended to thwart a presentation made by the former rector, Pontefract priory, which seems as late as May 1394 not to have known about the royal grant (244–5).

It was presumably not until 1399 that the vicars acquired full possession of the church, on the death of the rector inducted in 1395.[33] The vicars' chamberlain included a receipt from St. Sampson's for the first time in his account for Pentecost to Martinmas 1401,[34] and by 1405 a separate account had been set up for the church.[35] Meanwhile, the statute enforcing the ordination of vicarages for appropriated churches was reissued in 1402, but the vicars petitioned Henry IV and he confirmed their exemption (254–5).

---

[28] N. Saul, 'Richard II and the City of York', *The Government of Medieval York*, ed. Sarah Rees Jones (Borthwick Studies in History 3, 1997), 5.

[29] *Historians of the Church of York and its Archbishops*, ed. J. Raine, ii (Rolls Series), 425.

[30] Ibid. The service took place on St. Laurence's day 1393 (i.e. either 10 August 1393 or 3 February 1393/4).

[31] Ibid. 426.

[32] M. Aston, *Thomas Arundel* (1967), 285–6.

[33] *Historians of the Church of York*, ed. Raine, ii. 425 (giving rector's name as John 'Breen').

[34] VC 6/2/41 (50s. for the repair of houses, as stipulated in the 1399 arbitration). Nothing relating to St. Sampson's occurs in the preceding accounts for 1395, 1398–99, and 1399: VC 6/2/36–8.

[35] The surviving accounts, which cover spans of years up to 1514, have been expertly transcribed by A-M. Imbornoni in her 1999 York University M.A. dissertation, 'The parish account rolls for St. Sampson's, York, 1405–1514'.

Even before 1399, however, the vicars evidently received enough financial benefit from the church for them to resume their common life, as had been the intention behind the original grant. Nonetheless, the precise form of the disbursement of funds was disputed. Some vicars evidently believed that there should be an equal division of income, so that each got a share even if absent from meals in the common dining hall. In 1396 and again in 1397 the king had to insist that the whole income should be applied to common expenses (248–50). The dispute was arbitrated in 1399 by the dean and chapter, which stipulated that £6 13s. 4d. should be assigned each year to the common expenses of the vicars' hall, and that individual vicars would benefit only if they attended the royal obits and the antiphon; the remaining income from St. Sampson's was to be applied to the costs of repairing common property and parish expenses (251). The arrangement was confirmed by the new king, Henry IV, in January 1400 (253).

No financial account survives giving the overall costs to the vicars of securing St. Sampson's, although as late as 1408–9 the officer responsible for its revenue included a payment of ½ mark (6s. 8d.) to agents travelling on the business (*ambassiatoribus transeuntibus pro unione ecclesie*) and for expenses incurred in entertaining two legal advisors, once in a tavern and on another occasion in the succentor's house.[36] Further costs for travelling to London (in the 1411–12 account) and for agents (in 1414 and 1416) may also have been connected with securing the appropriation.[37]

A payment made, on the succentor's order and almost certainly about the time of the 1399 arbitration, for lighting candles before St. John's altar may indicate a resumption of the antiphon after a lapse in its observance.[38] The antiphon was still celebrated in 1415, but apparently not in 1416 and later years;[39] at least, no further payments for it are recorded in the St. Sampson's accounts, even though there were sufficient funds at hand. Instead, in the years up to 1420 the money accrued to the church's general profits, which were then shared out amongst the vicars,[40] a policy that may still have been followed in the late 15th and early 16th century (although not explicitly stated in the accounts). The candles, however, continued to be lit, by the Minster choristers until at least 1472, and afterwards by one of the cathedral staff.[41] The royal obit survived longer than the antiphon. It was still celebrated for both Richard and Anne in 1419–20, but for Richard only by 1489–90 (each vicar getting 12d. rather than 2s.) and even that failed in the early 16th century.[42]

Nether Wallop

According to the 15th-century continuation of the history of the archbishops of York, the church of Nether Wallop in Hampshire was appropriated to the vicars by Archbishop William Booth, at his own costs and in return for the vicars' prayers for his soul.[43] Indeed, the first stage of the process was the grant in 1459 of the advowson of the church by the archbishop's kinsman John Booth, treasurer of York Minster, to a group of trustees who were closely associated with the archbishop, three

[36] VC 4/2/Sam/1, m. 2.
[37] VC 4/2/Sam/2, mm. 1 and 3.
[38] VC 6/2/37.
[39] VC 4/2/Sam/2, mm. 3–4.
[40] The payments are conveniently tabulated in Imbornoni (p. 23 of dissertation).
[41] The point is highlighted by Imbornoni (p. 33 of disseration).
[42] VC 4/2/Sam/2, m. 4; VC 4/2/Sam/4–6.
[43] *Historians of the Church of York*, ed. Raine, ii. 435–6.

of them being his executors (**262**). The timing may have been connected with John Booth's forthcoming transfer to the archdeaconry of Richmond and the need to secure the grant before he vacated the treasurership. Having secured a royal licence later in the same year, the trustees in 1460 assigned the advowson to the dean and chapter, at whose request the bishop of Winchester authorised the appropriation of the church to the vicars in 1461 (**264–6**).

The incumbent rector, William Fenton, resigned in October 1465 and the vicars should then have acquired possession of the church (**268–9**). The death of Archbishop Booth in 1464, however, seems to have caused problems, and in 1466 Hugh Pakenham, the lessee of the Hampshire properties belonging to the York treasurership, presented his own candidate, Thomas Paslew, to the bishop of Winchester for induction as rector (**270**). Pakenham claimed the advowson, even though it had evidently been the intention to exclude it from a lease made by Booth (**261**) and from another made by his predecessor as treasurer (**260**). Both leases, however, reserved the advowson of 'Overwallop' (rather than Nether Wallop), and it was on that ground that Pakenham argued that the advowson of Nether Wallop belonged to him. According to a memorandum concerning the descent of the advowson, apparently drawn up by the vicars, both leases had in fact originally referred to 'Nether Wallop', but Pakenham, having acquired the one made by Booth, erased the word 'Nether' and substituted 'Over' in its place.[44] The surviving copy of the lease, however, shows no sign of being tampered with, and nor does that made by Booth's predecessor. Presumably the account given in the memorandum was the vicars' explanation of Pakenham's actions.

The bishop of Winchester refused to admit Paslew, who was also opposed by the dean of York, Richard Andrew, and the chapter. Although Paslew died while the cause was still pending, the dean and chapter were sufficiently unsure about the 1461 grant of appropriation that they petitioned the pope in January 1471 to authorise a confirmation.[45] That had evidently been made by June 1471, when the vicars, in gratitude for Dean Andrew's financial and legal support, promised to maintain his obit (**272**). For a further benefaction, the vicars also bound themselves in 1472 to commemorate the dean with an antiphon to the Virgin Mary before her image in the Minster and an antiphon in honour of the name of Jesus before the crucifix in the loft on the south side of the nave (**273**). Special prayers and the provision of candles by the vicars to represent the Five Wounds of Christ (together with the Five Sorrows of the Virgin Mary) reveal Dean Andrew's particular devotion to Christ.[46]

It was not until the autumn of 1472 that all the necessary legal business had been completed, the vicars' warden, William Hoton, having spent most of August and September travelling to Wallop and Salisbury and then on to London.[47] Even so the vicars probably did not begin to receive a regular income from the church until 1474, when they leased it to the parochial vicar (**276**). It was also in 1474 that the vicars entered into an agreement with Archbishop Booth's brother-in-law and executor, Sir Robert Clifton, to celebrate an obit for Booth, Clifton, and Clifton's wife Alice (the

[44] In September 2000 the memorandum (a loose sheet) was inside the back cover of VC 3/1/2. It is discussed in *The Cartulary of the Treasurer of York Minster*, ed. Janet E. Burton (Borthwick Texts and Calendars, no. 5, 1978), pp. 78–9.
[45] *Cal. Papal Letters*, xii, pp. 367–8.
[46] On this devotion and Andrew's career as dean of York, see S. Walker, 'Between Church and Crown: Master Richard Andrew, King's Clerk', *Speculum*, vol. 74, no. 4 (October, 1999), 956–91 (esp. 984–5).
[47] VC 3/4/NW/15. Besides Hoton's travelling and subsistence expenses, incidental costs included alms for the parishioners of Nether Wallop and expenses for winnowing the recently gathered rectory crops.

archbishop's sister) each year on 14 September.[48] The agreement probably confirmed an arrangement already in place, at least as regards the archbishop: the 1471 expenses account includes a section recording the payment for Booth's obit.[49]

If financial accounts were kept for the church none survive, but totals of income and expenditure were included in the succentor's accounts, the profits being distributed amongst the vicars in a weekly common.

ECONOMIC BACKGROUND

With all the charters relating to the vicars' property now edited, and especially in view of the details concerning their financial problems given in the inquiries held in connection with the appropriation of Fryston and Huntington churches, it is convenient here to provide a general overview of the level of the vicars' common income from endowments.

The earliest surviving rental in the archive is that for Pentecost to Martinmas 1309,[50] but totals of rents were entered on the accounts of the vicars' chamberlain and so details are given on the earliest surviving chamberlain's roll, that for Pentecost to Martinmas 1304.[51] The 1304 account gives a half-yearly income of £32 12d. 4d. 'as shown on the rental' and the 1309 rental one of £36 9s. 6½d. (comprising £27 0s. 9d. from property in York and £9 8s. 9½d. from property outside the city). These figures, however, are the totals of rents due and not what was actually collected: in 1304 the chamberlain included an arrears section in his account, which reveals that unpaid rents amounted to £2 16s. 8d. and had been £1 16s. 4d. in the previous half-year.[52]

Income came from both assized (or fixed) rents and farms (that is, rents which reflected economic values).[53] The former were paid by free tenants, who might sub-let parts of their tenement to tenants-at-will without passing on the extra income to the vicars as landlord. Indeed, one of the main features of the vicars' management of their estate in the 14th century was the extension of their control over tenements formerly held by tenants owing assized rents. As a result the number of rents owed directly by tenants-at-will increased significantly, even though the vicars did not physically enlarge their holding in the city.[54] Reflected in the purchase of multiple rent charges with which some properties were burdened,[55] this policy of recovering direct control over properties that had been alienated was a practice common to most ecclesiastical corporations in the period.

---

[48] VC 3/3/14. The date was presumably that of Booth's death.

[49] VC 3/4/NW/15.

[50] VC 4/1/1. The vicars' rentals have been used to illustrate patterns of prosperity and decline in York's economy by Sarah Rees Jones in her 1987 York university D.Phil. thesis, 'Property, Tenure and Rents: some aspects of the topography and economy of medieval York'. The thesis provides an important critique (volume i, chapters 5 and 6) of the conclusions (also based mainly on the vicars' rentals) made by J. N. Bartlett in his 1958 London university Ph.D. thesis 'Some Aspects of the Economy of York in the Later Middle Ages, 1330–1550' (partly written up in 'The expansion and decline of York in later Middle Ages', *Economic History Review*, 2nd ser. xii (1959), 17–33).

[51] VC 6/2/1.

[52] The section, in fact, refers merely to an indenture made with the succentor (the vicars' warden) regarding the money, but its origin is made clear in the comparable section in the chamberlain's account for 1310: VC 6/2/2.

[53] It is not until the mid 1360s, however, that rentals distinguish between assized rents (*redditus assisae*) and farms (*firma*): VC 4/1/14 (rental of 1371); VC 6/2/25 (chamberlain's account of 1366, referring to a rental no longer surviving).

[54] The point is made in Rees Jones thesis, i. 200–3.

[55] For an example see *Chs. Vicars Choral*, i, nos. 295–300.

More particularly affecting the York vicars, however, in the early 14th century were the Scottish raids in northern England following the defeat of the English at Bannockburn in 1314.[56] The invaders penetrated as far as the Vale of York, and the threat of attack in September 1319 caused panic in the city: for five nights the vicars themselves took part in a watch on the city walls.[57] The Scottish danger also resulted in the temporary relocation of the royal household and government departments to York, and the influx (and then departure) of personnel may have had some effect on the letting of the vicars' property in the city.[58]

According to the chief witness who deposed on the 1332 articles drawn up to investigate the appropriation of Fryston church (**156**), the vicars' income before the Scottish troubles had amounted to £83 3s. 7d. a year, of which £9 9s. 6d. had been lost, leaving only £73 14s. 1d. The same evidence was repeated by other witnesses (**157–9**), although one gave the loss as £8 19s. (**160**) and two as £10 (**161, 168**). The articles themselves itemise the losses from particular places or properties, giving a total of £7 7s. 2d. (**155**).[59]

The losses incurred in country properties were most severe at Warthill, where a rent of 26s. 8d. from two bovates with tofts and crofts had been diminished by 12s. (**133, 135**). The cause was given specifically as the Scottish raids by the man who had actually inhabited one of the houses, along with his father: they had been forced to abandon their home and live elsewhere in the village (**164**). Nonetheless, the vicars had tried to distrain the tenant, and in 1331–2 they had engaged the bailiff of Bulmer wapentake to help them enforce warranty of the land.[60] It seems that one of the tenements at Gildhusdale near Thirsk was similarly abandoned, and as late as 1342 the vicars were still trying to recover its rent (**118–19**). At Bubwith the vicars' land had been occupied by 'powerful men' (**155**), possibly as a result of the disturbance caused by the Scots: a 12d. rent there was recovered in 1334 along with a fine for arrears going back to 1316.[61]

The refusal to pay rents was also a difficulty in certain parts of York (**155** e and j), although there the main problem was that houses had either been abandoned or were inhabited by 'the lowest sort of people and paupers' (**161**). The vicars were unable to attract better tenants because they could not afford to repair their properties, especially the larger houses, such as the 'great hall' called Cambhall (or Romaynhall: **167**) in Goodramgate, standing opposite the entrance to the Bedern. Cambhall was one of a group of stone houses there, probably dating from the 12th century, which were among the vicars' earliest endowments.[62] It was their size which made such houses difficult to keep in repair and to let, and eventually, in the 1360s, Cambhall at least was demolished and a court of eight timber-framed houses

[56] J. A. Tuck, 'War and society in the medieval North', *Northern History*, xxi (1985), 34–7. For the extent of the raids of 1318 and 1319 see I. Kershaw, 'A note on the Scots in the West Riding, 1318–19', *Northern History*, xvii (1981), 231–9.

[57] VC 6/2/4 (chamberlain's account itemising payments for candles and ale).

[58] For tables showing periods of government residence in York see W. M. Ormrod, 'Competing Capitals? York and London in the fourteenth century', in *Courts and Regions in Medieval Europe*, ed. Sarah Rees Jones, Richard Marks, and A. J. Minnis (York Medieval Press, 2000), 80–1, 83.

[59] The arrears and decayed rents sections of the chamberlain's account for Martinmas 1331 to Pentecost 1332 give a combined figure of only £2 9s. 11d., but that omits the unpaid income which the vicars were trying to reclaim at Gildhusdale and Warthill: VC 6/2/11.

[60] VC 6/2/11.

[61] VC 3/1/1, fo. 52v.

[62] Cambhall was named after Canon John de Caen, to whom it was let in 1298; the vicars had acquired it by the bequest of Archbishop John de Romeyn (d. 1296), so accounting for its alternative name: *Chs. Vicars Choral*, i, nos. 162 note and 268 note.

built on its site.[63] In the late 1320s the house was in fact fully tenanted (possibly as a consequence of parliaments being held in York in 1328) and produced a rent of 5 marks (£3 6s. 8d.) a year, although the rent had been 40s. in 1325 and as low as 24s. in 1321.[64] The other large house mentioned by name in the inquiry was Hustwaitehall in Ogleforth (155, 167; otherwise the houses of Roger de Cawood: 161), probably the house occupied by John de Hustwaite in 1311, when the vicars received an annual rent of £4; it yielded only 15s. in 1321 and 26s. 8d. in 1325 and 1330.[65]

Several witnesses (all former chamberlains) provide figures for the amount of money spent by the vicars on repairing their properties, ranging from 'sometimes £30' but usually £20 (160) to £17 (158) or £13 6s. 8d. (161); in one year a chamberlain spent as much as £10 on a palisade (157). There is no means of verifying these figures, because payments recorded in the surviving chamberlains' accounts for the period usually amount to only a few shillings, although exceptionally 'the expenses of the pavement and buildings' section of the account for Pentecost to Martinmas 1319 total over £11 (including a little over £1 spent on 'the great hall').[66] Most probably, large sums were indeed spent in other years but were recorded in separate accounts, possibly because the building work was funded on an *ad hoc* basis. Certainly, in the late 14th and early 15th century accounts for building work on particular houses show that the necessary funds came mostly from cash gifts for the support of obits.[67] The inclusion (in the vicars' articles) of building costs as a call on income from rents is, therefore, somewhat misleading and was presumably intended to maximise their plight. Indeed, the emphasis on loss of rents from certain older properties in York masks the fact that in the years leading up to 1332 (and afterwards) the vicars got additional income from more profitable, newly built rows of cottages, notably in Aldwark and the area around the Bedern.[68] Constructed with funds given to endow obits, these cottages attracted low-paid workers,[69] with the result that the vicars' half-yearly rental in York in fact rose from £37 6s. 9d. in 1325 to £39 12s. 3d. in 1328-9, although falling slightly to £38 14s. 2d. in 1330.[70]

The figures for income from property outside York, in contrast, show a loss from £7 5s. 11½d. (1325) to £2 13s. 9d. (1328-9). The figure of £7 5s. 11d. given in the 1330 rental, however, is suspiciously similar to that of 1325, and it seems that the vicars had reverted to an earlier list of tenants, as may have been the case with the list of city tenants. The total half-yearly income as given in the 1330 rental, therefore, was £46 0s. 1d., which when doubled is nearly £10 a year more than the figure given by the witnesses questioned in 1332. The explanation is presumably that not all the rents listed in 1330 were in fact collected, so that the rentals give a misleading picture of the

---

[63] The 1359-62 building accounts (VC 6/9/1) have been studied by Christine Fraser in her 1994 York University M.A. dissertation, 'The building accounts of the vicars choral: Benet Place and Cambhall Garth, 1360-64'. The same account roll also covers the cost of building houses in 1362-4 in Benetplace, in Patrickpool.

[64] VC 4/1/3-5; VC 6/2/9 (giving half-yearly sums).

[65] VC 4/1/3-5; VC 6/2/3; VC 6/2/9 (giving half-yearly sums).

[66] VC 6/2/4.

[67] VC 6/6/1; VC 6/9/1-5. A college officer called the repairer emerged in the early 15th century to administer routine building work: VC 6/6.

[68] *Chs. Vicars Choral*, i, p. xxxii; R. A. Hall, H. MacGregor, and M. Stockwell, *Medieval Tenements in Aldwark, and other Sites* (being *The Archaeology of York*, ed. P. Addyman, volume 10, fascicule 2, 1988), 56-7 (text by Sarah Rees Jones).

[69] Many were women, on whom see P. J. P. Goldberg, *Women, Work, and Life Cycle in a Medieval Economy: Women in York and Yorkshire c. 1300-1520* (1992), 299, 304.

[70] VC 4/1/4-5; VC 6/2/9.

vicars' actual income: a number of entries in the rental for Pentecost to Martinmas 1342 (which gives a total of £59 8s. 9¼d.) have 'vacat' against the rent which was claimed.[71] A truer figure is probably provided by a rental for Martinmas 1347 to Pentecost 1348, in which the total income is given as only £40 11s. 5d.[72]

The Black Death struck York in May 1349,[73] killing not only some vicars[74] but also their tenants, with a consequent reduction in rents: income for the half-year ending at Martinmas 1351 was only £34 19s. 6d.[75] As with the investigation which preceded the appropriation of Fryston church, further details are provided by the inquiry held in 1351 in advance of the appropriation of Huntington church in 1354. According to the chief witness (208), the vicars' income before the plague was £93 14s. a year but now only £69 6s. 6d., a loss of £24 7s. 6d. Other witnesses gave the loss as £24 (215) or £25 6s. 8d. (216). Their figures, however, are less than that calculated by totalling up the itemised losses given in the articles on which the witnesses deposed, namely £29 10s. 8d. inside York and £2 3s. 0d. outside the city (207).

The greatest reductions were from properties in Goodramgate and Stonegate, notably from 'the great hall' opposite the Bedern. Cambhall, however, had been uninhabited since at least the mid 1340s,[76] so that the decline in its income had only been exacerbated by the effects of the Black Death and was rather the result of a continued decline in the value of the vicars' larger houses in the city. Some of the vicars' meaner properties were evidently also abandoned as a consequence of the plague: in rentals of the early 1350s the vicars seem once more to be using conventional lists of tenants rather than naming actual occupants.[77]

Investment by the chamberlain in repairing older properties in the 1360s, and the acquisition of some new property, accounts for a steady increase in the vicars' income from rents in the second half of the 14th century,[78] although there was also some inflation:[79] by 1395 half-yearly income had risen to £81 19s. 6d.[80] Most of the cash used in improving the estate had come from gifts made as endowments for obit services,[81] with the result that over two-thirds of the chamberlains' real income had to be disbursed in obit distributions by the late 1370s, and the proportion continued to rise.[82] Although individual vicars benefited from such payments, there was a shortfall in funds available for the general upkeep of the vicars' common life in the Bedern and it was in that respect that Richard II granted St. Sampson's church to the vicars in 1394. The grant itself carried with it the obligation to celebrate commemorative services, but interestingly provision was made for a scaling down of the expenditure if the church's income was reduced (251).

---

[71] VC 6/2/13.

[72] VC 4/1/8.

[73] It lasted until 25 July: A. Hamilton Thompson, 'The pestilences of the fourteenth century in the Diocese of York', *Archaeological Journal*, lxxi (1914), 97–154 (at p. 105).

[74] There were apparently only 29 vicars in the autumn of 1352: VC 6/2/17 (section relating to distribution of money at obit services).

[75] VC 4/1/6.

[76] VC 4/1/7–8 and 10.

[77] Rees Jones thesis, i. 243 (commenting on VC 4/1/6 and VC 6/2/14).

[78] *Chs. Vicars Choral*, i, pp. xxi, xxxvi.

[79] Rees Jones thesis, i. 211, 214.

[80] VC 6/2/36.

[81] For a table of such gifts see *Chs. Vicars Choral*, i, pp. xxxii–xxxv, to which should be added two bequests, both of 1354, made in connection with the foundation of obits: (i) £10 left by a York merchant, John de Butterwick (H 1/2, fo. 80) and (ii) £10 left by a York cutler, Adam of Ireland (H 1/3, fo. 10). Also omitted from the list is the gift made in 1453 noted below in the text on note 105 (below).

[82] Rees Jones thesis, i. 221–2. The proportion had been less than half in the early 14th century.

The financial benefit to the vicars from the appropriated churches of Fryston and Huntington is revealed in accounts which survive for 1351 and then for a spread of years between 1377 and 1453.[83] The bulk of the income for both churches came from tithes of grain and hay, Fryston being the more profitable: in the 1380s Fryston's income was around £31 and Huntington's around £22, with a similar ratio (£29 and £20) in 1414–15. Moreover, apart from the annual stipend of £3 13s. 4d. payable to the parochial vicar at Fryston, other payments which the vicars were obliged to make from that church's revenue were not entirely lost: the money spent on maintaining the two obits for Henry Vavasour and his wife and on Henry's chantry mostly benefited the vicars choral who shared in the 36s. that was usually distributed at each obit, and the two chaplains who celebrated the chantry in the Minster (for which each was paid £3 6s. 8d.) were invariably vicars choral. At Huntington the vicars were not obliged to provide a stipend for the parochial vicar,[84] and so the outgoings there were usually quite low (between £5 and £2)[85] and the net profit greater than Fryston's. In 1383–4, for example, surplus income from Huntington was £20 5s. 5d. compared to Fryston's £9 4s. 3 ½d. and in 1414–15 £17 13s. 0d. compared to £9 1s. 0d. The residue of both churches' income was divided equally among the vicars, augmenting their personal finances in a good year by over 16s. in the late 14th and early 15th century. No distributions, however, were recorded in the 1434–5 account for Fryston nor in the 1452–3 account for Huntington (being the last for each church), and the surplus income was evidently being paid directly into central funds. That was still the case with Fryston in the later 1540s,[86] but by 1470 the Huntington money (then £30 18s. 11d.) was the principal income of the officer in charge of repairing college property.[87]

Accounts also survive for St. Sampson's church following its appropriation in 1395, the first dating from 1405 and the series continuing (with breaks) until 1514.[88] In the early 15th century the income (mostly from personal tithes)[89] averaged around £34 a year, but it fell dramatically during the century as the city suffered a general economic decline and was only £6 6s. 8½d. in 1513–14. Because the vicars as rector were exempted from endowing a parochial vicarage for the church, their main outlay on behalf of the parishioners was a chaplain's stipend, which was only £2 10s. a year in 1405. By 1472 even that was no longer being paid, and the employment of a priest may have become the churchwardens' responsibility.[90] As in the case of Fryston church, some of the income from St. Sampson's had to be used to commemorate the donor, in the form of an antiphon and an obit at which individual vicars benefited from doles of money.[91] The antiphon ceased in the early 15th century and the obit in the early 16th century, but the vicars as a whole enjoyed a share of the church's overall profit, if there was one. The payment of £6 13s. 4d. to the vicars' common hall,

[83] VC 4/2/FF and Hun/1, 4–12, 14–18 (nos. 2–3 and 13 are vacant). The details were entered in the warden's general accounts, at least in the later 14th century, and so also survive for 1370–2 (VC 6/1/1, 2, and 5).
[84] They had to pay the last rector a pension of £10 a year, but he had died by the time of the 1377 account.
[85] The exceptional expenses in 1415–16 were the result of legal and other costs incurred in the dispute over the archdeacon of Cleveland's claim to visit the church.
[86] VC 6/1/27.
[87] VC 6/6/7.
[88] VC 4/2/Sam/1–8 (the main run is from 1405 to 1420). For a transcription and general introduction see Imbornoni dissertation, on which much of this paragraph is based.
[89] The tenement in Thursday Market leased by the vicars in 1420 (Chs. Vicars Choral, i, no. 513) is identified as the rectory house in a marginal note against the copy of the lease in VC 1/1.
[90] As suggested by Imbornoni (dissertation, p. 24).
[91] For details see the Appropriated Churches section, above.

stipulated in 1399 (**251**) was the most stable item on the expenses of St. Sampson's, and it was still being paid when the surviving run of accounts ends in the early 16th century.

Although the vicars' nominal income from rents continued to rise in the first half of the 15th century, actual income declined as properties were abandoned and tenants no longer paid full rents. York's economic problems have been linked with population decline,[92] and specifically with return visitations of plague;[93] the extent of the problem is revealed by sections on decayed (reduced in value) and defective (unpaid) rents entered into the chamberlains' accounts.[94] Thus, of the £87 9s. 10d. nominally due from farms and assized rents in the half-year Pentecost to Martinmas 1409 nearly one-sixth (£14 7s. 8d.) was unpaid.[95] The accumulated decayed and defective rents were apparently written off in the 1410s,[96] but they mounted up again and were a similar proportion in the early 1430s; by the mid 1450s the losses had shot up to over one-third of the nominal rent (£38 9s. 5d. / £94 17s. 2d.).[97] Once again, the losses were written off, probably in the later 1460s, and a new rental drawn up.[98] Income from farms and rents was a realistic £46 2s. 1½d. in the half-year Martinmas 1471 to Pentecost 1472, falling to £43 19s. 1½d. when collected at Pentecost 1480.[99] Of that income, however, a substantial portion was spent on repairing college property, for which the vicars usually retained responsibility,[100] and so receipts from rents rarely exceeded the expenses accounted by the chamberlain, and when a profit did occur it was usually only a few shillings.

As earlier, the vicars were crucially dependent on the generosity of benefactors. In 1417 a canon, mag. William Cawood, agreed to give them 546 marks (£334) in return for maintaining his chantry,[101] and when the vicars received the money (in fact, £337 6s. 8d.) from his executors in 1420 they embarked on an ambitious programme of repairing houses (spending £172 5s. 10s.) and buying new property in York.[102] (They also spent money on repairing college buildings and acquiring a grant of incorporation from the Crown.) In 1422 an undisclosed (but undoubtedly much smaller) sum of money was given to the vicars 'in their great necessity' by the widow of a York apothecary to support an obit, and in 1424 the executors of Stephen le Scrope, archdeacon of Richmond, gave £41 for an obit.[103] In 1442 the subdean of York gave them £20 for the repair of a tenement in North Street 'almost destroyed by the negligence or poverty of the vicars' predecessors'.[104] The executors of William Duffeld, archdeacon of Cleveland (d. 1453), gave the vicars

---

[92] D. M. Palliser, *Tudor York* (1979), 201–6.

[93] Rees Jones thesis, i. 254–5.

[94] Ibid. 216–17, and graph facing p. 207.

[95] VC 6/2/44.

[96] The relevant allowances section of the chamberlain's account for Martinmas 1415 to Pentecost 1416 was started but abandoned: VC 6/2/45.

[97] VC 6/2/51 and 58.

[98] VC 6/2/61 and 62.

[99] VC 6/2/62 and 66.

[100] The costs of building work undertaken by the chamberlain and the repairer are conveniently tabulated in Rees Jones thesis, i, pp. 234–5.

[101] Agreement of 12 May 1417: VC 1/1, pp. 60–3 (ink pagination).

[102] VC 1/1, pp. 30, 35, 43–5 (ink pagination); *Chs. Vicars Choral*, i, no. 443 note. The account in VC 1/1 (pp. 29–39, 42–5) dealing with the expenditure following Cawood's bequest was drawn up by his own vicar, Richard Ulleskelf: L 2/4, fo. 195 (Cawood's will). Ulleskelf seems to have resumed office as the vicars' warden for the period 1419–22 specifically in order to oversee the task.

[103] VC 3/3/43; VC 6/1/8.

[104] VC 1/1, pp. 104 and 95 (ink pagination; corrected order of pages).

£40 for his obit,[105] and further 'notable sums' in connection with obits were given in 1475 by the executors of John de Saxon, a clerk, and in 1496 by Sir Richard York, merchant of York and twice its mayor; the latter gift was given to the vicars 'in their great necessity'.[106]

Despite the injection of such funds, the severe downturn in York's economy prevented the vicars from recouping a commensurate income, and they had to seek other ways of achieving solvency. This was done mainly by reducing their numbers, from 36 still in 1425 to 30 in 1469 and 26 in 1476, after which there was a recovery to 30 again by 1487 followed by a further decline.[107] The appropriation of Nether Wallop church in 1461 was intended to enhance the vicars' 'slender and meagre' resources (266), and the abortive appropriation of Cottingham church in 1485 was made specifically to increase their numbers (145). When Cottingham rectory became vacant in 1499, the vicars immediately tried to pursuade the king to appropriate the church, but to no avail,[108] and in 1501 they also unsuccessfully tried to obtain a royal licence to appopriate Broughton church in Hampshire.[109] Such was their financial plight in 1500 that the vicars petitioned the archbishop to be excused from having to pay subsidies levied by convocation.[110]

Given its distance from York, the church at Nether Wallop was understandably held by lessees, the first being the parochial vicar and two husbandmen, jointly paying £30 a year (276). As had originally been the case with the surplus income of Fryston and Huntington churches, the Nether Wallop money was not applied to the college's general expenses but was disbursed to individual vicars: each received 15s. 1d. in 1490, 23s. 3d. in 1507, and 30s. in 1547, the share increasing as the number of vicars declined.[111]

Income from rents began to stabilise in the 16th century. Just over £41 for the half-year in 1500 and £40 in 1521, it was £40 11s. 1d. in 1531 and £42 14s. 1d. in 1539.[112] No longer responsible for repairs to college property, the chamberlain was even able to resume the disbursement of surplus funds to individual vicars: each of 22 vicars received 12d. at Pentecost 1494 and 15d. at Martinmas 1500.[113] In later years, however, there was rarely a surplus, and disbursements were again being made only by the later 1530s.[114] Even so, when the vicars were reprieved from having their college dissolved by the chantry commissioners in 1546, they were still suffering from 'poverty and destitution'.[115]

EDITORIAL METHOD

The documents have been edited in the same manner as in the companion volume of York city charters.

A full Latin text, preceded by a brief English caption, is given for those charters

[105] VC 6/1/9.
[106] VC 3/3/45 and 46.
[107] VC 6/4/22, 27, 30, and 34. The 36 figure given for 1473 in *Chs. Vicars Choral*, i, p. xviii is the result of a mistaken reading of VC 6/4/29.
[108] VC 6/1/13.
[109] VC 6/1/14.
[110] VC 1/1, p. 113 (ink pagination).
[111] VC 6/1/10, 15, and 27.
[112] VC 6/2/70, 82, 87, and 90 (all Pentecost to Martinmas accounts).
[113] VC 6/2/69–70.
[114] VC 6/2/88–90.
[115] *Chs. Vicars Choral*, i, p. xix and no. 580.

which date from before *c.* 1230. The original spelling has been retained, except that 'i' and 'j' have been standardised as 'i'; 'u' when used as a consonant has been transcribed as 'v'; and 'c' has been transcribed as 't' in such words as *exactio*. Modern usage has been adopted in respect of capital letters and punctuation. Christian names have been extended but not names indicated only by initials. The suspended form of abridged place-names has been kept.

In calendared texts place-names in Latin have been translated but those in English retain their original spelling; for identifying such places, the reader should consult the index.

Warranty, distraint, and sealing clauses appear as 'Warranty', 'Distraint', and 'Seal', unless peculiarities require a fuller rendering.

Dates which have been supplied for charters by the editor are given in square brackets and the reasons for the choice appear in a note which follows the text. A number are determined by the dates of early canons or dignitaries of York Minster, for which the reader should consult the recent York volume of the revision of *Fasti Ecclesiae Anglicanae*.

In the case of original documents (rather than cartulary copies) the critical notes which accompany each document include medieval endorsements, and ones of later date if of special interest. In the description of the seal, 'impression' and 'legend' with no further comment indicate that neither the exact form of the impression nor the wording of the legend is decipherable; 'tag' means that a single tag survives from which the seal has been detached and is now lost; and 'slit' means that there is a single slit through which a tag was formerly inserted.

The Charters

Schedule

Appropriated churches

Yorkshire

ACASTER MALBIS
(parish in Ainsty wapentake WR)

1.   Grant by William son of Ralph de Malo Lacu and his wife Joan to Ranulph de Catton of York and his wife Joan of their meadow in the meadow of Acastre Malbys called Suthheng', namely a moiety of 3½ a. of meadow which were once of Robert Verdenell' de Marisco citizen of York and which descended by inheritance to William's wife Joan; to be held by Ranulph and Joan of the chief lord of the fee for the customary service; paying a rose at the time of roses if asked for. Warranty. Seal.
Witnesses: John the clerk de Acastre, Alan Greedeken of the same place, Thomas Jeukyn of the same place, John de Camsale of the same place, Roger son of Robert of the same place, Henry the clerk de Co[u]pmanthorp,[1] Michael de Knapton', Adam de Thorp, Thomas son of Nicholas de Northfolk, and others.   [early 14th century]

SOURCE: VC 3/Vv 2 (228 mm. × 110 mm.; top left-hand corner missing).
ENDORSEMENT: (in a ? 16th-cent. hand) *Acast' Malb'*.
SEAL: two slits.

[1] MS. rubbed; one letter missing.

DATE: The suggested date is derived from the handwriting.
NOTE: The meadow is presumably that granted in 2.

2.   Confirmation by William Malebys knight of the grant made by charter by John Malebys to John Catton' of York and his wife Emma of 1 a. 3 r. of meadow in the meadow of Acast' Malebys in a place called le Mersk, lying in length from the Ouse to the church of the vill and in breadth between the meadow of Richard de Godishalve and the meadow called Fubbeheng'; to be held with free entry and exit for mowing his meadow and removing and carrying away its crop. Warranty. Seal.
Witnesses: Henry Sampson, William de Friston' of York, Henry son of Peter de Coupmanthorp', Laurence son of . . .,[1] Richard de Campsale, and others.
Acast', Thursday after the feast of St. Barnabas the apostle [15 June] 1335.

SOURCE: VC 3/Vv 3 (227 mm. × 103 mm.)
ENDORSEMENT: *pratum*.
SEAL: evidence lost as a result of document repair.

[1] MS. rubbed; one word missing.

NOTE: The meadow granted here to Catton later passed to Roger de Weel, whose executors conveyed it to trustees. They transferred it in 1411 to the vicars (5). For property in York which similarly passed from Weel's executors through the same trustees to the vicars, see *Chs. Vicars Choral*, i, no. 491.

3.   Grant by John de Catton' of York and his wife Emma to John son of Adam de Catton' of York of 1 a. 3 r. of meadow in the meadow of Acastre Malebys in a place called le Mersk, which they have of the gift and enfeoffment of John Malebys, lying as

in 2 (reading Godishalf for Godishalve) and to be held with right of entry and exit as in 2. Warranty. Seal.

Witnesses: dom. William Malebys knight, Henry Sampson, Henry son of Peter de Coupmanthorp', Richard de Camsale, John de Soureby of York, Andrew le Bower of York, John de Egton' of York, John de Drynghouses of York, and others.

Acastre Malebys, Sunday after feast of blessed Peter in cathedra 1346, 21 Edward III [25 February 1346/7].

SOURCE: VC 3/Vv 4 (239 mm. × 125 mm.)
ENDORSEMENT: *pratum Acast' Malb'*.
SEAL: one slit, one tag.

NOTE: See 2.

4.   Grant, in the form of a cirograph, by John son of Adam de Catton' of York to Emma widow of John de Catton' of York for her life of 1 a. 3 r. of meadow in the meadow of Acastr' Malebys in the place called le Mersk, which John has of the gift and enfeoffment of John de Catton' and Emma, lying as in 2 (reading Godishalf for Godishalve and Fubbheng for Fubbeheng') and to be held with right of entry and exit as in 2; paying a rose on the day of the nativity of St. John the Baptist if asked for. After Emma's death the meadow shall revert to John and his heirs and remain with them. Sealed with John's seal and Emma's seal alternately on each part of the cirograph.

Witnesses: as 3 (reading Sourby for Soureby).

Acastr' Malebys, Sunday before feast of St. Mark the evangelist [22 April] 1347, 21 Edward III.

SOURCE: VC 3/Vv 5 (230 mm. × 115 mm.). Indented at top, with letters.
ENDORSEMENT: *pratum*.
SEAL: tag.

NOTE: See 2.

5.   Deliverance and grant by Richard Horneby, Thomas Martyn, and Robert Appilton, chaplains, to Robert Feriby, warden of the house of vicars, and the college [of vicars], of 1 a. 3 r. of meadow in the meadow of Acastre Malbys which they have of the gift and enfeoffment of William de Ottelay chaplain and William Hugate citizen and merchant of York, executors of the testament of Roger de Wele once citizen of York, lying between the meadow of the lord of Acastr' Malbys on both sides and in length from the ditch (*a fossato*) of the churchyard of the parish church of Acastre Malbys in front to the water of Use behind; to be held of the chief lord of the fee for the service owed and according to customary law (*de iure consueta*). Seal.

Witnesses: Richard Katterton de Acastre Malbys, John Catterton of the same place, John Mosse of the same place, Richard Broune of the same place, William Duffeld, and others.

Acastre Malbys, on the feast of relics 12 Henry IV [12 July 1411].

SOURCE: VC 3/Vv 6 (302 mm. × 118 mm.)
ENDORSEMENT: *Evidenc' de un' acr' prati*; *in Acast' Malbis*.

Seals: (left) round (14 mm. dia.), red, impression of 'R' with a crown over it and palm leaves on either side; (centre) oblong (21 mm. long × 6 mm. across), red, impression of a standing figure with left arm raised, set in a border; (right) slit.

NOTE: See 2. The three grantors were themselves vicars choral.

BARTON
(parish in Gilling East wapentake NR)

6. Grant, in free alms, by Robert de Marske for the salvation of his ancestors and his successors to God and the vicars in the church of blessed Peter of York of a furlong at Nichinacr' in Barton with the adjoining meadow, a furlong at Wluekelde, land at Milnestan, land at Riuelighou, land at the Odeline acre, land at Stanhou' and half of his toft next to St. Mary's chapel in Barton on the east.   [1220 × 1228]

Sciant presentes et futuri quod ego Robertus de Mersc divine pietatis intuitu pro salute antecessorum meorum et successorum concessi et dedi et hac carta sigillo meo inpressa confirmavi Deo et vicariis in ecclesia beati Petri Ebor' servientibus totam culturam meam apud Nichinacr' in territorio de Barton' cum prato adiacente et totam culturam meam apud Wluekelde et totam meam terram apud Milnestan et totam meam terram ad Riuelighou et totam terram meam ad acram Odeline et totam terram meam ad Stainhou et dimidietatem tofti mei iuxta capellam sancti Marie in Barton' versus orientem cum omnibus pertinenciis et aisiamentis predictis terris pertinentibus infra villam de Barton' et extra sine aliquo retinemento, tenendas illis et eorum successoribus in puram et perpetuam elemosinam. Et ego Robertus et heredes mei predictam terram cum pertinenciis illis sicut puram et perpetuam elemosinam warantizabimus in perpetuum. Hiis testibus magistro R. de Insula decano, magistro Johanne Romano, Nicholao de Stapelton', Radulpho de Uckerbi, Halnad de Halnadebi, Galfrido de Coleburn', Galfrido de Huceswell', Nicholao de Didreston', Hugone de Selebi, Adam Flur, Willelmo tinctore, Helia Boschettar', et aliis.

SOURCE: VC 3/3/82a (184 mm. × 103 mm.)
ENDORSEMENT: *Barton'*.
SEAL: tag.

DATE: When Roger de Insula was dean of York and before John Romeyn became subdean.
NOTE: Robert de Marske is presumably the Robert son of Alan de Marske who made another grant to the vicars (7), possibly intended to replace 6.

7. Grant by Robert son of Alan de Marske for the souls of his father, mother, ancestors, and successors to God and the blessed Mary and the vicars in the church of St. Peter at York of [a furlong] at Breches in Barton, a furlong at Nichinacre, [land] at Pinnedrane, land at Wl[uekelde], land at [Ri]uelighou', a furlong at Milnestanflat', with his house in the vill of Barton, except half an acre on the west which Robert gave to God and the canons of [St.] Agatha.   [1220 × 1228]

Omnibus sancte matris ecclesie filiis has literas visuris vel audituris Robertus filius
Alani de Mersc salutem. Noveritis me concessisse et dedisse et hac pres[enti cart]a mea
confirmasse Deo et beate Marie et vicariis in maiori ecclesia sancti Petri apud Ebor'
Deo servientibus [unam cultur]am apud Breches in territorio de Barton' et totam
culturam [meam] apud Nichinacre et [totam terram me]am apud Pinnedrane et totam
terram meam apud Wl[uekelde] et totam terram meam apud [Ri]uel'ighou et totam
culturam meam apud Milnestanflat cum [? toto] mesuagio meo in villa de Barton'
extra dimidia acra terre versus occidentem quam dedi Deo et canonicis de [sancte]
Agatha cum omnibus libertatibus et pertinenciis suis sine aliquo retinemento pro
animabus patris mei et matris mee et omnium antecessorum et successorum meorum,
tenendas adeo libere et quiete in puram et perpetuam elemosinam sicut aliqua
elemosina in toto regno liberius vel melius tenetur vel possidetur. Et ego Robertus
et heredes mei predictas terras et mesuagium cum pertinenciis Deo et beate Marie et
beato Petro apostolo et prenominatis vicariis contra omnes warantizabimus [et
defendemus] in perpetuum. Hiis testibus magistro R. de Insula tunc de[cano],
Johanne Romano ca[nonico], ..., Ada Flur, Willelmo tinctore de Richemund',
[? Helia] Boschettar', Nor[mano] . . ., Rogero de Barton', Alexandro Mansell',
Simone Mansell', et [aliis].

SOURCE: VC 3/3/82c (171 mm. × 121 mm.; right-hand side and two diamond-shaped
    areas left of centre missing).
ENDORSEMENT: none.
SEAL: remains of wax on tag.

DATE: As 6.
NOTE: See 6.

8.   Confirmation by Ralph son of Thomas de Barton of the grant of land in Barton
which Robert son of Alan made to the vicars serving God in the church of St. Peter.
                                                                        [1220 × 1228]

Sciant presentes et futuri quod ego Radulphus filius Thome de Barton' concessi [et
hac] presenti carta confirmavi Deo et vicariis in ecclesia sancti Petri Deo servientibus
totam terram quam Robertus filius Alani [? de Mersc] in puram et perpetuam
elemosinam in territorio de Barton' dedit et carta sua confirmavit sicut co[ntinetur in
carta quam] ipsi habent de prenominato [R]oberto. Hiis testibus R. de Insula decano,
magistr[o ? Johanne Romeyn, Nicholao] de Stapelton', Radulpho [de Uc]kerbi,
Roberto de Clesebi, Alano de Clesebi, Willelmo tinctore [? de Richemund', Helia
de] Boschettar', et aliis.

SOURCE: VC 3/3/82b (152 mm. × 63 mm.; left- and right-hand sides missing).
ENDORSEMENT: *Carta Radulphi filii Thome [de] Bartona*.
SEAL: tag.

DATE: After 6 and 7, but when Roger de Insula was still dean.
NOTE: See 6.

BUBWITH
(parish in Harthill wapentake ER)

9.   Grant by Cecily de Bubwiht widow of William de Langetona, in her free
widowhood and lawful power, to mag. Simon, archdeacon of the Estrithing', and to
whomever he wishes to assign, of that part of her toft which adjoins the courtyard
(*curie*) of the canons of blessed Peter of York in Bubwiht on the north, containing in
length from the canons' court the space of 100 feet (*quinquies viginti pedum*) and in
breadth the width of the toft (*in latitudinem quantum continet toftum predictum*). [The
grant is made in return] for 3 marks which Cecily has received from mag. Simon.
Warranty. Seal.
Witnesses: German Hay, Nicholas his brother, Robert de Mustroil, Walter son of
William de Bubwiht, Richard de Gunneby, Roger de Hugat', William son of Walter
de Herletorp, Richard and Jordan his brothers, Roger de Grendale, Walter Bricchric,
Peter de Hugat', and others.   [1247 × 1261]

SOURCE: VC 3/Vv 11 (178 mm. × 92 mm.)
ENDORSEMENT: *De terra in fine curie de Bubwith*; *Bubwith*; *pro vj^d*.
SEAL: tag.

DATE: When Simon de Evesham was archdeacon of the East Riding, and probably *c.*
   1260.
NOTE: All the Bubwith charters relate to a holding which the vicars had from Simon
   de Evesham, canon of York and archdeacon successively of the East Riding and of
   Richmond.
     Cecily's toft (9), together with other land in Bubwith, was assigned to the vicars
   by Evesham in 1261 for the support of his obit (11). On the same day Evesham also
   assigned land in York to the vicars for the obit (*Chs. Vicars Choral*, i, no. 412).
     Evesham later increased his holding in Bubwith (buying a windmill from Oliver
   de Middleton, a bovate from Maud Base, meadow from Roger de Grendale, and 4
   a. of arable from Nicholas de Mundevyle), and he revised the obit arrangements
   (*Chs. Vicars Choral*, i, no. 413). Maud Base may have been Cecily's daughter, and a
   group of charters (12–15) show how in 1258 and again in 1260 and 1261 she was
   forced by economic hardship to lease out part of her inheritance in return for the
   advance payment of the rent (that being the implication of her receiving 'the
   whole farm'). The leases were made in her husband's absence, but he confirmed at
   least one of them on his return (16). Maud sold her land to Evesham after her
   husband's death, when she was still in financial difficulty (17). Roger de Grendale
   was also having financial problems when he sold his meadow to Evesham (18).
     The vicars subsequently acquired confirmations of parts of their holding in
   Bubwith (19, 20).
     The church at Bubwith was divided into moieties (presumably because the
   manor was divided tenurially between two tenants-in-chief), although both halves
   of the church were acquired by the chapter of York Minster in the mid 12th
   century (*YMF*, i, pp. 51–3). References to the lessee of one of the moieties (11, 20,
   21) indicate that the vicars' land lay in that part of the manor which had been held
   in 1086 by the Mortemer family (20).

10.   Quitclaim by Thomas son of Thomas de Cottingwith and his wife Alice to mag.
Simon de Evesham, archdeacon of the Estriding', and his heirs or assigns, of a toft

which John the marshal (*mariscall'*) once held of Adam Batayl in the vill of Bubwith. Because Alice is a bastard and not born in matrimony, she has placed her seal on this document with her husband's consent, together with his seal.
Witnesses: dom. William de Geveldale, Robert Mustroyl, Walter son of William, Richard de Gunneby, Roger de Grendale, Walter Brictryc, Peter de Hugate, Hugh Blanchard, Walter son of Robert de Bubwith, and others.   [1247 × 1261]

SOURCE: VC 3/Vv 12 (128 mm. × 79 mm.)
ENDORSEMENT: *De tofto ante januam de Bubwith.*
SEAL: two tags.

DATE: As 9.
NOTE: The toft quitclaimed here is presumably that granted to Evesham by Cecily de Bubwith (9).

11.   Notification by mag. Simon, archdeacon of the Estriding', that he bequeaths and assigns to God and the minster (*monasterio*) of St. Peter of York and the vicars of the same land which he bought in Bubwyth, lying between the land of Robert de Mustroyl and the Derewent, [and] land which he bought at the far end of the chapter's courtyard (*in extremitate curie capituli*), so that the farmer [i.e. lessee] of the moiety of the church of Bubwyth which appertains to the chapter has the lands from the vicars for the whole term of the farm [i.e. lease] if he wishes, as long as he gives them surety (*si fecerit eos securos*) for paying them 5s. a year within eight days before the anniversary of Simon's death; the money is to be given to the succentor of the vicars and be distributed by him personally (*per manum ipsius*) thus: 12d. to the lesser clerks (*clericulis*) of the third form, 12d. to the lesser clerks of the second form, and the residue to the vicars, on condition that only those present at Simon's exequies have portions. If the farmer does not give the vicars surety as above or fails (*cessaverit*) [to pay the rent] at any term, and if he does not pay double at the next term (*nisi firmam illius termini dupplicaverit*), the vicars may transfer the land to another man of their choice for his lifetime (*ad terminum vite alteri cui voluerit tradere*), for him to hold under the same condition; after that man's death, whoever is then the farmer shall be chosen [to hold the land] before others, according to the aforesaid condition (*ita quod post mortem illius firmarius qui pro tempore fuerit secundum formam prescriptum aliis preferatur*). Whoever holds the land shall pay the chief lords the annual rent owed for it. So that this assignment and ordinance shall be preserved fixed and valid Simon affixes his seal and asks (*supplico*) that the seal of the chapter of York be similarly affixed.
Bubwyth, 3 Kalends June [30 May] 1261.

SOURCE: VC 3/Vv 13 (182 mm. × 97 mm.)
ENDORSEMENT: *Ordinacio terre de Bubwiz.*
SEAL: tag.
COPY: VC 3/1/1, fo. 40r.

NOTE: See 9.

12.   Grant, in the form of a cirograph, made at Pentecost [12 May] in the year of the Incarnate Word 1258, by Maud daughter of William son of Alice de Bubwit to Roger son of Thomas de Grendale of 4 a. of arable in Bubwiht, lying in 5 selions, namely: one selion lying under Hirst on the east next to Roger's land on the west; one selion called Buldayle, lying nearer (*propinquiorem*) the east next to Haverlandesik; one selion

at Hesilrowe, lying next to the land of the lady of Wrtlay, as much as appertains there to 2 bovates of land; one selion of land in the old moor, lying in a place called Wytheker next to the land of Richard de Wixstowe, as much as appertains there to 2 bovates of land; and one selion in Estbro[d]es in the middle of the doles (*ad daylas medio loco*), as much as appertains to 2 bovates of land; to be held for 20 years by Roger, his heirs, and anyone to whom he wishes to assign or bequeath at whatever time of his life or where and when he wishes, for the whole farm which he gave Maud in her urgent need (*in mea urgente nescessitate*); when the term of 20 years is complete, Roger, his heirs, or assigns shall pay Maud and her heirs 2s. a year for each acre, namely 12d. at Pentecost and 12d. at Martinmas. Warranty of the land with free entry and exit against the chief lords and all people. If Roger, his heirs, or assigns fail to pay the farm, Maud and her heirs may enter and possess the land as if it were their demesne. Sealed in plighted faith (*fide media*) with the seals of the parties of the cirograph.

Witnesses: Robert de Mustroil, Walter son of William de Bubwit, Richard de Guneby, Peter de Hugat', Walter Brictric, Hugh Blanchard, Walter Helebald.

SOURCE: VC 3/Vv 9 (198 mm. × 156 mm.). Indented at top, CYROGRAPHA-TUM.

ENDORSEMENT: *Bubwith'*; *Bubwyth iiij*^{ar} *acras terre*.

SEAL: slit.

NOTE: See 9.

13. Agreement, in the form of cirograph, between Maud daughter of William son of Alice de Bubwiht and Alexander de Crancewiht carpenter that Maud has demised to Alexander 4 selions of arable in Bubwiht, namely: 2 selions in a place called Croftis, lying between the land of Richard de Wyxstowe and Hungirhyl; one selion lying above Thwayt in the north field, as much as appertains there to 2 bovates of land; and one selion in the old moor, lying towards Aldithehou next to the land of Richard de Wyxstowe, as much as appertains to one bovate of land in Bubwiht. Moreover, Maud has demised to Robert the carpenter of Bubwiht ½ a. of land, lying above Newehyl next to the land of Richard de Wixstowe towards the south, and pasture for one beast anywhere in the fenced-off lands (*ubique in defensis*), except in the meadows and corn fields (*bladis*). Alexander and Robert and their heirs and assigns are to hold the lands for 12 years from Easter [4 April] in the year of the Incarnation 1260, paying the whole farm which they have given Maud. Warranty against the chief lords of the fee and all people. If Maud or her heirs try in any way overturn this agreement (*contra hanc convencionem in aliquo venire attemptaverit*) or withhold the warranty and acquittance, they shall give (*exhibebunt*) 20s., namely 10s. to Alexander, 5s. to Robert, and 5s. to the fabric of the church of blessed Peter of York, and the dean and chapter of the church of blessed Peter can compel Maud and her heirs by ecclesiastical censure to observe this agreement. Maud in plighted faith (*fide media*) has renounced for herself and for her heirs all remedy of law, both civil and canon. The parts of the script are sealed reciprocally (*mutuo*) with the seals of the parties.

Witnesses: dom. Thomas de Guneby, Robert de Mustroil, Walter son of William, Richard de Guneby, Walter Bricctric, Peter de Hugat', Hugh Blanch', Richard the clerk, and others.

SOURCE: VC 3/Vv 14 (195 mm. × 132 mm.). Indented at top, CYROGRAPHUM.
ENDORSEMENT: *vij. s. . . . de Alexandro*; *Bubwith*; *de vij*^{tes} *selion'*.

SEAL: tag.

NOTE: See **9**. Robert may have been Alexander's father or brother; it was possibly because of his death that Maud made a new lease in 1261 (**14**).

14.   Grant, in the form of a cirograph, by Maud daughter of William son of Alice de Bubwit to Alexander the carpenter of 7 selions of her land in the territory of Bubwit, namely: one selion which she has at Thwait in the north field; 2 selions at Croftis in the same field, lying at the western end (*capud*) of Hungirhyl; one selion in the old moor, lying in a place called Wytheker; one selion in the new moor, lying at the southern end between the land of Richard de Wixstowe and the land of Roger de Grendale; and 2 selions in Bircles, lying at the southern end next to the land of Richard de Wixstowe towards the south (*versus solem*); to be held by Alexander, his heirs, or assigns for 24 years from Easter [24 April] in the year of grace 1261 for the whole farm which Alexander paid Maud; when the term of 24 years is complete, Alexander, his heirs, or assigns shall pay Maud 2*s*. a year for each acre, half at Pentecost and half at Martinmas. Warranty of the 7 selions with free entry and exit and with the pasture belonging to Maud in Bircles against the lords of the fee and against all men and women. If Alexander, his heirs, or assigns fail to pay the farm at any term within the 24 years, Maud and her heirs may enter the land and possess it as if it was demesne. The parts of the cirograph are sealed reciprocally (*mutuo*) with the seals of the parties.
Witnesses: Robert de Mustroil, Walter son of William de Bubwit, Richard de Gunneby, Roger de Grendale, Richard ad Flet, Peter de Hugat', Walter Brictric, Hugh Blanchard, Richard the clerk, and others.

SOURCE: VC 3/Vv 15 (188 mm. × 160 mm.). Indented at top, CARTA CYRO-GRAPHATA.
ENDORSEMENT: none.
SEAL: tag.

NOTE: See **9**.

15.   Grant, in the form of a cirograph, made at Easter [24 April] in the year of grace 1261 by Maud daughter of William son of Alice de Bubwit to Philip de Bynington' of a dole (*daylam*) of meadow appertaining to the 2 bovates of land which belonged to her father William, lying in the great meadow of Bubwit at the northern end between the meadow of Roger de Grendale and that of Richard de Wixstowe, and extending from the Derewente up to the boundary (*divisam*) towards Acton'; and [also of] 2 selions of arable in Bubwit, namely: one selion lying at Fonthelehes between the land of Richard de Wixstowe and that of Roger de Grendale, as much as appertains there to 2 bovates of land; and one selion in Hestecroft extending across the path (*in traverso vie*) at the northern end between Roger's and Richard's lands, as much as appertains to 2 bovates of land. [The land is] to be held for 20 years by Philip, his heirs, or assigns for the whole annual farm of ½ mark [6*s*. 8*d*.], which Philip paid Maud in her severe hardship (*in meo arduo negocio*); when the term of 20 years is complete, Philip, his heirs, or assigns shall give Maud, her heirs, or assigns ½ mark a year, in equal parts at Pentecost and Martinmas. Warranty of the meadow and 2 selions with free entry and exit and with the pasture which appertains to the meadow and land against the lords of the fee and against all people. If Philip, his heirs, or assigns fail to pay the farm at any term during the 20 years, Maud, her heirs, or assigns may enter the meadow and land and possess them as if they were demesne. If Maud, her heirs, or assigns default in the warranty or wish in any way to overturn this agreement (*contra istud instrumentum in aliquo venire voluerimus*), they bind themselves by plighted faith to pay one mark as a debt (*nomine debiti*) to Philip, his heirs, and assigns and one mark on account of the offence (*ratione transgressionis*) to the dean and chapter of blessed Peter of York, and they shall have no entry to the land or meadow until the said 2 marks have been fully paid. The dean and chapter can bind Maud, her heirs, and assigns to implement this agreement by whatever coercion pleases them, notwithstanding any remedy at law (*non obstante aliquo iuris remedio per quacumque eis placuerit cohercionem*). The parts of the script are sealed alternately with the seals of the parties.

Witnesses: dom. Thomas de Guneby, Richard his brother, Robert de Mustroil, Walter son of William de Bubwit, Roger de Grendale, Roger de Hugat', Henry son of Peter de Herlethorp, Walter Brictric, Peter de Hugat', Hugh Blanchard, Walter Holebald, Richard de Guneby clerk, and others.

SOURCE: VC 3/Vv 18 (202 mm. × 158 mm.). Indented at top, CARTA CYRO-
GRAPHATA.

ENDORSEMENT: *Bubwith'*; *dailam prati cum duabus bavatis* [sic] *terre*.

SEAL: tag.

NOTE: See 9.

16.   Grant made on the feast of the translation of blessed Thomas the martyr [7 July] by Adam son of Benet de Cotingwit to Alexander the carpenter de Bubwit of those 7 selions of land in the territory of Bubwit which his [Adam's] wife Maud demised at term to Alexander by a cirograph made in Adam's absence for the support of herself and their children (*ad sustentacionem illius et pueorum nostrorum*), namely: one selion lying above Thwait; 2 selions at Croftis; one selion at Wytheker in the old moor; one selion in the new moor; and 2 selions in Bircles; to be held by Alexander, his heirs, and assigns as the cirograph made between Alexander and Maud details (*representat*). Warranty of the 7 selions with free entry and exit against all people up to the end of the term given in their cirographs. Seal.

Witnesses: Robert de Mustroil, Walter son of William de Bubwit, Richard de Gunneby, Roger de Grendale, Richard ad Flet, Peter de Hugat', Hugh Blanchard, Philip de Gunneby, Richard the clerk, and others.   [possibly 1261 or 1262]

SOURCE: VC 3/Vv 16 (151 mm. × 101 mm.)

ENDORSEMENT: none.

SEAL: tag.

DATE: After 15.

NOTE: See 9.

17.   Quitclaim by Maud daughter of William son of Alice de Bubwiht, in her full power and free widowhood, to mag. Simon de Evesham, then archdeacon of Richemund', and his heirs and to whomsoever he wishes to assign, of 6 a. of arable in Bubwiht, part of that bovate of land which her father William gave with her in marriage (*mecum in maritagio*), and of a dole (*daylam*) of meadow appertaining to the same bovate, namely: a selion in the old moor, lying in a place called Wytheker containing 1½ a.; a selion at Waitecroft containing ½ a.; a selion lying at Gaytebrig' containing ½ a.; 2 butts on the boundary (*super divisam*) of Gunneby containing 1 p. ; 3 selions of land in Walbainemor at the eastern edge containing 1 a.; a selion in Thwerdail' in the same moor containing ½ a.; a selion at Mickeldayl' in Hestecroft towards Haverlandesic containing 1 a.; a selion at Thwerdayl in Hestecroft containing 1½ p. ; a selion between the ditches (*inter fossata*) containing 1½ p. ; and a dole of meadow in the great meadow of Bubwit at the northern end, lying next to the meadow of Richard de Wixstowe on the south and containing 1 a. 1 p. [The land is] to be held by mag. Simon and his heirs or assigns for money which he gave Maud in her severe hardship (*in meo arduo negocio*). Warranty of the 6 a. with meadow against all people.

Witnesses: Thomas de Guneby knight, Ralph de Ryhe bailiff of Beverley (*de Beverlac'*), Matthew de Bridlingt', Richard de Guneby, William son of Walter de Bubwit, Richard ad Flet of the same place, Peter de Hugat', Hugh Blanchard, Robert son of Alan de Brihton', Richard de Guneby clerk, and others.   [1262 × 1269–71]

SOURCE: VC 3/Vv 10 (213 mm. × 131 mm.)
ENDORSEMENT: *Bubwith*; *magna* [? pra]*ta . . . acris terre et j. bovat'*.
SEAL: vesica (39 mm. × 20 mm.), impression rubbed out.

DATE: When Simon de Evesham was archdeacon of Richmond.
NOTE: See 9.

18.   Grant by Roger son of Thomas de Grendale to mag. Simon de Evesham, then archdeacon of Richemund', of a dole (*daylam*) of meadow in the southern part of the great meadow of Bubwiht between the meadow of Richard de Wyxstowe and the ditch (*fossatum*), namely as much [as appertains] there to the half carucate of land which was once of William son of Alice in the same vill, [and] which Roger bought from William's son and heir Robert in demesne and in service; to be held by mag. Simon and his heirs and assigns for his and their lives. [The grant is made in return] for a sum of money which mag. Simon gave Roger in his severe hardship (*in meo arduo negocio*). Warranty of the land with free entry and exit against the lords of the fee and against all men and women. Seal.

Witnesses: Thomas de Guneby knight, Thomas his son, German Hay de Acton', Roger de Hugat', Richard de Gunneby, William son of Walter de Bubwit, Richard ad Flet of the same place, Peter de Hugat', Hugh Blanchard de Bubwit, and others.
                                                                    [1262 × 1269–71]

SOURCE: VC 3/Vv 17 (200 mm. × 92 mm.)
ENDORSEMENT: *Bubwit*; *de prato de Bubwith'*; *una dayland prati*.
SEAL: round (24 mm. dia.), brown, impression of ? a standing figure.

DATE: When Simon de Evesham was archdeacon of Richmond.
NOTE: See 9.

19.   Grant in free alms by Robert son of William de Ros to God and the warden of the vicars of blessed Peter of York and the vicars serving God there of a windmill with its site and appurtenances in the vill of Bubewit, namely that windmill which the vicars have from mag. Simon de Evissham once archdeacon of Rychemund', as a charter which they have for it fully shows. Neither Robert nor his heirs nor anyone on their behalf may exact any distress or claim in the mill for any loss (*pro aliquo defectu*) or sell [it]. Seal.

Witnesses: dom. Peter de Ros, dom. William de Ros, dom. Herbert de Ros, dom. Alexander de Kyrketona, knights, German le Hay, Nicholas de Meltona, William de Lyvirseg', Roger de Hugate, and others. [early 1270s]

SOURCE: VC 3/Vv 8 (197 mm. × 133 mm.)
ENDORSEMENT: *Molendinum de Bubwith.*
SEAL: tag.

DATE: Probably not long after Evesham's death (by August 1271).
NOTE: See 9.

20.   Notification by John del Flete de Bubwytht recording that in the time of king Henry the son of king John mag. Simon de Levessam granted to the warden of the house of vicars and the vicars of the church of blessed Peter of York a parcel of a messuage in Bubwyth as inclosed in a place (*in vico*) called Mustrellan, lying on the north side next to the chief messuage of the farmer [i.e. lessee] of the moiety of the church of Bubwyth which belongs to the church of blessed Peter. The vicars have held the parcel of John and his ancestors because John's grandfather Richard del Flete, whose heir John is, acquired it from the demesne by the grant of dom. Humphrey de Veyly knight. John confirms the grant of that place which mag. Simon made in free alms to the warden and vicars. Warranty. Seal.
Witnesses: dom. William de Scwynton perpetual vicar of the church of Bubwyth, John de Guneby, Thomas de Bubwyth, Richard his brother, Richard de Her-lyethorpe, Richard de Kardoile, Stephen son of William, and others of Bubwyht. York, in the house of the vicars called the Bedern, Tuesday in Pentecost week [13 May] 1326.

SOURCE: VC 3/Vv 19 (267 mm. × 150 mm.)
ENDORSEMENT: *Carta de Bubwyth'; ex dono Symonis de Levessam custodi domus vicariorum, Bubwit, tempore Henrici regis filii Johannis regis; An° domini m¹ ccc vicesimo vj^to.*
SEAL: remains of wax on tag.

NOTE: See 9. In the earlier 13th century the Veilly family held fees in Yorkshire of the Vescy honor, and they presumably held that half of Bubwith which descended to the Vescys from Ralph de Mortemer, the owner in 1086 (*EYC*, iii, p. 256; *YMF*, i, pp. 51–2).

21.   Indenture witnessing that Ellis de Walkyngton, warden of the house of vicars of the church of blessed Peter, and the vicars of the same church have demised at farm to dom. William de Burton', vicar of a moiety of the church of Bubwith, 4 a. of arable and 2½ a. of meadow in the territory and meadow of Bubwyth', lying thus: a selion containing 1 a. 1 r. in a field called 'le alde more', lying between the land of Robert de Gunby on the north and the royal way on the south; 1½ a. in 'the lingis' between the land of Robert de Gunby on the south and that of John Cardole on the north; ½ a. in 'the est felde landis' between Robert's land on the east and John's land on the west; and 3 r. in 'the awnehomys' between the land of William de Aldburgh knight on the south and John's land on the north; the meadow lies in the great meadow of Bubwith next to the south ditch (*fossam australem*), that is the whole of the south of the great meadow of Bubwith. [The land is] to be held from Pentecost 1380¹ for 10 years, paying the vicars 8s. a year in equal portions at Pentecost and Martinmas, the first payment to be at Pentecost in the said year. William is bound to the vicars by a deed

of obligation for £4 of silver payable next Pentecost, to be void if William pays the annual farm at the said terms or within 15 days. Seal.
York, on the feast of St. Michael [29 September] 1379.

SOURCE: VC 3/Vv 20 (274 mm. × 104 mm.). Indented at top with letters.
ENDORSEMENT: *Vicar' de Bubwith*; *vj acras terre et . . . duarum acrarum prati.*
SEAL: remains of one slit.

¹ Altered in same hand from '1370', possibly because the scribe was copying from an earlier lease.

NOTE: See **9**.

CLIFTON
(in Overton parish, Bulmer wapentake NR)

22.   Demise at farm by Robert de Haldenby to Robert de Feryby, warden of the house of vicars of the cathedral church of York, and the vicars of 3 selions of land in the fields of Clyfton' called Langelandes, lying between the land of Ellen widow of John de Ingelby and that of William de Lynton and stretching from Wyllyghbiygfyld to the water of Use, with free entry and exit to the land and also carriage of clay, however much and whenever it seems necessary to the warden and vicars or the farmers [i.e. lessees] of their house of Tyllehos outside the walls of the city; the selions are to be held for 10 years from next Pentecost, paying 8s. a year.
York, Sunday after the feast of Corpus Christi 12 Henry IV [14 June 1411].

SOURCE: VC Box XII, misc. 26 (302 mm. × 150 mm.). Indented at top.
ENDORSEMENT: none.
SEAL: tag.

NOTE: The vicars acquired the tile works beyond North Street in 1410 (*Chs. Vicars Choral*, i, no. 514 note), and operated it to produce bricks and tiles used in repairing their own property in York (see Introduction: Economic Background). The necessary clay came from nearby Clifton, where *c.* 1420 the vicars rented 1 r. belonging to John Lynton for digging up sufficient clay for 'the Tilehous beyond the Use': VC 1/1, p. 35 (ink pagination).
   When the lease of Haldenby's land was up in 1421, his son William, alleging that the lease was invalid, brought an action against the vicars for carrying away 100 cartloads of clay in 1416 (VC 3/1/2, enclosing loose sheet = memorandum of process heard in the king's bench in 1421).

EARSWICK

(in Huntington parish, Bulmer wapentake NR)

23.   Grant, in free alms, by Thomas de Drentona to God and blessed Peter of York and the vicars ministering to God there, for the salvation of his soul and [the souls] of his ancestors and successors, of a bovate of land in Everheswyk with toft and croft, which Robert son of Ralph once held of him, and with all its appurtenances in and outside the vill, namely that [bovate] which William Scoticus once held of him, lying near the land of the prebend of Stranshale. Warranty. Seal.
Witnesses: dom. Simon de Lillink knight, David the lardener (*lardinario*), Nicholas and Gervase de Rou . . ., Henry son of Gamel de Everistevike, Walter de Thoutorp, Robert Sel, Robert de Blaketoft, Ralph Russel, Walter the clerk, and others.
[later 13th century]

SOURCE: VC 3/Vv 24 (217 mm. × 100 mm.; the top 15 mm. of the document is attached with string, having been cut off).
ENDORSEMENT: *Carta de Ethertheswic'*; *una bovata terre cum tofto et crofto.*
SEAL: no evidence as the foot of the document is missing.
COPY: VC 3/1/1, fo. 40v.

DATE: Simon Lilling witnessed another grant to the vicars, dated 1260: *Chs. Vicars Choral*, i, no. 169.
NOTE: For a confirmation see 24.

24.   Confirmation by dom. Robert de Nevill' of the grant of a bovate of land in the vill of Ericewyc which William Scoticus held in the same vill and of a toft which Simon de Hundintona held in the same vill; Thomas de Drenthona made the grant in free alms to God and the church of blessed Peter of York and the vicars serving God there.
Witnesses: dom. Gerard Salvayn and Simon de Lillink, knights, Robert de Sancto Paulo, Richard de Torny, William the stabler (*stabulario*), Henry and Walter de Ericewic, Walter the clerk de Wiltona, and others   [later 13th century]

SOURCE: VC 3/Vv 25 (141 mm. × 66 mm.)
ENDORSEMENT: *Ercewyke*; *pro una bovata terre.*
SEAL: round (22 mm. dia.), green, impression of a running man, legend + SIGILLVM SECRETI

DATE: After 23. Robert de Neville died in 1282: *Yorkshire Inquisitions*, ed. W. Brown, i (YASRS xii, 1892 for 1891), p. 254.
NOTE: See 23.

25.   Letter of Thomas Thurkell' citizen of York and his wife Alice recording that the vicars of the cathedral church of blessed Peter of York are seised of a rent of 12*d*. a year from 3 tofts, 3 crofts, and 2 bovates of arable once of Peter de Tadcastr' of Evercewyk'; the 3 tofts with crofts lie in length and breadth between land once of John Algare and that of Adam Scote and the 2 bovates lie [dispersed] in the field (*per totum campum*) between the land of the prebend of Strenshall' and that once of Peter de Tadcastr'. Thomas and Alice are seised of the land in the right of Alice's mother but they have not paid the 12*d*. rent to the vicars for the past 11 years; they

acknowledge that they owe the vicars the rent, which was charged on the land by
Peter's charter to his son William, namely:

Grant by Peter de Tadcastre of Evercewyk to his son William of 3 tofts, 3 crofts,
and 2 bovates of arable in the vill and territory of Evercewyk (lying as given above
but reading Scot for Scote); paying Peter and his heirs 30s. a year, half at Pentecost
and half at Martinmas, and the vicars of blessed Peter of York 12d. a year.
Warranty. Seal.

Witnesses: Thomas de Stodley, Robert Haget, Roger de Thornton clerk, John le
stabler, William de Crakall' of Touthorp', John son of Nicholas of the same place,
Robert son of Simon de Huntyngton, Nicholas son of Benet of the same place,
Henry at the water (ad aquam) de Evercewyk', William de Wygynton of the same
place, and others.   [later 13th century]

Sealing clause of Thomas and Alice's letter.
12 May 1407, 8 Henry IV.

SOURCE: VC 3/Vv 26 (414 mm. × 187 mm.)
ENDORSEMENT: *Eweryswyke xij^d.*

SEALS: (left) round (24 mm. dia.), red, impression of a shield, legend; (right), square (8
mm. sides), red, impression.

DATE: Peter de Tadcaster held property in York in the later 13th century: *Chs. Vicars
Choral*, i, no. 420.

GRIMSTON

(in Dunnington parish, Ouse and Derwent wapentake ER)

26.   Grant by Eudes de Punchardun knight, son of Roger de Punchardun, to God
and blessed Mary, blessed Peter of York, and the altar of the holy virgins Agatha,
Lucy, and Scholastica in the great church of St. Peter of York in the crypt (*in criptis*)
towards the south next to the door (*hostium*), and to two chaplains and their successors
serving God and blessed Mary, blessed Peter, and the said virgins [and celebrating
mass] each day except Saturday, on which day they celebrate the mass of the blessed
Virgin, in perpetuity for the soul of dom. James de Kawrd once canon of the church
of blessed [Peter], the souls of James's father and mother, the soul of dom. Ralph son
of Nicholas, the souls of all [who were] once James's parishioners, Eudes's soul, and
the souls of all his predecessors and successors and of all the faithful departed, of [the
following]: all Eudes's manor and free chapel in the vill and territory of Grymmeston
between York and Pons belli [i.e. Pontefract]; 6 bovates of land from his demesne
with tofts and crofts, gardens, and all appurtenances; a rent of 12d. a year . . . (? in
Grymmeston) which (? Gilbert) the reeve held of him; 2 bovates of land which Peter
de (? Sut)ton' his neif held with all his offspring (*sequela*), chattels, and possessions; (? 2
bovates) of land which Mariot widow of John de Grimmiston his neif held with all
her offspring, chattels, and possessions; one bovate of land . . . [two or three illegible
words] his neif held with all his offspring, chattels, and possessions; a rent of 6d. a year
from one acre of land which Alan . . . [three illegible words]; and 3 tofts and 3 crofts
. . . [three or four illegible words]. [The land is] to be held in pure and perpetual alms

from the nuns of Mollesby by God and blessed Mary, blessed Peter, and the virgins and by the chaplains and their successors serving God there in perpetuity; paying Eudes . . . [two or three illegible words] a year, half at Pentecost and half at Martinmas. Warranty. Seal.

Witnesses: *dominis* John de Haulton' sheriff of Yorkshire, John de Ocketon', John de Raignate, Geoffrey Aguilum and Roger de Lascels, knights, John de Seleby mayor of York, Robert Blund, John Speciar', and Roger Basy, bailiffs of the same place, Walter de Stokes, John Speciar', Gilberto de Fenton', Simon le Graunt', Robert de Sexdecim Vallibus, Thomas de Hewrd', William de (? Sto)ketton', Benet de Hewrd', Richard de Murers, Walter de Hemelsay, William Darel, Nicholas de Naburn', Robert de Hewrd', Serlo de Stai[ne]gat', William le Graunt', John de Clervaus, and others.

[1265 or 1266]

SOURCE: VC 3/3/79 (310 mm. × 218 mm.; damaged by water)
ENDORSEMENT: *Carta de Grimston; sine data; carta de Grymston iuxta Ebor'.*
SEAL: round (32 mm. dia.), plain, impression of ? the paschal lamb, legend.

DATE: Probably soon after Cawood's death (see note below). Selby was mayor with Blund, Spicer, and Coniston as bailiffs in October 1265 (*Chs. Vicars Choral*, i, no. 307); Basy may have replaced Coniston either before the end of that mayoralty or when a new mayoralty was formed in 1266.
NOTE: By the early 14th century all, or part, of the land had been assigned to the vicars (VC 4/1/1), presumably by Cawood's executors (who included a leading vicar choral, Alan Salvator); they certainly assigned them a rent charge on property in York in return for maintaining the canon's obit: *Chs. Vicars Choral*, i, no. 509.

According to the vicars' rental for 1309 Cawood's obit was celebrated on 7 November (VC 4/1/1), making 1265 the probable year of his death: his successor was collated to the vacant prebend on 10 November 1265 (*Fasti, York*, 101).

NORTH GRIMSTON
(parish in Buckrose wapentake ER)

27. Grant, in pure alms, by Richard son of Walter de Grimston to God and blessed Peter of the church of York and the vicars serving God there, for the salvation of his soul and the souls of his ancestors and successors, of 2 bovates of land in Grimston next Malton with toft and croft, which Robert son of Hugh held, lying on the west near Richard's demesne; to be held with the pasture of 3 bovates of land in the same vill and with all easements appertaining to the 2 bovates in and outside the vill.

[earlier 13th century]

Sciant presentes et futuri quod ego Ricardus filius Walteri de Grimestona dedi, concessi, et hac presenti carta sigillo meo inpressa confirmavi Deo et beato Petro Eborac' ecclesie et vicariis ibidem Deo servientibus pro salute anime mee, antecessorum, et successorum meorum duas bovatas terre in Grimestona iuxta Maltonam cum tofto et crofto, illas scilicet quas Robertus filius Hugonis tenuit et illas que iacent ex parte occidentali propingwiores dominico meo; tenendas et habendas eisdem vicariis et eorum assingnatis in puram et perpetuam elemosinam libere, quiete,

integre, et honorifice cum pastura trium bovatarum terre in eadem villa et cum
omnibus aysiamentis in acris, in viis, in semitis, in planis, et in omnibus aliis
libertatibus et liberis consuetudinibus infra villam et extra predictis duabus bovatis
terre pertinentibus. Et ego predictus Ricardus et heredes mei adquietabimus,
defendemus, et warantizabimus predictas duas bovatas terre predictis vicariis et
eorum assingnatis contra omnes homines cum omnibus pertinencibus suis in
perpetuum sicut aliqua elemosina melius et liberius poterit adquietari, defendi, et
warantizari. Hiis testibus Radulfo de Friby, Thoma de Luttona, Roberto filio Nigelli,
Roberto filio Willelmi, Waltero Grumet', Thoma filio Galfridi, Orm de Berthetorp',
Ada de Alna, Ada de revest', Reginaldo, Thoma sacrista, diaconibus, Thoma de
Tumba, Willelmo feru', Ricardo caretario, et multis aliis.

SOURCE: VC 3/Vv 31 (164 mm. × 91 mm.)
ENDORSEMENT: *Carta de Grimmestona.*
SEAL: tag.

DATE: Before 28.
NOTE: All the Grimston charters relate to the same land, granted to the vicars by
    Richard son of Walter de Grimston (27). What happened after the original grant
    was made is unclear. The land was presumably conveyed to a tenant, Henry le
    mercer, who reserved a 2s. rent charge payable to the vicars when he later granted
    the land to John son of Stephen de Westbrunne (28). That grant was confirmed by
    Robert de Grimston, possibly the heir of the original grantor, although evidently
    not his son (29). Robert's son, Walter, however, challenged John's right to the
    land and renounced his claim only after a plea in the county court (30). Despite his
    confirmation of Henry's grant, Robert de Grimston (as Robert son of Thomas de
    Watton) separately conveyed the land to Alan de Watton (31).
        By the 1260s the land had come to Walter de Towthorpe, who received a
    quitclaim from John de Westbrunne (32) and who in 1266 conveyed possession to
    the vicars, having secured his claim to the land before royal justices at York (33).
    The acquisition of the land cost the vicars a considerable amount of money and
    was probably made in connection with securing an endowment to fund an obit for
    Roger Pepin (d. 1266), subdean of York (34); the money presumably came from
    Pepin's executors or from funds administered by one of Pepin's fellow canons,
    John le Cras (cf. *Chs. Vicars Choral*, i, no. 323). By 1309, however, rent from the
    land supported an obit on 3 September for Roger de Holderness, otherwise de
    Skeffling, dean of York (VC 4/1/1, giving the name as 'Sciftelings'); Holderness
    evidently died on 3 September 1260 or 1261.
        In the 1280s the vicars had to prove their right to the land before royal justices
    against Alan de Watton's son Walter de Grimston (35). The final charter in the
    group is a lease of 1420 (36).

28.   Grant by Henry le mercer de Gartona, validated (*roborata*) by his seal, to John
son of Stephen de Westbrunne, for his past service and a payment of 12½ marks
[£8 6s. 8d.] of sterling, of 2 bovates of land in Grimestona next to the land of
Maltona, which Richard son of Walter de Grimestona gave to the vicars of the
church of York; to be held by John and his heirs or assigns, except religious men and
Jews, with toft and croft and with the pasture of 3 bovates of land in the same vill;
paying 2s. a year in equal portions at Pentecost and Martinmas to the vicars of the

church of York at York and one pair of white gloves or ½d. at Christmas to Henry and his heirs at Grimestona. Warranty.

Witnesses: mag. John Roman then subdean of York, John le Sauner', Gilbert de Sancto Dionisio, William de Gerfortheby, vicars of St. Peter of York, William de Aurelianis chaplain, Richard de Burgo, John de Hesel, Richard de Aquila, Hamo the marshal (*marscallo*), Robert the cook, clerks, the clerks and servants of mag. J. Roman.

[1228 × 1240–1]

SOURCE: VC 3/Vv 33 (176 mm. × 127 mm.)
ENDORSEMENT: none.
SEAL: tag.

DATE: When John Romeyn the elder was subdean of York.
NOTE: See **27**.

29. Grant by Robert de Grimestona son of Thomas de Wattona, marked (*signata*) with his seal, to John son of Stephen de Westbrunne of 2 bovates of land with toft and croft and the pasture of 3 bovates of land in Grimestona, which Henry le mercer de Gartona gave to John and which he confirmed at Robert's request (*ad peticionem et ad instanciam meam*).

Witnesses: as **28** (with addition at end of list of Thomas of the churchyard (*de cimiterio*) and others). [1228 × 1240–1]

SOURCE: VC 3/Vv 35 (169 mm. × 90 mm.)
ENDORSEMENT: none.
SEAL: round (*c.* 25 mm. dia., damaged), green, impresssion of a wheel, legend.

DATE: Probably on the same occasion as **28**.
NOTE: See **27**.

30. Quitclaim by Walter Grimet son of Robert de Grimestona of all right and claim in 2 bovates of land in Grimestona to John de Brunne and his heirs and assigns, namely those bovates which John bought from Robert de Wattona and from Henry de Gartona, concerning which (*unde*) there was a plea between Walter and John in the county [court] of York (*in comitatu Ebor'*) by a writ of right, namely that John held the bovates from the vicars of the church of York, who had them from the gift of Richard de Grimestona in free, pure, and perpetual alms. For this quitclaim John gave 5 marks [£6 6s. 8d.] of silver. Seal.

Witnesses: dom. Ralph de Friby, Robert de Bulford, Geoffrey de Thurgrimthorp, William de Thurgrimthorp, William le Bret, Geoffrey de Ken'thorp, Geoffrey de Fribi, and enough others (*satis aliis*). [1230s or 1240s]

SOURCE: VC 3/Vv 34 (187 mm. × 89 mm.)
ENDORSEMENT: none medieval.
SEAL: tag.

DATE: After **29**.
NOTE: See **27**.

31. Grant by Robert son of Thomas de Wattona to Alan de Wattona and his heirs or assigns, for money which Alan gave him, of a messuage and 2 bovates of land in

Aclingrimmiston, namely that messuage and those 2 bovates of land which Robert bought from the vicars of St. Peter of York, paying 2s. a year to the vicars of St. Peter of York. Warranty.

Witnesses: dom. Ralph de Fritheby knight, Walter Gimmech, Walter then chaplain of Grimmistona, Robert son of William of Grimmistona, his brother Geoffrey the clerk, William de Bukton', Geoffrey son of Thomas de Grimmiston', William son of Simon de Setrington', Geoffrey son of Gerard de Setrington', William Crisping de Scakelthorp, Simon the chamberlain de Setrington', Adam de Dukilby, William Sleyth de Warrum, and many others.   [1230s or 1240s]

SOURCE: VC 3/Vv 30 (198 mm. × 58 mm.)
ENDORSEMENT: none.
SEAL: tag.

DATE: Possibly about the same date as 30.
NOTE: See 27.

32.   Quitclaim by John son of Stephen de Westbrunne to Walter de Thoutorp son of Richard the chaplain of Strensale and his heirs of 2 bovates of land in Grimestona which he held of the vicars of St. Peter of York with all appurtenances in and outside the vill, toft and croft, and all the pasture of 3 bovates of land in the same vill; doing the service that appertains to the 2 bovates to the vicars of the church of St. Peter of York. Seal.

Witnesses: dom. Simon de Lilling, Robert Guer, knights, Robert Daniel, Geoffrey de Fridebi, Thomas de Wattona, Robert the clerk of Edbristona, Walter de Thouthorp, William son of Simon, Robert de Torni, and many others.   [possibly earlier 1260s]

SOURCE: VC 3/Vv 28 (222 mm. × 74 mm.)
ENDORSEMENT: *Grimeston'*.
SEAL: tag.

DATE: Before 33.
NOTE: See 27.

33.   Grant, release, and quitclaim, by Walter de Thowethorp' son of Richard de Streneshale the chaplain, validated by his seal, to God and blessed Peter of the church of York and the vicars serving God there of 2 bovates of land in Grymestona next to Maltona with toft and croft in the same place, which Walter once held from the vicars and which the vicars have from the gift and feoffment of Richard son of Walter de Grymestona; to be held in pure alms with the toft and croft and all the pasture of 3 bovates of land in the same vill. Neither Walter nor his heirs nor anyone on their behalf may claim or sell the property. Roger Grimet released (*remisit*) the land to Walter before the king's itinerant justices at York, as is more fully contained in a cirograph made in their presence. For this grant, confirmation, and quitclaim the vicars have given Walter 56 marks [£38 6s. 8d.] of sterling in his great need (*in mea magna necessitate*).

Witnesses: dom. John de Vescy baron, dom. William de Vescy his brother knight, dom. William le Latimer then sheriff of York, Roger Grimet de Grimestona, Henry le mercer de Gartona dwelling in Grimestona, Walter Wacelyne de Brideshal', Reynold Luvel de Langtona, and others.

Dated in the month of September 1266.

SOURCE: VC 3/Vv 32 (209 mm. × 193 mm.)
ENDORSEMENT: *Carta de terre de Grimeston iuxta Malton; An° domini m[l] ducentisimo sexagesimo sexto.*
SEAL: slit.

NOTE: See **27**.

34. Release and quitclaim by Peter de Brus to the vicars of the church of blessed Peter of York, out of charity (*caritatis intuitu*) and for the soul of mag. Roger Pepin once subdean of the church of York, of the 2 bovates of land and one messuage in Grimeston' next to Seterington', which the vicars have of the gift of Walter de Touthorp; to be held in pure and perpetual alms and free of all secular service and suit at his [Brus's] court. Seal.
Witnesses: dom. W. de Rotherfeld dean of the church of York, dom. Stephen de Suttona, and mag. Thomas Passeleue, canons of the same church, *dominis* John de Oketona, John de Raygate, and Geoffrey Agelun, knights, Geoffrey de Menetorp', Henry de Garton, and others.   [1269 × 1272]

SOURCE: VC 3/3/2 (182 mm. × 104 mm.)
ENDORSEMENT: *Grimston.*
SEAL: slit.

DATE: After Thomas Passelew was collated to his canonry on 5 December 1269 and before his elevation to the archdeaconry of Richmond by 23 July 1272. Peter de Brus died in 1272 (*EYC* ii, p. 15).
NOTE: See **27**. Roger Pepin died in 1266.

35. Release and quitclaim by Walter de Grimeston' son of Alan de Watton', corroborated by the impression of his seal, to God, the church of blessed Peter of York, and Richard son of Stephen, warden of the house of vicars of the cathedral church of blessed Peter of York, and the vicars of the church and their successors of 2 bovates of land with toft and croft in Haclyngrimton' next to Seterington, which the vicars have of the gift of Richard son of Walter de Grimeston'; Walter impleaded Richard [son of Stephen] and the vicars concerning the bovates of land with toft and croft by writ of mort d'ancestor before Geoffrey Aguylum and Alan de Walckingham, justices [on eyre]. [Walter quitclaims] all the right he has in the bovates of land with toft and croft to the vicars for them to hold in free alms, together with the pasture of 3 bovates of land in the same vill with all easements in waters, ways, paths, open country (*planis*), and in all liberties and free customs appertaining to the 2 bovates with toft and croft in and outside the vill, according to the charter which the vicars have from Richard son of Walter de Grimeston'. Neither Walter nor his heirs may claim or sell the property. Warranty. Seal.
Witnesses: dom. Geoffrey Aguyllum and Adam de Walclyngham, king's justices, mag. Thomas de Corebryg' chancellor of York, mag. Thomas de Grimeston' archdeacon of Clyveland', mag. Thomas de Hedon' canon of the cathedral church of York, *dominis* William Burdon' and William de Belkesthorp', knights, Baldwin de Schipton, Roger de Hewurth, William Sklethe de Suarrum, Roger le Spenseyr de Langton', Henry de Wythton' of the same place, Thomas le Iuuen of the same place, and many others.   [1281 × 1286–89]

SOURCE: VC 3/Vv 29 (243 mm. × 134 mm.)

ENDORSEMENT: *Quietaclamacio de terra de Grimeston'*; *Walterus de [Grime]ston dedit custodem [vicariorum]*. (The medieval text is obscured by 19th-cent. labels.)

SEAL: tag.

DATE: When Thomas de Corbridge was chancellor and Thomas de Grimston was archdeacon of Cleveland.

NOTE: See 27.

36.   Indenture witnessing that Richard Ulskelfe, warden of the house of vicars in the choir of the cathedral church of blessed Peter of York, with the assent and consent of all the vicars, has granted and demised at farm to John Geffeson de Northgrymston those 2 bovates of land with one toft and croft in the vill and territory of Northgrymston' iuxta Setryngton' lately held by the widow of Nicholas Wetewang for the term of her life; to be held for 20 years from the day of the making of this indenture; paying to Richard and the vicars 15s. a year at Pentecost and Martinmas in equal portions. If the farm is in arrears 40 days after either of the feasts, then the vicars may distrain the 2 bovates with toft and croft and take distress and retain the land until the farm and arrears have been fully paid. Geffeson may build a new kiln (*kilne*) and shall maintain (*reparabit, sustentabit, et supportabit*) the toft with the kiln (*le kylne*) at his own costs and expenses during the term of the lease. Warranty. Seal.

York, on the feast of St. Martin in winter 7 Henry V [11 November 1419].

SOURCE: VC 1/1, p. 52 (ink pagination).

NOTE: See 27.

HUNTINGTON

(parish in Bulmer wapentake NR)

37.   Grant by Geoffrey de Clifford, with the advice of his friends and the consent of his heir William, to Nicholas the parson of the church of Huntington and his chosen heirs of a toft and croft in Huntington which John held of Geoffrey; paying Geoffrey and his heirs 12d. a year.   [early 13th century]

Omnibus sancte matris ecclesie filiis Galfridus de Cliffordia salutem. Noverit universitas vestra me consilio amicorum meorum et consensu Willelmi heredis mei dedisse et concessisse et hac presenti carta mea confirmasse Nicol' persone ecclesie de Huntintona et illis quos sibi elegerit heredes unum toftum et croftum in Huntint' pro servicio suo illos scilicet quos Johannes tenuit de me tenendos illi et ipsis quos sibi heredes elegerit de me et heredibus meis honorifice, libere, et quiete; reddendo mihi et heredibus meis tamen duodecim denarios per annum pro omni servicio videlicet sex denarios ad Pasca et sex ad festum sancti Michaelis. Hiis testibus Adam de Brideshale domino meo, Willelmo, Gileberto, fratribus suis, Willelmo decano de Tiuerintona, Ivone, Gileberto, fratribus meis, Willelmo Aguillum, et Ingeramno et Amalrico, fratribus suis, Simone filio Gileberti fratris mei, Gileberto de Torinni, Roberto de Sigillo et Simone filio suo, Arundello, Alexandro succentore, Willelmo de Huntint', Willelmo Morel, Roberto de sancto Salvatore, Petro, capellanis, Waltero clerico, Nicol' de Buggetorp, et multis aliis.

SOURCE: VC 3/Vv 36 (164 mm. × 84 mm.)

ENDORSEMENT: *Galfridus de Cliffordia dedisse Niclo' parsone ecclesie de Huntyngton'*; *G' de Clifford*.

SEAL: round (30 mm. dia.), plain, impression of a large bird, legend.

DATE: Before **38**.

NOTE: Most of the Huntington charters (**37–57**) concern 3 tofts and crofts and a bovate of land granted in 1497 by Thomas Wandesford of York to Richard Godson, a clerk acting on behalf of his fellow vicars (**51, 55**). Other Huntington charters (**58–61**) relate to further land which the vicars also acquired from Thomas Wandesford.

Of the first group seven charters describe the earlier history of a toft and croft which lay between the village street and the river Foss (**37–46**), and three charters the earlier history of a toft and croft which lay between the street and a ditch called the Felddyke (**47–49**).

The earliest is the grant by Geoffrey de Clifford to Nicholas, the parson [i.e. rector] of Huntington church (**37**), who in turn granted the land to Peter the chaplain (**38**). The toft which Nicholas had once held was included in the grant of 2 bovates of land with a toft by William son of Ives de Johnby to Matthew the nephew of Matthew the clerk (**39**). One of the bovates was presumably that given by Matthew to his daughter Emma as her marriage portion; Emma as a widow later quitclaimed the land in favour of her brother Simon and his wife Edusa (**40**). Simon's son was probably the Robert son of Simon de Huntington who in 1291 granted 2 bovates and 2 tofts in Huntington to his intended wife Cecily for life; the bovates were described as lying on the east side of the Foss (**41**). In 1320 Robert granted to his daughter Alice a messuage which lay between the village street and the Foss and was bounded on another side by the lane leading to Huntington church (**42**), a description that fits one of the tofts and crofts granted by Wandesford in 1497 (**50**). In 1321 Robert granted the reversion of Alice's land (should she die without heirs) to his son Thomas and Thomas's wife Emma, and by the same grant also gave to Thomas and Emma his chief messuage in Huntington and 2 bovates, all lying on the west side of the Foss, and 3 tofts and a bovate on the east side of the river (**43**). It was the land on the west side that Thomas in 1331 charged with a rent of 8*s*. a year, payable to William de Huntington, a York apothecary, and secured by a bond of £5 (**44**); the bond was raised to £10 in 1347 (**45**). No further charters can be connected with the bovates on the west side of the Foss, but by 1366 the messuage granted in **42** was held by John de Rawcliffe (**46**), whose wife Margaret may have been Thomas's daughter.

In the second group of charters (**47–49**) the earliest is the grant of a toft and croft by a vicar choral, John de Alkborough, to Thomas de Cawton (**47**). The description of the property as lying between the village street and a ditch fits that of one of the tofts and crofts granted in 1497 (**50**). In 1362 Thomas's widow Alice quitclaimed the property to John de Rawcliffe (**48**), who in 1363 acquired an adjoining toft (**49**).

Rawcliffe's heir was his daughter Alice, whose grandson Thomas Wandesford in 1497 granted 3 tofts and crofts to Richard Godson (**51**). A bond to secure the grant was made at the same time (**52**) and a final concord in 1498 (**53–4**). In 1505 Godson transferred the property to a group of vicars choral (**55**).

38. Grant by Nicholas rector of the church of Huntington to his kinsman Peter the chaplain and his heirs of his toft and croft in the vill of Huntington which he holds of Geoffrey de Clifford; paying Geoffrey and his heirs 12*d.* a year.   [1199 × 1216]

Omnibus has literas visuris vel audituris Nicol' rector ecclesie de Huntingt' salutem in Domino. Noverit universitas vestra me dedisse et concessisse et hac presenti carta confirmasse Petro capellano consanguineo meo toftum unum et croftum in villa de Huntingt' quos teneo de domino G. de Clifford', tenendos sibi et heredibus suis de G. de Cliffordia vel illis quos sibi heredes elegerit; reddendo annuatim predicto G. vel heredibus suis tamen duodecim denarios pro omni servicio et exactione. Hiis testibus H. thesaurario Ebor', Anketillo de capella, Matheo clerico, A., Jordan, Waltero Jord', Juliano, Ricardo, servientibus domini thesaurarii, Matheo nepote Mathei clerici, Astino, Waltero, Willelmo de Bolton', et pluribus aliis.

SOURCE: VC 3/Vv 37 (130 mm. × 55 mm.)
ENDORSEMENT: *Nicol' rector ecclesie de Huntyngton' dedisse Petro capellano consanguineo meo.*
SEAL: remains of wax bound in cloth.

DATE: When Hamo was treasurer of York; and probably before **39.**
NOTE: See **37.**

39. Grant by William son of Ives de Johnby to Matthew the nephew of Matthew the clerk and his heirs, for his homage and service, of 2 bovates of land in Huntington with a toft, namely those which Gilbert once held, and of another toft beyond the ditch, which Nicholas once the parson of the church of Huntington held; paying William and his heirs 5*s.* a year, half at Pentecost and half at Martinmas, and doing the forensic service due from the 2 bovates, where 14 carucates make one knight's fee.
[1199 × 1214]

Universis sancte matris ecclesie filiis hanc cartam visuris vel audituris Willelmus filius Ivonis de Iohanneb' salutem in Domino. Noverit universitas vestra me dedisse et concessisse et hac presenti carta mea confirmasse Matheo nepoti Mathei clerici et heredibus suis pro homagio et servicio suo duas bovatas terre in Huntington' cum uno tofto, illas scilicet quas Gilebertus quondam tenuit, et unum alium toftum super fossam quod Nicol' quondam persona ecclesie de Huntingt' tenuit, tenendum sibi et heredibus suis de me et heredibus meis in feodo et hereditate, libere, et quiete, in bosco, in plano, in viis, in aquis, in moris, et in pasturis, et in omnibus aliis aisiamentis predictis bovatis terre et predictis toftis pertinentibus; reddendo mihi et heredibus meis quinque solidos annuatim ad duos terminos, medietatam ad Pentec' et medietatem ad festum sancti Martini, pro omni servicio et exactione; faciendo forinsecum servicium quantum pertinet ad predictas duas bovatas terre unde quatuordecim carucate terre faciunt feodum unius militis. Ego etiam et heredes mei warantizabimus prefatas bovatas terre cum duobus predictis toftis predicto Matheo et heredibus suis contra omnes homines inperpetuum. Et ne ista mea donatio et concessio de cetero possit infirmari, sigilli mei appositione presentem paginam corroboravi. Hiis testibus Simone decano Ebor', H. thesaurio, Rad' rectore hospitalis sancti Petri Ebor', Johanne Romano, magistro Waltero rectore hospitalis Ierulimitani in Ebor' Syria, Fulcone de Ruhford, Adam de Multorp, Galfrido de Ecton', Willelmo de Clifford', magistro Martino, Philippo de Cop'll'a, Alano, Jordano, Waltero fratre eius, Juliano, Ricardo de Alneburg', Herberto de Huntingt', Petro capellano, Rannulfo filio Willelmi de Johannebi, Matheo clerico, Waltero nepote eius, Hamone, Waltero, clericis, Johanne de Esiguald, Anketino, et multis aliis.

SOURCE: VC 3/Vv 41 (240 mm. × 72 mm.)
ENDORSEMENT: *Evidenc' de Huntyngton' iuxta Ebor' duas bovatas terre.*
SEAL: tag.

DATE: When Simon de Apulia was dean of York and Hamo was treasurer.
NOTE: See **37**.

40.   Release and quitclaim by Emma widow (*relicta*) of Walter le frere de Untingth-ona, in her widowhood and lawful power, to her brother Simon and his wife Edusa and their heirs or assigns of any right or claim she has by reason of her free dowry (*ratione liberi maritagii mei*) in that bovate of land with toft and croft in the vill and territory of Untingthon, which her father Matthew gave to her husband Walter le frere in free dowry. Emma has also sworn and declared (*iuravi etiam et affidavi*) for herself and her heirs that they will never move a plea, device, trick, or suit (*placitum, artem, nec ingenium vel querelam*) against Simon and Edusa and their heirs or assigns by which they could dispossess or disturb them. [Emma has done this] for a sum of money which Simon gave her in her necessity. Seal.
Witnesses: John de Kirkeby, Thomas de Johanby, Nicholas Bret, Matthew de Sigillo, ... son of Thomas, William his brother, Stephen de Holdernes clerk, Richard Pruddum, Henry de Arne'hale, Walter son of Peter, Henry Saubree, and others.

[earlier 13th century]

SOURCE: VC 3/Vv 38 (195 mm. × 91 mm.)
ENDORSEMENT: *Emma relicta Walteri le frere confirmasse Simon' fratri meo et Educe uxori sue;*
   evidenc' de una bovata terre cum uno tofto et uno crofto in Huntyngton.
SEAL: remains of wax wrapped in cloth.

DATE:
NOTE: See **37**.

41.   1291 on the feast of the nativity of St. John the Baptist [24 June]. Agreement, in the form of a cirograph, between Robert son of Simon de Huntingtona and Cecily daughter of John son of Ralph de Stoketon. Robert has granted and confirmed to Cecily 2 tofts and crofts and 2 bovates of land in the vill and territory of Huntingtona; the tofts lie at the south end of the vill between the toft of William once the servant . . . (? *sp'uer*) and that of Thomas Prudome, and the 2 bovates lie on the east side of the water of Fosse. Cecily is to hold the land for her life, and after her death it is to revert to Robert and his heirs. Cecily's heirs or assigns may not sell, demand, or hold (*habere*) the land. That part of the cirograph held by Cecily is sealed with Robert's seal and that part held by Robert with Cecily's seal.
Witnesses: mag. William de Pothom then rector of the church of Huntington', Thomas de Joneby, Thomas de Aldwerk, Thomas Prudome, Nicholas de Arnale, mag. William de Touthorp, John Torny, Henry son of Nicholas de Everscewike, John son of Ralph de Stoketon', John his son, Robert the clerk, and others.
If Cecily has made a marriage with anyone else (*cum aliquo alio contraxerit*), there having been (*fiat*) a divorce between her and Robert, she shall have nothing from the said tenements, and these charters [i.e. the two parts of the cirograph] shall then be void (*iste carte pro nichilo habeantur ex tunc*).

SOURCE: VC 3/Vv 39 (182 mm. × 134 mm.). Indented at top, CIROGRAFFATUM.
ENDORSEMENT: *Duas bovatas terre ex parte orientali de Fosse.*
SEAL: slit.

NOTE: See **37**.

42.   Grant by Robert son of Simon de Huntyngton' next to York to his daughter
Alice of his messuage in Huntyngton', lying in breadth between the lane which leads
to the church of Huntyngton' and the messuage which Henry de Etton' once held,
and in length from the royal street in Huntyngton' in front to the water of Fosse
behind. Robert has also granted to Alice 4 a. of arable land in the territory of
Huntyngton', which he bought from John Prudomme. The lands and tenements are
to be held of the chief lord of the fee by Alice and the legitimate heirs of her body,
paying Robert and his heirs a rose at the time of roses if asked for. If Alice dies
without a legitimate heir, all the lands and tenements shall revert entirely to Robert
and his rightful heirs. Warranty. Seal.
Witnesses: William Gra, Bartholomew Bacoun, Thomas de Helperby, Alan de
Joneby, Nicholas de Arnale, Peter de Arnale, Nicholas Prudomme, Richard son of
Nicholas son of Benet, Nicholas son of William, Walter son of Ralph de Touthorp',
William de Appelby clerk, and others.
Huntyngton', 7 May 1320.

SOURCE: VC 3/Vv 40 (267 mm. × 187 mm.)
ENDORSEMENT: *Carta Roberti filii Simonis facta Alicie filie eius; Robertus filius Symonis de*
     Huntyngton pro uno domo iuxta venellam que ducat ad ecclesiam; in Huntyngton'.
SEAL: vesica (40 mm. × 26 mm.), red, impression of feathers forming a star, legend
★S. ROBERTI FIL' SIMONIS.

NOTE: See **37**.

43.   Grant by Robert son of Simon de Huntyngton' next to York to his son Thomas
and Thomas's wife Emma, daughter of Robert de Bouthum, of his chief messuage in
Huntington' on the west side of the water of Fosse, and of 2 bovates of land on the
same side of the water; the messuage lies in breadth between the churchyard of the
church of All Saints at Huntyngton' and the land of the rector of the said church on
the one side and the land of Richard de Sigillo on the other, and in length from the
water of Fosse in front to the royal street behind; the 2 bovates of land lie [dispersed]
in the field (*per totum campum*) between the land of Bartholomew Bacoun and that of
Richard de Sigillo. Robert has also given Thomas and Emma 3 tofts and one bovate
of land in Huntyngton' on the east side of the water of Fosse. The lands and
tenements are to be held of the chief lords of the fee by Thomas and Emma and the
legitimate heirs of their bodies. Robert has also granted that one toft, one croft, and
one bovate of land in Huntyngton', which Richard de Barton' and his wife Alice,
Robert's daughter, hold of Robert for themselves and the legitimate heirs of their
bodies, and that 4 a. of land which Richard and Alice hold of Robert for the term of
Alice's life shall pass to Thomas, Emma, and their legitimate heirs after the deaths of
Richard, Alice, and their legitimate heirs. Warranty. If Thomas and Emma die
without legitimate heirs, all the lands and tenements shall revert entirely to Robert
and his heirs. Seal.

Witnesses: Bartholomew Bacoun, William Gra, John le stabeler, Robert son of Roger de Thornton', Patrick de Barton', Richard Bernard, Richard de Huntyngton', Thomas de Helperby, Nicholas de Arnale, Peter de Arnale, Nicholas Prudomme, Walter son of Ralph de Touthorp', William de Appelby clerk, and others.
Huntyngton, 5 July 1321, 14 Edward II.

SOURCE: VC 3/Vv 42 (234 mm. × 224 mm.)
ENDORSEMENT: *Carta feofamentis*; *Evidencia de duobus bovatis terre in campo de Huntyngton iuxta Ebor'*; *ex parte occedent' de Fosse.*
SEAL: tag.

NOTE: See **37**.

44. Indenture witnessing that since Thomas son of Robert son of Simon de Huntyngton next to York, living in Stoketon, is bound to William de Huntyngton apothecary of York for 100s. of silver, payable at Martinmas 1331, William has granted that if he, his heirs, or assigns shall receive 8s. a year from all of Thomas's lands and tenements in the vill and territory of Huntyngton on the west side of the water of Fosse for 20 years from the date of this indenture, as is more fully contained in indentures made between the said parties concerning the 8s., then the bond for 100s. shall be void. If William, his heirs, or assigns are dishonestly deprived (*maliciose eiectus seu eiecti fuerint*) of the 8s. during the term of 20 years by Thomas or his heirs or anyone else, then William, his heirs, or assigns may claim (*petere*) the debt of 100s. and use the bond with all right of the law. The parts of this cirograph are sealed alternately with their seals.
Witnesses: Richard de Huntynton', Richard Brett', Nicholas Broun, Thomas de Allerton', Richard the cook (*koco*), Laurence son of William, William de Appelby, and others.
York, 10 March 1330, 5 Edward III [1330/1].

SOURCE: VC 3/Vv 43 (248 mm. × 103 mm.). Indented at top, CIROGRAF'.
ENDORSEMENT: illegible.
SEAL: remains of red wax.

NOTE: See **37**. Thomas son of Robert and William de Huntington were probably cousins: for William's family see *Chs. Vicars Choral*, i, nos. 117 note, 120.

45. Indenture witnessing that since Thomas son of Robert son of Simon de Huntington next to York, living in Stockton, and his daughter Margaret are bound by a bond to William de Huntington' of York apothecary for £10 of good and legal sterling, payable at the feast of the purification of the blessed Virgin Mary [2 February] next after the making of the bond, William de Huntington' has granted that if he, his heirs, or assigns fully receive, from Martinmas 1347 to the end of 24 years, a rent of 8s. a year from all of Thomas's lands and tenements in the vill and territory of Huntington' on the west side of the water of Fosse, according to the form of an indenture made between Thomas and William, [then] the bond shall be void.
York, Friday after the feast of St. Valentine 1346, 21 Edward III [16 February 1346/7].

SOURCE: VC 3/Vv 44a (278 mm. × 107 mm.). Indented at top, CYRO . . .
ENDORSEMENT: none medieval.

SEAL: traces of wax on a cue.

NOTE: See **37**.

46. Release and quitclaim by Stephen Leper vicar of the church of Bubwith for himself and his heirs to John de Rouclif clerk and his wife Margaret of a tenement in the vill of Huntyngton' next to York, lying in breadth between the lane which leads to the church of Huntyngton' and the land of John de Snawshill', and in length from the royal street in Huntyngton' in front to the water of Fosse behind. Warranty. Seal. Witnesses: Hugh atte Water, John de Sadyngton, Thomas Lovell' de Skelton', George de Coupemanthorp', John del Strinsall', Richard del See, Thomas de Siggeston', and others.
Huntyngton', 13 February 1365, 40 Edward III [1366].

SOURCE: VC 3/Vv 46 (232 mm. × 98 mm.)
ENDORSEMENT: *pro uno tofto iuxta le layne in Huntyngton.*
SEAL: tag.

NOTE: See **37**.

47. Grant by John de Alkebarow chaplain, vicar of the cathedral church of blessed Peter of York, to Thomas de Caulton', citizen and butcher of York, of one toft in Huntyngton' next to York which John recently had of the gift and feoffment of Richard de Mar' cook de Strensale and his wife Emma, lying in breadth between the messuage once of Richard Dunpole de Barton' and land once of John de Snaweshill', and extending in length from the royal street in Huntyngton' in front to a certain ditch (*fossatum*) behind; paying 2s. of sterling a year to Margaret, daughter of Thomas son of Robert son of Simon de Stocton', her heirs, and assigns at Martinmas and Pentecost in equal portions. Warranty. Seal.
Witnesses: Hamo de Hessay, William de Huntyngton', Thomas Lovel de Skelton', Hugh atte Water, John de Sadyngton', Henry de Coupmanthorp' the elder, John Godbarne de Haxeby, John de Staunton' clerk, and others.
Huntyngton', 2 September 35 Edward III [1361].

SOURCE: VC 3/Vv 44b (284 mm. × 162 mm.)
ENDORSEMENT: *Johannes Alkebarow capellanus dedi Thome Caulton; Huntyngton.*
SEAL: round (14 mm. dia.), red, impression of two hands holding a ball, legend.

NOTE: See **37**.

48. Release and quitclaim by Alice widow of Thomas de Calton' of York for herself and her heirs to mag. John de Rouclif' clerk of a toft in the vill of Huntyngton' which she has of the gift of John de Alkebarowe chaplain and which Richard Coke formerly held, lying in breadth between the toft of Richard Dunpole and that lately of John de Snawsill', and in length from the royal street in front to a certain ditch (*fossatum*) behind. Seal.
Witnesses: Robert de Huntyngton', Hugh Attewat', Thomas Lovell', John de Sadyngton', John de Snawsill', William Sampsoun, William Carter, and others.
York, 28 January 1361, 35 Edward III [1361/2].

SOURCE: VC 3/Vv 45 (242 mm. × 115 mm.)

ENDORSEMENT: *uxor Thome Caulton remisi Johanni Roucliff clerico heredibus et assingnatis suis*; *Huntyngton*.

SEAL: round (22 mm. dia.), red, impression of a shield, legend.

NOTE: See **37**.

49. Grant by Nicholas Jeff' de Huntyngton' next to York to John de Rouclyff' clerk of one toft in Huntyngton', lying in breadth between John's land and that once of John Wyseman, and in length from the royal street in Huntyngton' in front to le Felddyk' behind; to be held by John, his heirs, and assigns of the chief lords of the fee for the customary service. Warranty. Seal.

Witnesses: dom. Brian de Rouclyff' knight, Thomas Lovell' de Skelton', Hugh atte Watre, William Latymer de Tyveryngton', John de Sadyngton', John Godebarn', Robert de Huntyngton', Thomas Parchemyner, and others.

Huntyngton next to York, Friday after the feast of St. Mark the evangelist [28 April] 1363.

SOURCE: VC 3/Vv 47a (286 mm. × 122 mm.)

ENDORSEMENT: *Nicholaus Jeff' de Huntyngton' dedi Johanni de Rouclyff; pro uno tofto quondam Johannis Rouclyffe.*

SEAL: remains of red wax wrapped up in cloth.

NOTE: See **37**.

50. Indenture made on 20 May 3 Henry VII [1488] witnessing that Thomas Wandesford of York gentleman (*gentilman*) has demised at farm to Robert Suthewik' de Huntyngton husbandman a messuage and a barn (*oreum*) with an adjoining garden and a bovate of land in the vill and territory of Huntyngton; the messuage lies between the land of William Snawsell' alderman and citizen of York on the north side and that of William Towthorp chaplain on the south side; Robert is to hold the property from next Pentecost up to the end . . .[1] years; paying [Thomas and his heirs and] assigns 14s. of legal English money a year, at [Martinmas] and Pentecost in equal portions. Distraint. Robert shall maintain the messuage and barn during the term at his own expense. Seal.

Witnesses: John (? Ch)ert, John Lo[n]esdale, Thomas Lelegrave, and others.

SOURCE: VC 3/Vv 52a (288 mm. × 188 mm.). Indented at top.

ENDORSEMENT: *Una indentura Thome Wandesford pro una bovata terre quod d . . . ad firmam . . .*

SEAL: round (12 mm. dia.), red. impression of 'T' with a crown above.

[1] Hole in MS.; one word missing.

NOTE: See **37**.

51. Grant by Thomas Wandesford of York gentleman (*generosus*), son and heir of Richard Wandesford the son and heir of William Wandesford and his [Richard's] wife Alice, daughter and heir of John Roclyff, to Richard Godson de York clerk, his heirs, and assigns of 3 tofts and 3 crofts and a bovate of land in the vill and territory of Huntyngton next to York; one of the tofts with a croft lies in breadth between the land of mag. John Haryngton on the south side and that of Seth Snawsell esquire

(*armigeri*) on the north side, and in length from the royal street in Huntyngton in front to the field of Huntyngton behind, and is now in the holding of Robert Suthewyk; another toft with a croft lies in breadth between the land of John Gower knight on the east side and that of William Gascoign knight on the south [*sic*] side, and in length from the royal street in Huntyngton in front to le Felddyke behind, and is now in the holding of John Awger; the third toft with a croft lies in breadth between the lane which leads to the church of Huntyngton on one side and the land of Seth Snawsell' on the other side, and in length from the royal street in Huntyngton in front to the water of Fosse behind, and is now in the tenure of William Wylton; the bovate of land lies in the fields of Huntyngton and is now in the holding of Robert Suthewyk. Warranty. Thomas has made Laurence Herryson and Peter Symson of York, chaplains, his attorneys in taking seisin of the tofts, crofts, and bovate. Seal.
Witnesses: William Wylson, John Awger, Robert Suthewyk, John Acastr' de Huntyngton, husbandmen (*husbondmen*), William Lasynby of the same place parish clerk (*parisshclerk*), and others.
Huntyngton, 27 November 13 Henry VII [1497]

SOURCE: VC 3/Vv 53a (344 mm. × 192 mm.)
ENDORSEMENT: *Evidenc' Thome Wandesford' heredis Ricardi Wandisford'.*
SEAL: round (10 mm. dia.), red, impression.

NOTE: See **37**. Herryson was the vicars' warden and Symson also a vicar choral.

52. Obligation whereby Thomas Wandesford of York gentleman (*generosus*) is bound to Richard Godson of York clerk for £40, payable to Richard, his heirs, or assigns next Christmas. Seal. Dated 27 November 13 Henry VII [1497].
The condition of the bond is that Richard Godson, his heirs, and assigns shall peacefully hold and enjoy 3 tofts, 3 crofts, and a bovate of land lying in the vill and territory of Huntyngton next to York, according to a feoffment made by Thomas to Robert.

SOURCE: VC 3/Vv 53b (329 mm. × 146 mm.)
ENDORSEMENT: *Obligacio Thome Wandesford domino Ricardo Godson.*
SEAL: traces of wax on tag.

NOTE: See **37**.

53. Final concord made in the king's court at Westminster at Easter 13 Henry VII [1498] between Richard Godson, plaintiff, and Thomas and Margaret Wandesford, deforciants, concerning 3 messuages, 13 a. of land, and 2 a. of meadow with pasture in Huntyngton, which Thomas and Margaret have released and quitclaimed to Godson for 20 marks [£13 6s. 8d.] of silver.

SOURCE: VC 3/Vv 53c (380 mm. × 96 mm.)
ENDORSEMENT: *Deliberatur per proclamacionem secundum formam statuti.*

NOTE: See **37**.

54. Counterpart of **53**.

SOURCE: VC 3/Vv 53d.
ENDORSEMENT: *Ebor'* . . . *Ricardus Godson.*

55.   Grant by Richard Godson of York clerk to Peter Symson, Thomas Uttersall',
Roger Brampton, Thomas Harpham, Laurence Herryson, John Nosterfeld, and John
Ussher, chaplains, their heirs, and assigns of 3 tofts and 3 crofts and a bovate of land
lying in the vill and territory of Huntyngton next to York; Richard has the property
of the gift and feoffment of Thomas Wandesford of York gentleman (*generosi*).
Warranty. Seal.
Witnesses: Thomas Newark, Thomas Holme, esquires (*armigeris*), William Chawm-
bre, William Wright the elder of Huntyngton, husbandmen (*husbondmen*), William
Lasynby of the same place parish clerk (*parysshclerk*).
Huntyngton, 29 January 20 Henry VII [1504/5].

SOURCE: VC 3/Vv 53e (279 mm. × 162 mm.)
ENDORSEMENT: *Evidenc' de Huntyngton iuxta Ebor' ex dono domini Ricardi Godson pro*
   tribus toftis et tribus croftis cum una bovata terre arrablis; nuper Thomas Wandesford.
SEAL: round (15 mm. dia.), red, impression.

NOTE: See 37. All the grantees were vicars choral.

56.   Final concord made in the king's court at Westminster on the morrow of the
purification of the blessed Mary 8 Henry VII [3 February 1492/3] before Thomas
Bryan, Roger Touneshend, William Banners, and John Vavasour, justices, and others
of the king's faithful men, between Laurence Herryson clerk, Peter Symson clerk,
William Cleveland clerk, and John Louunesdale clerk, plaintiffs, and Thomas
Wandesford and his wife Margaret, deforciants, of a messuage, 31 a. of land, and 1
a. of meadow with pasture in Huntyngton in the forest of Galtres, concerning which a
plea was heard between the parties, namely that Thomas and Margaret recognised that
the said tenements are to be of Laurence etc. and released and quitclaimed them
against John abbot of St. Peter, Westminster. For this agreement Laurence etc. gave
Thomas and Margaret £20 of sterling.

SOURCE: VC 3/Vv 52b (422 mm. × 113 mm.)
ENDORSEMENT: *Deliberatio per proclamationem secundum formam statuti.*

NOTE: See 37. The plaintiffs were all vicars choral. The land probably represents the
   one-third interest which Margaret had in Thomas's land.

57.   Draft agreement for a lease of 3 years by the subchanter of the vicars of York
with the consent of his brethren to Wilfrid Gra . . . of Huntyngton gentleman of 2
oxgangs of land in Huntington field on the west side of the Fosse; paying 20s. a year
29 August 14 Henry VIII [1522].

SOURCE: VC 3/4/Hun/8 (224 mm. × 252 mm.; document is damaged and the text
   very faint)
ENDORSEMENT: none.

NOTE: See 37.

58.   Demise and grant, in the form of an indenture, by Robert Bamburgh' of Scardeburgh' and William Scharpylles, the heirs of Robert Huntyngton', to the warden of the college of vicars in the cathedral church of blessed Peter of York and the college of vicars of a garden or place of land in Huntyngton', lying in breadth between the land of John Algar and that of Henry Preston', and in length from the royal street in front to John's land behind; the warden and vicars are to hold the land of the chief lords of the fee from the day of the making of the [indenture] to the end of 200 years; paying Robert and William and their heirs and assigns 2s. of silver a year, at Pentecost and Martinmas in equal portions. Distraint. Warranty. Seal.
Witnesses: William Darell', John Algare, William Kylburn', and others.
Huntyngton', 21 January 9 Henry VI [1430/1].

SOURCE: VC 3/Vv 48 (292 mm. × 144 mm.). Indented at top.
ENDORSEMENT: *de una placia in Hunti[n]gton; pro una placea in Huntyngton.*
SEAL: (left) oblong (16 mm. × 10 mm.), red, impression of a tree; (right) oblong (25 mm. × 20 mm.), red, impression of a prancing lion facing left, in a lozenge border.

NOTE: The vicars first acquired land in Huntington (besides the glebe of their appropriated church) in 1431, when they were leased a garden for 200 years (**58**). In 1452 they acquired a 30-year lease of what was probably adjoining land, consisting of a close and garden, together with 4 selions of new arable (**59**). That lease was made by Joan, the widow of Richard Wandesford (together with her second husband), and was renewed by her son Thomas in 1492 (**61**).

59.   Indenture witnessing that Richard Duffeld of York merchant and his wife Joan, lately wife of Richard Wandesford of York, have demised at farm to John Gauke, warden of the college of vicars in the choir of the cathedral church of York, and all the vicars of the college a close with adjoining garden and 4 selions of land lying newly-broken (*frisc'*) in the fields of Huntyngton next to York; the close and garden lie between the land of John Bolton and that of the warden and vicars, and the 4 selions lie together between John Bolton's land on the north and that of the vicars on the south, abutting on the royal way (*viam*) which leads to York in front and on the vicars' close and barn (*orreum*) and then to the water of Fosse behind; the warden and vicars are to hold the property from the feast of the annunciation of the blessed Virgin Mary (25 March) next up to the end of 30 years, paying Richard and Joan or their heirs and assigns 6s. 8d. of sterling a year, at Michaelmas and Easter in equal portions. If the farm is not paid in whole or in part within 6 weeks after either term, Richard, Joan, and their heirs may distrain the land; if there is insufficient distress from the land for the farm, then they may re-enter the land and retain it. The warden and vicars shall enclose (*fossabunt*) the close with the garden and shall plant, at their own costs when they first enter it, with a hedge (*whikfall*) of blackthorn and hawthorn, and they shall give up the close properly (*competenter*) enclosed at the end of the term. Warranty. Seal.
York, 7 November 1452, 31 Henry VI.
The warden or vicars and their successors shall not cut down any trees (*vastum seu destructionem in arboribus . . . facient*) growing in the said close with the garden and 4 selions during the said term, namely oak, ash, apple, bullace [i.e. wild plum], and crab apple (*ake, esshe, appiltr', bolestr',* and *crabtr'*).

SOURCE: VC 3/Vv 49 (278 mm. × 165 mm.). Indented at top with letters.
ENDORSEMENT: illegible.

SEAL: slit.

NOTE: See 58.

60. Counterpart of 59.

SOURCE: VC 3/Vv 50 (278 mm. × 138 mm.)

ENDORSEMENT: *Indentur' de clausura cum gardino et iiij^{or}* . . . *iuxta Hontington vic'* . . . *pro* . . . *reddendo* . . . *vj^s viij^d.*

SEAL: two slits, with remains of tag.

61. Indenture made between Thomas Wandesford of York gentleman (*gentilman*) and Laurence Herryson chaplain, warden of the college of vicars in the choir of the cathedral church of blessed Peter of York, and the vicars witnessing that Thomas has demised at farm to Laurence and the vicars a close and 4 selions of land lying in the fields of Huntyngton; the close lies between the land of John Bolton on one side and that of the warden and vicars and Huntyngton churchyard, and the 4 selions lie together between John Bolton's land on the north and the land of the warden and vicars on the south, abutting on the royal way (*viam*) which leads to York before and up to the vicars' close and barn (*orreum*) and then to the water of Fosse behind; Laurence and the vicars are to hold the property for 20 years from next Pentecost; paying Thomas, his heirs, and assigns 6s. 8d. of legal money a year, at Pentecost and Martinmas in equal portions, the first payment beginning next Martinmas. If the rent is not paid in part or in whole at any term, Thomas, his heirs, and assigns may re-enter the land and retain it. Laurence and the vicars shall enclose the close and shall plant at their own costs with a hedge (*whikfall*) of blackthorn and hawthorn, and they shall give up the close properly fenced at the end of the term. Seal.
16 June 7 Henry VII [1492].

SOURCE: VC 3/Vv 51 (293 mm. × 115 mm.)

ENDORSEMENT: *Obligacio Thome Wandesford ex una parte et Laurence Herison [custodis] vicariorum.*

SEAL: fragments of vicars' common seal [1421 matrix] in red wax (for description see *Chs. Vicars Choral*, i, p. xxii).

NOTE: See 58.

62. Notification by the warden of the spiritualities of Huntington that he absolves the executors of the testament of Richard Haxby of Huntington', having heard the account made by them before him at Martinmas 1420 in the chapel within the Bedern of the vicars of the cathedral church of York to the effect that they had faithfully administered the goods of the deceased.

SOURCE: VC 3/Vv 47b (317 mm. × 72 mm.)

ENDORSEMENT: none.

SEAL: remains of red wax on tag.

NOTE: The vicars evidently claimed the proof of wills of Huntington parishioners as the appropriators of the church.

KENNYTHORPE
(in Langton parish, Buckrose wapentake ER)

63. Release by the vicars of the church of York to William son of Robert de Kennetorp for his homage and service of that carucate of land in Kennetorp which Oliver de Buscy gave them in free, pure, and perpetual alms; paying the vicars 5s. a year, half at Martinmas and half at Pentecost.

Witnesses: R. dean of the church of York, G. precentor, W. archdeacon of Noti[n]gham, and mag. J. Romain, mag. Maurice, and mag. Godard the penitentiary, canons of the same church, mag. Nicholas, Richard the marshal (*mariscallo*), Walter of the vestry (*de vestiario*), Stephen the sacrist, Geoffrey de Ottelaye, Simon the tailor (*talliatore*), etc.   [1220 × 1228]

SOURCE: VC 8/Metcalfe notebks., Deeds in extenso, VIa, no. 65.

DATE: When Roger de Insula was dean of York and before John Romeyn became subdean.

KILHAM
(parish in Dickering wapentake ER)

64. Grant by William de Langeton, dean of York, for the salvation of his soul, the soul of Walter le Gray formerly archbishop of York, and the souls of all his benefactors, in free and perpetual alms, to dom. Robert de Fenton', priest celebrating at the altar of St. Stephen in the cathedral church of blessed Peter of York for William's soul and for the souls of his benefactors and all the faithful dead, and to Robert's successors appointed (*assumendis*) by the vicars of the church of York, of land which William bought in the vill and territory of Kyllum, namely: 5 bovates of land, of which 2 lie divided (*per partes*) in the south field and the other 3 divided in the north field, with the toft and croft which William bought in the same vill in Suthgate, and with all that land which William bought in the territory of Kyllum lying on both sides of Rostongate from the vill of Kyllum up to the cross and the way which extends towards Louthorp'; to be held by Robert de Fenton' and his successors celebrating perpetually at the altar of St. Stephen, having been chosen and placed (*eligendis et ponendis*) by the vicars within eight days of a vacancy occurring or by the chapter of blessed Peter of York after eight days; doing the service owed to the chief lords. Warranty. Seal.

Witnesses: mag. Thomas de Grymeston', dom. Henry de Milleford, Henry de Damiet, Nicholas de Crosseby, William de Burton', William Haget, Richard de Barton', Roger de Langeton', Henry Spervero, William Lahman, Stephen de Strenshale, Henry de Camera, dom. Alexander vicar of Kyllum, and others.

[probably 1279]

SOURCE: VC 3/3/4a (248 mm. × 197 mm.)
ENDORSEMENT: (in a 16th-cent. hand) *Lande in Kyllome of the wolde.*
SEAL: slit.

DATE: Probably shortly before Langton's death as dean of York on 15 July 1279: his nephew's confirmation has the same witnesses (65).

NOTE: This charter endowed a chantry at the altar of St. Stephen in York Minster. The chanty priest was collated by the vicars, who administered the endowment.

65.   Grant, in free and perpetual alms, by William de Langeton', nephew and heir of the venerable dom. William de Langetun' formerly dean of York, for the salvation of the souls of William [the dean], Walter le Gray formerly archbishop of York, and all their benefactors, to dom. Robert de Fenton' and his successors of the land which William the dean bought in the vill and territory of Kyllum, described as in 64; conditions as in 64. Warranty. Seal.

Witnesses: as 64 (reading Grimeston' for Grymeston' and Streneshal' for Strenshale).

[probably 1279]

SOURCE: VC 3/3/4b (261 mm. × 185 mm.)
ENDORSEMENT: illegible.
SEAL: slit.

DATE: See 64.
NOTE: See 64.

LINTON
(in Spofforth parish, Upper Claro wapentake WR)

66.   Grant by Robert son of Hugh de Bilton' of Wetherby to Robert de Nichol' burgess of Pontefract', his wife Beatrice, and the legitimate heirs of their bodies of a moiety of 3 a. of land in the field of Lynton' which Robert bought from Thomas son of Robert the chamberlain de Lynton' and of a moiety of 2 a. of land in the field of Suthditton' which he bought from John son of Adam the clerk de Suthditton', together with 3 r. of meadow lying in Melmire which Robert has by the grant of the said John the clerk as appears in the feoffment of Hugh de Bilton'. If Robert and Beatrice die without legitimate heirs, Robert [the grantor] wishes that the moieties shall revert to him and his heirs and assigns. Warranty. Seal.

Witnesses: Alan de Folyfayt, John Fayrfax, Thomas (T)ayas, Roger de Lynton', John de Bolyngbroke, Ellis de Fayrwath', William Scot, William Martel, Niel de Wetherby, Thomas Chamberl[ai]n.

Wetherby, Thursday on the feast of St. Laurence 1 Edward II [10 August 1307]

SOURCE: VC 3/Vv 56 (232 mm. × 134 mm.)
ENDORSEMENT: none.
SEAL: tag.

NOTE: Beatrice was most probably the grantor's daughter. The charter appears to be a stray in the archive, as the vicars are not known to have had property in Linton.

MANFIELD
(parish in Gilling East wapentake NR)

67. Grant, in free alms, by Agnes daughter of Thorphin de Manfield, in her widowhood, to God and the vicars serving God in the church of St. Peter of York of 5 furlongs, 3 tofts, and 2 bovates of land in Manfield; doing the forinsec service which appertains to the 2 bovates in the same fee, where 12 carucates of land make one knight's fee. [1220 × 1228]

Sciant presentes et futuri quod ego Agnes filia Thorphini de Manefeld in viduitate mea concessi et dedi et hac mea presenti carta confirmavi Deo et vicariis in ecclesia sancti Petri apud Ebor' Deo servientibus totam culturam meam apud Grenton' in territorio de Manefeld et totam culturam meam apud Elewaltebrigg' et totam culturam meam apud Spitelflat et totam culturam meam apud Reinaldeflat et totam culturam meam apud Cattemite et toftum Rogeri fabri et toftum Ade filii Acke et toftum Yvonis Rotincrune in eadem villa et duas bovatas terre scilicet unam quam Alanus King tenuit et aliam quam Rogerus filius Ricardi quondam tenuit, cum omnibus pertinenciis et aisiamentis predictis terris pertinentibus infra villam de Manefeld et extra, tenendas illis et eorum successoribus in liberam et puram et perpetuam elemosinam, faciendo tamen forinsecum servicium quantum pertinet ad dictas duas bovatas terre in eodem feudo ubi xii carucate terre faciunt feudum unius militis. Et ego Agnes et heredes mei predictas terras cum pertinenciis Deo et vicariis sancti Petri apud Ebor' et eorum successoribus contra omnes warantizabimus in perpetuum. Hiis testibus magistro Rogero de Insula decano, Johanne Romano, Alano de Manefeld, Willelmo parsona de Manefeld, Willelmo fratre suo, Roberto de Clesebi, Roberto de Hyppleswell', Alano filio Alexandri, Roberto filio Johannis, Willelmo filio Petri, et aliis.

SOURCE: VC 3/Vv 57 (213 mm. × 146 mm.)
ENDORSEMENT: *Carta Agnetis filia Torphini de Manefeld'*; *de multis terris ibidem datis vicariis Ebor'*.
SEAL: slit.

DATE: When Roger de Insula was dean of York and before John Romeyn became subdean.
NOTE: The vicars received no income from Manfield by the the early 14th century (VC 4/1/1), and had presumably either lost the land or exchanged it.

NORTHALLERTON
(parish in Allerton wapentake NR)

68. Grant, in free alms, by Hugh son of Richard de Nordaltona, for the souls of his ancestors and all the faithful departed, to God and the church of blessed Peter of York and the vicars serving God there of 3½ a. in the territory of Nordaltona, namely 1 a. in Rulanddail [lying] from Dikisgate up to Yorkisgate, [a further] 1½ a. in the same place, and 1 a. [lying] from Cleinggate up to the south; holding and having [? all that land] in Hunginildale, lying between the land of the convent of Wattona and that of Robert Wusse.

Witnesses: Roger Thomson chaplain de Nordalt etc.

[probably first half of 13th century]

SOURCE: VC 8/Metcalfe notebks., Deeds in extenso, V, no. 48.

NOTE: The vicars received no income from Northallerton by the early 14th century (VC 4/1/1), and had presumably either lost the land or exchanged it.

GREAT OUSEBURN
(in Claro wapentake WR)

69.   Grant, in free alms, by Richard de Scholes knight, for his soul and the souls of his ancestors and successors, made at the instance of Richard son of Roger succentor of York, to the cathedral's vicars of 2 bovates of land with toft and croft which Richard Anglicus held of Richard [the grantor] in Great Ouseburn, except for ½ a. of land in Flash; the grant is made with all liberties, except in the wood of Great Ouseburn, although reserving free pasture there for the vicars. Warranty.   [1220 × 1228]

Omnibus Christi fidelibus hanc cartam visuris vel audituris Ricardus de Scales miles salutem in Domino. Noveritis me dedisse, concessisse, et hac carta sigillo meo impressa confirmasse ad instanciam et pro procuracionem Ricardi filii Rogeri tunc subcentoris Ebor' ecclesie vicariis dicte ecclesie in puram, liberam, et perpetuam elemosinam illas duas bovatas terre cum tofto et crofto et aliis pertinenciis suis quas Ricardus Angl'ic' de me tenuit in villa de Grant Useburn' excepta una dimidia acra terre in Flasc, habendas et tenendas dictis vicariis in perpetuum libere et quiete et hono[ri]fice[1] pro anima mea et animabus antecessorum et successorum meorum sicut aliqua elemosina melius et liberius haberi potest cum omnibus pertinenciis, aisiamentis, et libertatibus et liberis consuetudinibus suis infra villam et extra sine aliquo retenemento excepto bosco eiusdem ville, salva dictis vicariis libera pastura in eodem bosco. Et ego et heredes mei warantizabimus et defendemus dictis vicariis predictam terram cum pertinenciis sicut liberam, puram, et perpetuam elemosinam contra omnes homines in perpetuum. Hiis testibus R. decano Ebor' ecclesie, G. precentore, magistris G. penitenciario, J. Romano, et Mauricio, eiusdem ecclesie canonicis, Herberto decano de Burcscire, Alano de Kirkeby, Willelmo de D[?isse]ford',[2] Ricardo de Wivelestorp, Johanne Mauleverer, Roberto de Munketon', Johanne de Fuleford, Ricardo dispensatore, et aliis.

SOURCE: VC 3/3/1 (160 mm. × 109 mm.)

ENDORSEMENT: *Carta Ricardi de Scales militis; Useburn'.*

SEAL: evidence lost as foot of document is mostly missing.

[1] MS. rubbed.
[2] Hole in MS.

DATE: When Roger de Insula was dean of York and before John Romeyn became subdean.

NOTE: Richard son of Roger was the succentor of the vicars.

SCARBOROUGH

(parish in Pickering Lythe wapentake NR)

70. Grant by Thomas son of William de Irton' and his wife Agnes, daughter of
William Broun de Scard', to Gilbert de Neusum of Scard' and his wife Margaret,
daughter of Bernard de Hundemanby, of land which was once William Broun's chief
dwelling-house (*capitalis mansio*), in which William died; paying 5s. sterling a year to
the lord of the fee, at Pentecost and Martinmas in equal portions, and [husgable][1] for
the land to the king. Warranty. Seal.
Witnesses: Henry de Roston', Roger le Carect', Reynold le Milner, Alan le Carect',
Henry de Brumpton', John le Nair, Robert de Norfolc', Roger ad Crucem, Robert
son of Nelle, Thomas Folck, William son of Nicholas, and others.
Sunday before the feast of St. Andrew the apostle [28 November] 1294, 23 Edward
son of king Henry.

SOURCE: VC 3/Vv 61 (215 mm. × 101 mm.)
ENDORSEMENT: *Reddit'* . . .
SEALS: (left) vesica (33 mm. × 20 mm.), green, impression of a star of petals, legend
+ S'. AG[NETI]S DE IRTVN; (right) round (22 mm. dia.), green, impression of a
star of petals, legend + S'. TOME D' IRTVZ.

[1] Hole in MS.

NOTE: The vicars held two properties in Scarborough, one in the new town (**70–86**)
and the other just outside it (**88**).
   In 1294 Gilbert de Neusum acquired land which included the house formerly
inhabited by William Broun (**70–71**). A 5s. rent charge on that land was transferred
to other land in Scarborough in 1300 (**72**) and was quitclaimed in Neusum's favour
in 1315 (**73**). Gilbert died leaving his land jointly to his sons Adam and Roger, and
in 1336 Adam quitclaimed his share to Roger (**74**). A memorandum in the vicars'
cartulary records a dispute in 1342 between Roger and Simon de Folkton, the
latter having ejected Roger from a strip of land which divided his land from
Roger's (**75**). Roger, a York barber, died in 1349, leaving the land he had
inherited from his father to a group of five vicars choral (**76**). One of the vicars
made a quitclaim in 1356 (**77**), although he was included with the other four vicars
when they transferred ownership to the vicars' college in 1358 (**78–79**; quitclaim
80; delivery of seisin **81**). That transfer was made in partial fulfilment of a licence to
acquire in mortmain, granted by the king in 1332 (*Chs. Vicars Choral*, i, pp. xxx–
xxxi).
   In 1359 the vicars granted the strip of land (in fact, a wall) disputed in 1342 to
the holder of the neighbouring property, presumably Simon de Folkton's successor
(**82**). It was possibly because of uncertainty caused by that surrender that the 1358
grant to the vicars' college was repeated later in 1359 (**83**). A 20-year lease made by
the vicars in 1385 (**84**) was not allowed to run its course and was renewed in 1390
(**85**). In 1400 the land was sub-let (**86**).
   The property can be identified as the burgage plot which in the early 19th
century was described as lying on the south side of Carrgate: BIHR, C.C. V/C 10,
Scar 5.

71. Grant by Thomas son of William de Irtona and his wife Agnes, daughter of William Broun de Scardeburgh, to Gilbert de Neusum of Scardeburgh' of land in the new town (*in novo burgo*) of Scard', lying in breadth between land once of John de Lindbergh and that of John Gerard and in length from the royal way to land once of John de Lindbergh; paying 5s. sterling a year to the lord of the fee, at Pentecost and Martinmas in equal portions, and husgable (*gabulag'*) for the land to the king. Warranty. Seal.
Witnesses: as 70 (reading Folc' for Folck, and adding John Upsek and John son of Hugh after Thomas Folc').
Sunday before the feast of St. Andrew the apostle [28 November] 1294.

SOURCE: VC 3/Vv 62 (254 mm. × 121 mm.)
ENDORSEMENT: *Concessio terre in novo burgo Gilberto Newsom*; *Scarburgh.*
SEALS: (left) round (20 mm. dia.; damaged), green, impression of a star of petals, legend; (right) tag.

NOTE: See 70.

72. Notification by John Gerard de Scard' that he binds himself and his heirs to have at hand (*paratum*) the charter of Gilbert de Neusum by which Gilbert was enfeoffed by John de Lindberg' of 5s. worth of rent charged on land in the new town of Scard', which rent John [Gerard] bought from Gilbert. Whenever Gilbert or his heirs are called to warranty by John or his heirs or by any other people, they [i.e. Gilbert and his heirs] shall have the charter for vouching its warranty should they so wish, lest by default of possessing the charter they lose the vouching of its warranty; neither Gilbert or his heirs are to be held to warrant on behalf of John and his heirs (*ad nos*). Seal. Scard' on the day of the purification of the blessed Virgin Mary 28 Edward [2 February 1299/1300].

SOURCE: VC 3/Vv 65 (182 mm. × 86 mm.)
ENDORSEMENT: *de terra in novo burgo.*
SEAL: slit.

NOTE: See 70.

73. Grant and quitclaim by Alan son of John Gerard (*Gerardi*) de Scardburgh' to Gilbert de Neusom of Scardburgh' and his heirs or assigns of a rent of 5s. a year which Alan has in that dwelling-house (*illa mansione*) which Gilbert inhabits, lying in the new town of the vill of Scardburgh', in length from the royal street on the north to the land once of John de Lymbergh' on the south and in breadth from the land once of John de Lymbergh' on the west to the land once of John Gerard on the east; to be held of the chief lord of the fee for the service owed. Warranty. Seal.
Witnesses: Robert Waweyn and Adam de Pykering, bailiffs of Scardburgh', Adam de Helperthorp', Henry de Roston', John de Neuton', Geoffrey de Folketon', John de Folketon', Thomas de Neuby, Robert Gedge, and others.
Scardburgh', Monday before the feast of blessed Peter ad vincula 1315 [28 July].

SOURCE: VC 3/Vv 67 (233 mm. × 112 mm.)
ENDORSEMENT: *Annuum redditum in Scarburgh' ass' quinque solidorum modo legal'.*
SEAL: vesica (30 mm. × 18 mm.), plain, impression of a fleur-de-lys.

NOTE: See 70.

74. Release and quitclaim by Adam son of Gilbert de Neusum of Scartheburgh', for himself and his heirs, to his brother Roger son of Gilbert de Neusum of Scartheburgh' and his heirs and assigns of a tenement in Scartheburgh' which Roger and Adam once held jointly by the gift and bequest of their father Gilbert de Neusum, as is expressed more fully in his testament, namely: lying in breadth between the land of Simon de Folkton' and that of dom. Thomas de la Ryvere knight and in length from the royal street to the land of Robert de Helperthorp' behind; to be held of the chief lords of the fee for the service owed. Warranty. Seal.
Witnesses: William Sage de Scartheburgh', Adam de Semere of the same place, William Cutt' of the same place, Robert de Helperthorp' of the same place, William de Selby of York (*Ebor'*), William de Bukyngham of the same place, William de Appelby of the same place clerk, and others.
Scartheburgh', Sunday after the feast of St. Hilary the bishop 1335, 9 Edward III [14 January 1335/6].

SOURCE: VC 3/Vv 63 (233 mm. × 125 mm.)
ENDORSEMENT: *Evidenc' do domo in Scarburghe*; *Acquietacio Rogero de Newsom*.
SEAL: ovoid (18 mm. across, 24 mm. long), red, impression of St. Laurence on left with a griddle on right, legend.
CARTULARY COPY: VC 3/1/1, fo. 140.

NOTE: See **70**.

75. Memorandum that Roger son of Gilbert de Neusom of Scardeburgh produced a writ of right in these words:
Precept of Edward III to the bailiffs of Scardeburgh ordering them to do justice to Roger over land in Scardeburgh 24 feet in length and 2 feet in breadth, which Roger claims to hold from the king for the free service of 1*d.* a year, being the land from which Simon son of John de Folketon de Scardeburgh ejected him. Westminster, 6 June 1342.
As a result of this writ Simon was impleaded before the bailiffs in court on Monday after the feast of St. James the apostle [29 July] to answer Roger over the land, and the same court-day was given to Roger, who appointed Thomas Heved as his attorney.
On that day Roger, through his attorney, and Simon, in person, came to court. Roger said that Simon unjustly ejected him from the land, which he has by inheritance: his father Gilbert was seised of the land from which he received rents and he is his father's heir. Simon asked for and was given a view of the land and a day on which to appear in court to answer Roger, Monday after the feast of St. Bartholomew [26 August], and the same day was given to Roger.
On that day Roger, through his attorney, challenged Simon's essoin: Simon against Roger on a plea of land through John de Hatwod pledges Thomas son of John; and a day was given for hearing judgment, Monday after the feast of the nativity of the blessed Virgin Mary [9 September].
On that day Roger, through his attorney, asked for judgment and Simon essoined as follows: Simon against Roger on a plea of land through John de Haterbergh pledges Thomas son of John. Roger challenged the essoin because the essoiner did not mention in the fine of his essoin the view of land, and he asked that the essoin be considered in default; because the court was not ready (*non est bene provisa*) to give judgment, a day was given for the essoin, Monday after the feast of St. Michael [30 September].

On that day Roger, through his attorney, asked for judgment and Simon came likewise; because the court was not in full session (*non est plena*) a day was given, Monday after the feast of St. Luke [21 October].

On that day likewise the court was not in full session and not ready for judgment and a day was given, Monday after the feast of St. Martin [18 November].

On that day Roger, through his attorney, asked for judgment and because Simon had nothing to say for himself it was judged that the essoin was in default and that Roger should recover seisin against Simon of the land 24 feet in length and 2 feet in breadth.

Roger procured the seal of the office of the bailiffs of the town to witness this text.

SOURCE: VC 3/1/1, fos. 140–141.

NOTE: See 70.

76. Testament of Roger de Neusum of Scardeburgh', barbour of York, made on Friday after the feast of St. Bartholomew [28 August] 1349. The bequests include:
to dom. Roger de Everton', dom. John de Alkbaroue, dom. Richard de Aslakby, dom. Ellis de Burton', and dom. William de Gerford, vicars of the minster church of blessed Peter, their heirs and assigns, land with buildings on it, lying in the vill of Skardeburgh' between the land of John de Folketon' on the east and land once of John de Ughtred knight on the west and between the royal way on the north and land once of Roger ad Crucem on the south; Roger has the land from the gift and enfeoffment of his father Gilbert de Neusom and of his brother Adam. Roger also wishes that his wife Gillian shall have and enjoy all his land in Skardeburgh' for her life. He also gives to William son of Adam de Skardeburgh' a rent of 3s. a year from land with buildings on it, lying in the vill of Skardeburgh' between land once of Ralph Sessor' on the west and the royal way on the east and between the land of John de Cropton' on the south and the royal way on the north. Roger also gives to Roger de Everton', John, Ellis, and William de Gerford a rent of 18d. a year from the tenement which was of Simon de Folketon' de Skardeburgh'.
Witnesses: William de Huntyngton', Niel Taillour, Robert son of William de Huntyngton', John de Cendale, and Robert de la Pantrye clerk, and others.

SOURCE: VC 3/Vv 68i (286 mm. × 160 mm.)
ENDORSEMENT: *Devacio terre in Skarburgh'*; *Testamentum Rogeri Newsom de ten' dat' vicariis et eciam de x s' reddit' ass'.*
SEAL: remains of red wax.
CARTULARY COPY: (part) VC 3/1/1, fo. 141.

(*Attached to testament*) Certificate of probate by the auditor of causes of the dean and chapter of York 30 August 1349 (246 mm. × 49 mm.; with capitular seal *ad citationes* in plain wax).

NOTE: See 70.

77. Release and quitclaim by Richard de Aslakby chaplain to dom. Roger de Everton' chaplain, his heirs and assigns, of land with buildings on it which were once of Roger de Neusom' of Schardbourgh', lying in the vill of Schardbourgh' between the land of John de Folketon' on the east and that once of John de Ughtred knight on

the west and between the royal way on the north and land once of Roger ad Crucem to the south. Seal.

Witnesses: Adam de Semer, Adam son of Diote, Henry de Roston',Gregory de Bridlyngton', John de Broun of Schardbourgh', and others.

Schardbourgh', on the [feast] day of the conversion of St. Paul the apostle 1355 [25 Jaunary 1355/6].

SOURCE: VC 3/Vv 68ii (281 mm. × 111 mm.)
ENDORSEMENT: *Evidenc' de Skarburghe.*
SEAL: tag.

NOTE: See 70.

78.   Grant by Roger de Everton', John de Alkbarowe, Richard de Aslakby, Ellis de Burton', and William de Gerford, chaplains, to the warden of the house of vicars of the church of blessed Peter of York and the vicars of a messuage in the vill of Scardeburgh', lying as described in 77; the grantors have the messuage of the gift and feoffment of Roger de Neusum of Scardeburgh', lately of York, barbour. Seal.

Witnesses: Adam de Semer, Adam son of Denise, Henry de Roston', Stephen Carter, Gregory de Bridelyngton', John de Brunne, Walter the painter (*pictore*) de Scardeburgh', and others.

Scardeburgh', Tuesday before the feast of St. George the martyr [17 April] 1358, 32 Edward.

SOURCE: VC 3/Vv 69 (303 mm. × 75 mm.)
ENDORSEMENT: *Concessio vicariis unius messuagii in Skarburghe*; *Alkbarow.*
SEALS: five tags.
CARTULARY COPY: VC 3/1/1, fo. 141v.

NOTE: See 70. The royal licence to assign the property in mortmain was granted to the four named vicars, at the request of John de Wynwyk, treasurer of York, on 28 February 1357/8: VC 3/2/11 (cartulary copy: VC 3/1/1, fo. 141r.–v; calendared in *Cal. Pat. R.*, 1358–61, 19).

79.   Copy of 78.

SOURCE: VC 3/Vv 70 (308 mm. × 85 mm.)
ENDORSEMENT: *Concessio unius messuagii in Skarburghe vic'.*
SEALS: five tags (one with remains of green wax).

80.   Letter of John de Alkbarowe, Richard de Aslakby, Ellis de Burton, and William de Gerford, chaplains, appointing Roger de Everton, vicar in the choir of the church of blessed Peter of York, as their attorney in delivering seisin of a messuage in Scardeburgh to the warden of the house of vicars and the vicars. Seal.

York, Monday before the feast of St. George the martyr, 32 Edward III [16 April 1358].

SOURCE: VC 3/1/1, fo. 142.

NOTE: See 70.

81. Release and quitclaim by Roger de Everton, John de Alkbarowe, Richard de Aslakby, Ellis de Burton, and William de Gerford, chaplains, to the warden of the house of vicars of the church of blessed Peter of York and the vicars of a messuage in Scardeburgh, described as in **77**. Seal.

Witnesses: John de Langeton mayor of York, William Ferour, Thomas de Strensalle, John de Acastr', bailiffs, William de Grantham, John Capron' the younger, and others.

York, Monday after the feast of St. Mark the evangelist [30 April] 1358, 32 Edward.

SOURCE: VC 3/1/1, fos. 141v.–142.

NOTE: See **70**.

82. Indenture witnessing that Ellis de Walkyngton, warden of the house of vicars of the church of blessed Peter of York, and all the vicars have granted and demised at fee farm to Thomas de Burton of Scardeburgh all the land which they have of the gift and feoffment of dom. Roger de Everton, namely the land which Roger de Neusom previously recovered by writ of right in the court of Scardeburgh against Simon de Folketon, lying in the vill of Scardeburgh in length 24 feet from the street on the north up to the vicars' land on the south and in breadth 2 feet between Thomas's land on the east and the vicars' land on the west; paying 12*d*. a year to the vicars. Thomas agrees that if the rent is in arrears at any term in part or in whole, the vicars may distrain his tenement which lies on the east. Thomas or his heirs or assigns may not remove or destroy anything built [on the land], but shall maintain and repair it at their own costs whenever necessary. Warranty. Seal.

Witnesses: Henry de Roston, Adam Carter, bailiffs, Adam son of Diote, Stephen Carter, Gregory de Briddelynton, John de Brunne, and many others.

Scardeburgh, Thursday after the feast of St. Matthias the apostle 1358, 33 Edward III [28 February 1358/9].

SOURCE: VC 3/1/1, fo. 142r.–v.

NOTE: See **70**. Rentals give the income as 'for the wall', which evidently ran along the land (e.g. VC 4/1/12).

83. Grant by Roger de Everton', John de Alkbarowe, Richard de Aslakby, Ellis de Burton, and William de [Gerford][1] to the warden of the house of vicars of the church of blessed Peter of York and the [vicars] of a messuage in the vill of Scardeburgh', described as in **77**; the messuage is to be held of the chief lord of the fee for the services owed and [husgable] for the land to the king. Seal.

Witnesses: Henry de Roston', Adam Carter, bailiffs of the vill of Scardeburgh', [Adam son of Denise, Stephen Car]ter, Gregory de Briddelyngton', John Brunne, Walter the painter de Scardeburgh', and others.

[Scardeburgh], the morrow of the annunciation of the blessed Virgin Mary [26 March] 135[9], 33 Edward III.

SOURCE: VC 3/Vv 71 (about a quarter of the MS. is missing on the left-hand side; the remainder is 189 mm. × 124 mm.)

ENDORSEMENT: *Concessio vicariis de uno messuagio in Skarburghe; tricesimo tercio.*

SEALS: five slits with four remaining tags.

CARTULARY COPY: VC 3/1/1, fo. 142.

NOTE: See **70**.

---
[1] The text in square brackets is supplied from the cartulary copy.

84.   Indenture witnessing that Ellis de Walkyngton', warden of the house of vicars of the church of blessed Peter of York, and the vicars, with the unanimous assent and consent of the whole college, have demised at farm to Richard Cowper de Scharburgh' and [his wife] Maud, lately the wife of John Coke of the same place, their heirs, and assigns, houses (*domos*) in the vill of Scharburgh' which the vicars have of the gift and feoffment of Roger de Everton' and John de Alkbarowe, chaplains, lying in breadth between the land of John de Folketon' on the east and that once of John de Ughtred knight on the west and in length from the royal street to the land once of Roger ad Crucem. Richard and Maud are to hold the houses from Pentecost [21 May] 1385 for 20 years, paying from Martinmas 1385 at York 24s. sterling to the vicars, at Pentecost and Martinmas in equal portions, and husgable (*gabulag'*) for the land to the king. Richard and Maud and their heirs and assigns are to repair and maintain the houses as regards roof timber (*in coopertura meremio*) and other necessities at their own costs and whenever repairs are needed. If the farm is in arrears 40 days at any term during the 20 years, the vicars may enter the houses and distrain. Warranty. Seal.
York, on the eve of Pentecost [20 May] 1385.

SOURCE: VC 3/Vv 72 (311 mm. × 115 mm.). Indented at top, INDENTURA.
ENDORSEMENT: *Indentur' de Skarburgh'*.
SEAL: tag.

NOTE: See 70.

85.   Indenture witnessing that John Bautre, warden of the house of vicars of the church of blessed Peter of York, and the vicars, with the unanimous assent and consent of the whole college, have demised at farm to Alan de Yedyngham and his wife Joan, their heirs and assigns, houses in the vill of Scardburgh, described as in 84 (reading Folkton' for Folketon'). Alan and Joan are to hold the houses from Pentecost [22 May] 1390 for 20 years, paying rent (to commence at Martinmas 1390) and husgable as 84. Clauses concerning repair and distraint as in 84. Warranty. Seal.
York, on the feast of the purification of the blessed Virgin Mary 1389 [2 February 1389/90].

SOURCE: VC 3/Vv 73 (264 mm. × 126 mm.). Indented at top.
ENDORSEMENT: *Scarburgh'*.
SEAL: tag.

NOTE: See 70.

86.   Grant by Alan Yedingham lately of Scardeburgh' to William Edeson of the same place of all that property leased to him for 20 years in 85. William or his assigns are to hold the property from the feast of the annunciation of the blessed Mary 1 Henry IV [25 March 1400] for the remainder of Alan's life; paying the warden and vicars both the farm and the king's husgable as Alan has paid them hitherto, and keeping (*faciendo*) the tenement in repair with roof timber and other necessities at their own costs, as Alan and his wife have maintained and repaired it. Warranty. Seal.

Witnesses: Thomas Carthorp, John Carter, bailiffs of Scardeburgh, Robert Schilbotil, Alan Waldik, John Anlaby, John Storrour, Robert Drewry, and others. Scardeb', the day and year abovesaid [25 March 1400].

SOURCE: CCA, DCc/Charta Antiqua, Y 22 (287 mm. × 74 mm.)
ENDORSEMENT: *Skarburghe.*
SEAL: round (26 mm. dia.), red, impression, legend.

NOTE: See **70**.

87. Grant by Bernard de Hundmanby of Scardeburg' to his daughter Margaret and her heirs or assigns of the land which he bought from Geoffrey son of Richard le Corder, lying in the new town of Scardeburgh' in length from Bernard's land on the west to the new ditch (*novum fossatum*) of the town on the east and in breadth between Bernard's land and that of Geoffrey de Folketon on some sides (*pro aliquibus suis partibus*) towards the south and the land of Robert de Northfolk towards the north; paying the king's husgable (*gabulagium*) due from the land. Warranty. Seal.
Witnesses: Henry de Roston' and John le Nayr, bailiffs of Scardeburgh', John de Lyndeberg', Robert Hamund, Alan Beaufrunt, Robert Beaufrunt, Alan le Carter, Roger le Carter, John Gerard, John son of William, Henry Sampson, William son of Thomas, and others.   [probably 1290s]

SOURCE: VC 3/Vv 66 (218 mm. × 94 mm.)
ENDORSEMENT: *Evidenc' de Skarburghe.*
SEAL: tag.

DATE: Bernard's daughter was married by 1294: **70**.
NOTE: This charter seems not to relate to either of the plots of land conveyed in the other Scarborough documents in the archive.

88. Grant by John de Swathorp of Scardeburgh' to Ellis de Walkyngton' and William Wygeard, chaplains, of land with buildings, lying outside the gate of the new town (*extra portam novi burgy*) of the vill of Scardeburgh' next to the chapel of St. Thomas, in length from the royal way on the south to the land of Gregory de Bridlington' and the land of the new ditch (*fossatum*) on the north and in breadth from Gregory's land on the west to the new ditch on the east; paying the king's husgable (*gabulagium*) due from the land. Warranty. Seal.
Scardeburgh', on the day of the conversion of St. Paul the apostle 1367 [25 January 1367/8].
Witnesses: Henry de Roston', Stephen Carter, bailiffs of Scardeburgh', Thomas de Neuby, Gregory de Bridlington', William Smyt, Richard de Kychin, and many others. At the start of ⸢anno . . . incipiente⸥ 42 Edward III.

SOURCE: VC 3/Vv 64 (289 mm. × 141 mm.)
ENDORSEMENT: . . . *Scarburgh' de terra extra portam*; *Novo burgo iuxta capellam sancti Thome.*
SEAL: ovoid (18 mm. across, 24 mm. long), green, impression.

NOTE: Both grantees were vicars choral. The chapel belonged to the hospital of St. Thomas, in existence by the late 13th century: *VCH Yorks.* iii. 330.

SELBY

(parish in Barkston Ash wapentake WR)

89. Grant by John de Goldale of Selby, kinsman (*consanguineus*) and heir of Thomas de Goldale of Selby, to John de Blakewell' of Selby chaplain of 1 a. of land in Selby, lying next to the pool (*stagnum*) of the lord abbot of Selby in a field called Damriddyng' between the land once of Agnes de Hensall' and that of the abbot of Selby; John inherited the acre after the death of his uncle Thomas; to be held of the chief lords of the fee for the service owed. Seal.
Witnesses: John de Brun, Richard de Drax, Robert de Grayngham, John del Brynde, William de Hathelsay of Selby, John Marsshall' de Selby who used to live (*morabat*) in Roucliff', and others.
Selby, 9 May 1408, 9 Henry IV.

SOURCE: VC 3/Vv 74 (274 mm. × 93 mm.)
ENDORSEMENT: none medieval.
SEAL: tag.

NOTE: This and the next four charters refer to land which John de Welwick, a Selby man who moved to York, gave in 1439 to two vicars, one of whom was possibly his son (**91**), and which was later conveyed to the vicars' college (**93**).

90. Grant by John de Blakwell' chaplain of Selby to John de Welwyk of Selby and John's wife Margaret of 2 a. of land in Selby, lying next to the pool of the lord abbot of Selby in a field called Damriddyng' between the abbot's lands on both sides; John has one of the acres of the feoffment of John de Goldall' of Selby and the other by the bequest (*ex legato*) of Agnes de Hensall' of Selby; to be held of the chief lords of the fee for the service owed. Seal.
Witnesses: Robert de Grayngham, John Marschall', William de Hadilsay of Selby, Richard de Esthorpe, Thomas de Osgodby, and others.
Selby, 10 July 1410, 11 Henry IV.

SOURCE: VC 3/Vv 75 (286 mm. × 87 mm.)
ENDORSEMENT: none medieval.
SEAL: remains of red wax on tag.

NOTE: See **89**.

91. Grant by John de Welwyk of York, once of Selby, to William Welwyk and John Houk chaplains, vicars in the choir of the cathedral church of blessed Peter of York, of 2 a. of land in Selby, lying as described in **90** (reading Damryddyng' for Damriddyng'); John has the acres of the gift and feoffment of John Blakwell de Selby chaplain; to be held of the chief lords of the fee for the service owed. Seal.
Witnesses: Robert Davyson, William Housom, Richard Scorton', and others.
19 October 18 Henry VI [1439].

SOURCE: VC 3/Vv 76 (264 mm. × 98 mm.)
ENDORSEMENT: none.
SEAL: round (10 mm. dia.), red, impression of 'I' with ? a crown over it.

NOTE: See **89**.

92. Grant by [John Hou]k[1] de York chaplain to Henry [Gowcell, John Hert, chaplains, and John] Thweyng lawyer (*legisperitus*), for a sum of money which they have given him, of 2 a. of land in Selby, lying as described in **91**; together with the late William Welwyk chaplain, John has the acres from the gift and feoffment of John de Welwyk once of York; to be held of the capital lords of the fee for the service owed. Warranty. Seal.

Selby, 13 September 36 Henry VI [1457].

SOURCE: VC 3/Vv 77 (298 mm. × 90 mm.)
ENDORSEMENT: *Litt' de terris de Selby.*
SEAL: slit.

[1] The MS. is worn in parts. The names in square brackets are supplied by inference from the text later in the charter and from the text of **93**.

NOTE: See **89**.

93. Release and quitclaim by Henry Gowcell, John Hert, chaplains, and John Thweyng' lawyer (*legisperitus*) to dom. John More, warden of the house of vicars of the cathedral church of York, and the vicars of 2 a. of land in Selby, lying as described in **91**; they have the acres of the gift and feoffment of John Houk de York chaplain. Seal.

Witnesses: Thomas Gowcell, Thomas Batty, William Eleson, and others.

24 August 36 Henry VI [1458].

SOURCE: VC 3/Vv 78 (327 mm. × 82 mm.)
ENDORSEMENT: (in a 16th-cent. hand) *A reles of two acres of lande in Selby per annum ij s.*
SEAL: three slits (one with tag).

NOTE: See **89**.

SHIPTON IN GALTRES

(in Overton parish, Bulmer wapentake NR)

94. Mention of a grant by John de Skydbrook to the vicars of property at Shipton in Galtres. 1349 [no text survives].

SOURCE: VC 8/Metcalfe notebks., introductory bk., list of charters on p. 53.

DATE: The date given by Metcalfe is possibly an error for 1359; cf. **95**.
NOTE: Described as three messuages and 7 a., the property was included in the licence to assign in mortmain to the vicars' college land and rents granted to Grayingham and Alkborough in 1376 (*Chs. Vicars Choral*, i, no. 568 note, where **95** is wrongly classed 'Vi' 79, and wrongly described as a grant *by* (rather than *to*) Skidbrook).

In the 19th century the messuages lay along the village street, two at the southern end and one at the northern end: BIHR, C.C. V/C 10 Ove 16, 40, 68, and 73.

95. Grant by Roger de Everton', Richard de Grayngham, and John de Alkebarow, vicars of the choir of the cathedral church of blessed Peter of York, to John de Skydbrok citizen of York of all messuages, lands, and tenements in Shupton' in Galtres which they have of the gift and feoffment of John de Skydbrok; to be held for the term of his life of the chief lords of the fee for service owed and by common law (*de iure consueta*). Warranty. Seal.

Witnesses: Roger de Shupton', Thomas Lovell' de Skelton', John Brock de Shupton', William de Haxby, Robert de Crayk of Shupton' and others.

Shupton' in Galtres, 23 May 1359, 33 Edward III.

SOURCE: VC 3/Vv 79 (252 mm. × 116 mm.)

ENDORSEMENT: *Schupton'*.

SEALS: three tags.

NOTE: See **94**.

SKELTON

(in Howden parish, Howdenshire wapentake ER)

96. Quitclaim by Robert Batayl de Balcolm' the younger and his wife Katherine to William Page de Skelton' of a rent of 11*d*. of silver a year which William used to pay Robert and Katherine at the four stated terms [of the year] in Houedenschir' for a tenement in Skelton' next to Houeden, lying between the drainage channel (*g[u]tt[er]am*) of Balcolm' and the messuage with croft of John de Skelton' clerk; the grant is made in return for a sum of money which William gave them. Seal.

Witnesses: Amiger de Skelton', John son of John son of Peter of the same place, John the clerk of the same place, John de Bekyngham, Thomas son of Peter de Balcolm', Robert de Crigelston, William de Skelton' clerk, and others.

Houeden, Monday after feast of annunciation of blessed Mary [26 March] 1302.

SOURCE: VC 3/Vv 80 (226 mm. × 85 mm.)

ENDORSEMENT: none.

SEAL: tag.

NOTE: The charter may be connected with the obit which the vicars promised in 1524 to celebrate for one of their number, John Thomson; the endowment included an 8*s*. rent from a tenement in Skelton (VC 3/3/17; cf. *Chs. Vicars Choral*, i, no. 341).

SKIRPENBECK
(parish in Buckrose wapentake ER)

97. Grant, release, and quitclaim, in free and perpetual alms, by Thomas de Yrton' living in Schyrtinbeck to God and the cathedral church of blessed Peter of York, and to Robert the dean and the chapter of the same church, and to the executors of the testament of William de Langton' of good memory, formerly dean of York, of land which Thomas has in demesne in the vill and territory of Schyrtinbeck of the fee of the said church, namely Thomas's chief messuage with buildings on it and 4 bovates of land; of a rent of 14s. 10d. a year received, at Pentecost and Martinmas in equal portions, from dom. Thomas de Chancy of Schyrtinbeck, baron of the lord king, and his heirs from that messuage and those 4 bovates of land which the baron's uncle Thomas de Chancy held in Schyrtinbeck; and of the homage and service of the baron and his heirs for the messuage and 4 bovates, with the rent and all rights and escheats. The grant is made for a sum of money which William de Langton's executors paid to Thomas, the money having been assigned for Langton's soul by the dean and chapter. The land is to be held in free and perpetual alms; paying to the canons of St. Agatha living at Schyrtinbeck 29s. 8d. of silver a year, at Pentecost and Martinmas in equal portions, and to Thomas and his heirs at Schyrtinbeck a rose in the time of roses, together with all service, customary aid, suit of court, and secular demand. Warranty. Seal.

Witnesses: dom. Thomas de Chancy baron of the lord king, dom. Thomas Burdun knight, dom. Paulin de Lilling', Thomas de Thorny, Peter de Lund, Thomas de Chancy of Schyrtinbeck the elder, Walter de Emelsay, Peter Thurthill', John Burdun, and others.   [probably 1281 or soon afterwards]

SOURCE: VC 3/Vv 82b (229 mm. × 160 mm.)
ENDORSEMENT: *De capitali messuagio in Scrythynbeke decano et capitulo.*
SEAL: tag.

DATE: Dean William de Langton died in July 1279, but this grant was probably made at about the same time as **98**, which must date from 1281 or soon afterwards.
NOTE: Thomas de Irton's house and land in Skirpenbeck were bought by Langton's executors in order to endow his obit. The property was let to the Premonstratensian abbey of St. Agatha at Easby, which was to pay the rent directly to the vicars (**98**). The abbey evidently had a grange at Skirpenbeck by the 1280s and in 1312 the rent was paid by the 'canons of St. Agatha living there'; there was only one canon, however, by 1321 (VC 4/1/2 and 3). The vicars later acquired a further 2 bovates in Skirpenbeck (**101–103**).

The vicar's rental for 1309 notes that the income from Skirpenbeck was assigned to Langton's obit on 6 Nones July [2 July] (VC 4/1/1). That day was St. Swithun's feast day, so given as the day of his death in 1279 on his tomb and mistakenly read as the saint's translation on 15 July in *Fasti, York,* 12 (with references for inscription on tomb).

98. Demise at perpetual farm, in the form of a cirograph, by William de Langton' rector of the church of Croft, Walter de Langton' rector of the church of Askham, [and] Henry de Mileford rector of the church of Berningham, executors of the testament of dom. William de Langton', formerly dean of the church of York, with the consent of mag. Robert de Scartheburg' . . [gemipuncti] dean of York and the whole chapter of the same church, to the abbot and convent of St. Agatha and the canons of the same house living at Skirtenbec, of a chief messuage in the vill of Skirtenbec and 4 bovates of land with meadow, which they have of the gift of Thomas de Hirton [and which belong to] the fee of the abbot and convent of St. Agatha. They also quitclaim to the abbot and convent and canons of Skirtenbec a rent of 14s. 10d. a year, payable at Martinmas and Pentecost, from those 4 bovates which Thomas Chauncy, uncle of the lord of Skirtenbec, holds of the same fee; the abbot and convent and canons shall in future receive the rent from dom. Thomas Chauncy, baron, and his heirs directly (*absque ullo medio*) and at their convenience (*suum comodum inde faciant*). They also grant to the abbot and convent and canons of Skirtenbec the homage and service of dom. Thomas, baron de Skirtenbec, and of his heirs for the messuage, 4 bovates, and 14s. 10d. rent. The abbot and convent and canons are to hold all the above in perpetual alms of the lord . . [gemipuncti] dean and chapter of York; paying 46s. 8d. a year at the feast of the nativity of blessed John the Baptist to the vicars of the church of York for the obit of dom. William de Langton formerly dean of York on the day of his anniversary. Warranty. For this grant and demise the abbot and convent and canons of Skirtenbec promise and by this cirograph bind themselves and their successors for the farm of 46s. 8d. payable to the vicars of the church of York, granting that if the farm is not paid the vicars may distrain the tenement and allowing the . . [gemipuncti] dean and chapter of York if necessary to compel them and their successors as canons at Skirtenbec to pay the full farm. To the part of this cirograph remaining with the abbot and convent the executors and the dean and chapter of York append their seals, and the part remaining with the executors and the vicars of the church of York is corroborated with the common seal of the chapter of St. Agatha.

Witnesses: mag. Thomas de Grimeston' archdeacon Clyvelandie, dom. Thomas Chauncy baron de Skirtenbec, dom. Ellis parson of the same place, Peter de Lund, Thomas Turnay de Sutton', Thomas Chauncy de Skirtenbec, John Burdun of the same place, Peter Thurkille of the same place, Roger Bacil of the same place, and many others.   [probably 1281 or soon afterwards]

SOURCE: VC 3/3/84 (267 mm. × 216 mm.). Indented at top with letters.

ENDORSEMENT: *Skirtenbeke*; *de obitus Willelmi Langton decani Ebor' in Skyrtynbeke xlvj s. viiij d. de manerio ibidem cum clausa destringendi.*

SEAL: (left) oblong (40 mm. × 27 mm.), plain wax, impression of St. Agatha standing under a canopy; (right) tag.

DATE: Thomas de Grimston became archdeacon of Cleveland in 1281.

NOTE: See **97**.

99.   Copy of **98**, written in a 15th-century hand probably in connection with **100**.

SOURCE: VC 3/3/83 (300 mm. × 262 mm.)

ENDORSEMENT: *Skyrtynbek*; *de xlvj s. viiij d. de Skyrtynbek.*

SEAL: no attempt to seal the document.

100.   Letter of John Hikling, warden of the college of vicars of the cathedral church of blessed Peter of York, and the vicars of the college stating that they have received from the abbot of St. Agatha in the archdeaconry of Richimundie 46s. 8d. owed for

1431 for the manor and lands of Skyrtenbec in the county of York, and that he shall be quit. Sealed with their common seal.

SOURCE: VC 1/1, p. 83 (ink pagination).

NOTE: See **97**.

101. Cirograph witnessing that John Burd' de Scirpinbek has granted to his son Thomas and Thomas's heirs 2 bovates of land in the vill (*willa*) and territory of Scirpinbek, lying from the longer part of the ground of John's land (*a longiore parte solis terre mee*), with 2 furlongs (*culturas*) of meadow, namely one furlong in the great meadow above the Derwent' opposite the ash tree (*contra fraxinum*) and John's other furlong called Waudayle; paying to the church and the vicars of St. Peter of York all the services due from the land, and 1*d.* a year to John at Easter. Seal.
Date at Scirpinbek on the day of St. Paul the apostle 1288 [30 June 1288 or 25 January 1288/9].
Witnesses: dom. Thomas de Schauncy, Peter Thurkil de Scirpinbek, Roger de Bacile of the same place, Thomas de Schauncy of the same place, William the clerk de Yolthorp, and others.

SOURCE: VC 3/Vv 82a (163 mm. × 130 mm.). Indented at top with letters.
ENDORSEMENT: *Skirpenbek.*
SEAL:

DATE: The feast day is either that of the decollation of St. Paul (30 June) or his conversion (25 January).
NOTE: John (or possibly his son John, Thomas's brother) later granted the land to the vicars (**102**).

102. Grant by John son of John Burdon', living in Skerpinbeck, to God and the church of blessed Peter of York and to Richard son of Stephen, warden of the house of vicars of the same church, and the vicars of 2 bovates of land in the territory of Skerpinbeck, lying on the west in that carucate of land which John holds of the chapter of the same church; the land is to be held in free alms. Warranty. Seal.
Witnesses: dom. Thomas de Chauncy knight, Thomas Chauncy his uncle, Peter Thurkel, Roger de Bathele, Robert Curtays, Thomas son of Adam Chau[n]cy, and many others.   [*c.* 1290]

SOURCE: VC 3/Vv 81 (205 mm. × 71 mm.)
ENDORSEMENT: *Carta Johannis Burdun de Scherpenbec; custod' domus vicariorum; Skyrtinbeke;* (in a 16th-cent. hand) *The dede of gifte of John Burdun of the ij oxgan of lande in Skyrtynbeke wiche he dyd hold of the churche of Yorke gyven . . . he to the vicars without any charge . . .*
SEAL: vesica (30 mm. × 22 mm.), plain, impression of ? a bird, legend.

DATE: Probably soon after **101**.
NOTE: See **101**.

103. Cirograph witnessing that dom. Simon de Botelsford, warden of the house of vicars of the choir of blessed Peter of York, and all the vicars of the same choir have granted and demised at farm to dom. Peter de Skyrpynbek chaplain two thirds of

those bovates of land which they have of the gift and enfeoffment of John Burdon in
the vill and territory of Skyrpynbek and the third of the same bovates which John's
wife Cecily held in dower [and which were] to revert [on Cecily's death or
remarriage] to the warden and vicars, [to hold for] 20 years from the making of
this indenture commencing at Martinmas 1309; paying for the two thirds 17s. 9½d.
and for the third part 8s. 10½d.

SOURCE: VC 8/Metcalfe notebks., Deeds in extenso, V, no. 27.

NOTE: See 101.

SUTTON-ON-THE-FOREST
(parish in Bulmer wapentake NR)

104.   Grant by Ralph son of Beatrice de Sutthon Husgate to God and the vicars of
the church of blessed Peter of York of a moiety of one toft and croft in the vill of
Usgate Sutthon, namely the moiety of the toft and croft which was of his aunt
(*materterae*) Isold, daughter of Pain de Sutthon Usgate, lying between the toft and croft
of Walter the vicar of Folkethon and the moiety of the toft and croft of Isold's sister
Sybil and stretching from the great street (*magna strata*) to the Derewent; to be held for
the souls of his father and mother and his ancestors and successors and all the faithful
departed.
Witnesses: William de Gernen etc.   [probably first half of 13th century]

SOURCE: VC 8/Metcalfe notebks., Deeds in extenso, V, no. 62.

NOTE: This charter is probably a confirmation of a grant made earlier by Isold, whose
       two sisters also granted land to the vicars (106). The vicars no longer received
       income from the property, however, by the early 14th century (VC 4/1/1).

105.   Grant by Robert son of Sybil daughter of Pain de Husgate Sutthon to God and
the vicars of the church of blessed Peter of York of a toft with croft in the vill of
Husgat Sutthon which his mother Sybil conveyed (*contulit*) to God and the vicars in
free, pure, and perpetual alms, lying between two tofts and crofts which Beatrice and
Isold, Sybil's sisters, conveyed to the vicars; of a selion of land lying in Hungithill [?
recte Hungirhill] between the land of Ralph son of Beatrice de Husgate Sutthon and
Robert's land which extends from the meadows above (*super*) the Derewent to the
moor of Butercramb; and of 2 a. of land in the territory of Husgate Sutthon, namely 1
a. lying in the eastern field of Husgate Sutthon above Langlandis and extending from
'Hesdland' [? *recte* the headland] of William Gernun up to Halleflat de Buttercramb
and 1 a. lying in the western field of Husgat Sutthon at Smalerornedikis and extending
from the meadows to the moor of Smalerornedikis.
Witnesses: William Gernun etc.   [probably first half of 13th century]

SOURCE: VC 8/Metcalfe notebks., Deeds in extenso, VIa, no. 63.

NOTE: See 104.

106. Grant by Gilbert son of John de Camera to Alice daughter of Roger Blund de Evercewych of all his land with tofts and crofts which William de Langetoft gave Gilbert's mother Agnes in the vill of Osgat Sutton; paying Gilbert and his heirs one pair of white gloves at Christmas, the vicars of blessed Peter of York 12*d.* a year, namely 6*d.* at Pentecost and 6*d.* at Martinmas, and the lord of the fee 1 lb. of cummin at Christmas.

Witnesses: Walter de Hemelsay, Thomas de Joneby of Huntington, Peter de Tadcaster etc. [probably later 13th century]

SOURCE: VC 8/Metcalfe notebks., Deeds in extenso, VIa, no. 64.

NOTE: The rent charge was the only income that the vicars received from land in Sutton in the early 14th century (VC 4/1/1).

SUTTON-UNDER-WHITESTONECLIFF
(in Felixkirk parish, Birdforth wapentake NR)

107. Confirmation by Robert Fossart of the gift which his father Adam Fossart gave to his sister [i.e. Adam's daughter] Eleanor, namely a carucate of land in Gildehusdale. She and her heirs are to hold the land of Robert and his heirs. [early 13th century]

Omnibus tam presentibus quam futuris Robertus Fossart salutem. Sciatis me concessisse et hac presenti karta mea confirmasse donum quod Adam Fossart pater meus dedit Alyenor sorori mee, scilicet unam carrucatam terre in Gildehusdale cum pertinenciis ut ipsa et heredes eius eam teneant in feodo et hereditate de me et heredibus meis libere et solute et quiete ab omnibus serviciis sicut karta patris mei purportat. Hiis testibus Adam Fossart, Galfrido Fossart, Galfrido de Coi'gneres, Thoma Fossart, Andr' de Magnebi, Arnulfo de Upsale, Thoma de Laceles, Willelmo Malebisse, Stephano de Menul, Roberto de Kerebi, et multis aliis.

SOURCE: VC 3/Vv 83 (194 mm. × 118 mm.)
ENDORSEMENT: *Gildusdale.*
SEAL: round (35 mm. dia.), hung on cord, plain, impression of a star of petals, legend [..]G[. . .] ROBERTI FOSSA[..]
DATE: Robert Fossard had succeeded his father by 1209; he was still alive in 1220 but dead by January 1226/7: *EYC,* ix. 153. Before **111.**
NOTE: Robert Fossard probably made this charter (**107**) in order to give his sister secure title to the carucate, which she had from her father Adam as a marriage portion. She gave half of it to the dean and chapter of York to support prayers for her parents (**108**). That grant was later confirmed by her other brother Thomas Fossard (**109**) and by her son Robert Ridel (**110**). In the 1220s or early 1230s the dean gave the half carucate to William de Laneham, a canon of York and archdeacon of Durham (**111**). William also acquired the other half of the carucate on lease from Eleanor, and he continued to pay a rent for it to her son (**112**). At William's request the abbot of Byland, lord of the fee in which the land lay (cf.

119), granted one of the half carucates to the vicars (113). The vicars evidently also possessed the other half: in the earlier 1240s they leased the whole carucate to Roger de Stretton for a rent of 3½ marks [£2 6s. 8d.] (114–115). In 1273 the same rent was evidently paid to the vicars by Thomas son of Robert de Stretton, who that year granted the land to William Cook (116). Cook still held at least half of the carucate in 1308 (117).

In 1342 the vicars were forced to recover the land by plea, a process recorded by documents copied into their cartulary. In April justices of the king's bench at Westminster heard a claim by the vicars to 4 bovates of land and 4 bovates of wood, which Tessanta de Darlington had held of them. She had failed to pay the rent for the past 2 years, thereby being considered to have withdrawn her service (118). Tessanta acknowledged the vicars' claim, but because there was suspicion of collusion between the two parties an inquisition was held. It was there recorded that Tessanta had half the vicars' carucate in Gildhusdale from her father William Cook on her marriage to John de Darlington (119). A further three documents relate to the delivery of seisin of the half carucate to the vicars (120–122). In September 1342 the vicars claimed the other half of the carucate from William son of John de Kilvington, who (like Tessanta) had failed to pay the past 2 years' rent for the land (123). Presumably the land had descended to William as a result of William Cook's grant to Peter de Kilvington in 1308 (117). A further three documents relate to an inquisition into the vicars' claim (124–125) and the delivery of seisin (126). The final three charters are leases by the vicars, after they had recovered the carucate: for 12 years in 1408 (127), for 39 years in 1468 (128), and for 15 years in 1532 (129).

108.   Grant, in free alms, by Eleanor daughter of Adam Fossard, in her widowhood, to God and blessed Peter and the dean and chapter of York, for the souls of her father, mother, and ancestors, of half a carucate of land in the fields of Sutton, lying near Thirsk in a place called Gildusdale; the land is from the carucate which her father gave her as her marriage portion.   [early 13th century]

Universis sancte matris ecclesie filiis Alienor filia Ade Fossard salutem in Domino. Noverit universitas vestra me in viduitate mea et libera potestate mea existentem dedisse et concessisse et hac presenti carta mea confirmasse Deo et beato Petro et decano et capitulo Eboracensi pro animabus patris et matris mee et omnium antecessorum meorum in puram et liberam et perpetuam elemosinam dimidiam carucatam terre in campis de Suttona cum pertinenciis infra villam et extra sine aliquo retenemento, videlicet illam quam iacet in loco qui vocatur Gildusdale et que est propinquior ville de Tresch, que quidem dimidia carucata terre est de carucata terre quam Adam Fossard pater meus dedit mihi in liberum maritagium, tenendam et habendam libere et quiete ab omni servicio et exactione seculari in puram et liberam et perpetuam elemosinam sicut unquam aliqua elemosina liberius et melius potest dari et teneri. Et ego predicta Alienor et heredes mei predictam dimidiam carucatam terre cum omnibus pertinenciis sine retenemento ut puram et liberam et perpetuam elemosinam nostram Deo et beato Petro et decano et capitulo Ebor' contra omnes homines de omnibus sectis et consuetudinibus defendemus et warantizabimus et adquietabimus. Hiis testibus magistro Nicholao capellano, Serlone de Staingate capellano, Johanne bovar', Rogero de Esinwaud capellano, Philippo de Colevile, Jordano Heirun, Stephano de Menull' de Turkelby, Thoma le Maunsel, Galfrido de

Otteleia, Thoma aurifabro, Waltero de Roma, Eustachio ad portam, Willelmo de Dunewiz, et multis aliis.

SOURCE: VC 3/Vv 84 (139 mm. × 151 mm.)

ENDORSEMENT: *Carta Alienor Fossard*; *De Gildhusedale*; *Carta capitulo Ebor' de Gildhus-dall'*; *Donacio capituli, sine date.*

SEAL: tag.

DATE: See dating note to 107.

NOTE: See 107.

109. Confirmation by Thomas Fossard son of Adam Fossard of the gift which his sister Eleanor made, in free alms, of half a carucate of land in the fields of Sutton to God, blessed Peter, and the dean and chapter of York, namely the half carucate lying near Thirsk in a place called Gildusdale; the land is from the carucate which Adam Fossard gave Eleanor as her marriage portion, and it is to be held as described in Eleanor's charter which Thomas has seen and inspected. [early 13th century]

Universis sancte matris ecclesie filiis Thom' Fossard filius Ade Fossard salutem in Domino. Noverit universitas vestra me ratam et gratam habere donacionem et concessionem quam Alienor filia Ade Fossard soror mea fecit de dimidia carucata terre in campis de Suttona cum pertinenciis infra villam et extra sine aliquo retenemento Deo et beato Petro et decano et capitulo Eboracen' in puram et liberam et perpetuam elemosinam, que scilicet dimidia carucata terre iacet in loci qui vocatur Gildusdale et que est propinquior ville de Tresch; que quidem dimidia carucata terre est de carucata terre quam Ada Fossard pater meus et suus dedit ei in liberum maritagium. Istam siquidem predictam dimidiam carucatam terre cum omnibus pertinenciis infra villam et extra sine retenemento Deo et beato Petro et dictis decano et capitulo Eboracen' hac presenti carta mea confirmavi; tenendam et habendam libere et quiete ab omni servicio et exactione seculari in puram et liberam et perpetuam elemosinam sicut unqua aliqua elemosina liberius et melius potest dari et teneri, prout in carta predicte Alienor sororis mee quam vidi et inspexi continetur. Hiis testibus magistro Nicholao capellano, Serlone de Steingate capellano, Johanne bovario, Rogero de Esingwald capellano, Stephano de Manull' de Turkelby, Thoma le Maunsel, Galfrido de Otteley, Willelmo Turchil, Thoma aurifabro, Waltero de Roma, Eustachio ad portam, Willelmo de Dunewiz, et multis aliis.

SOURCE: VC 3/Vv 85 (138 mm. × 135 mm.)

ENDORSEMENT: *Carta Thom' Fossard*; *de Gildusdale*; *Carta Willelmo capitulo Ebor' gildhusdal'.*

SEAL: vesica (36 mm. × 27 mm.), green, impression of a bird, legend.

DATE: At the same time as 108 (the charter is written in the same hand).

NOTE: See 107.

110. Confirmation by Robert Ridel knight of the gift which his mother Eleanor made in her widowhood, in free alms, to God, blessed Peter, and the dean and canons of York of half a carucate in Sutton, which was from her marriage portion and lies at a place called Gildehusdale. [early 13th century]

Omnibus sancte matris ecclesie filiis Robertus Ridel miles salutem in Domino. Noverit universitas vestra me donacionem et concessionem quam Alienor mater mea in sua libera viduitate existens fecit Deo et beato Petro et decano et canonicis Ebor' in puram et perpetuam elemosinam de dimidia carucata terre cum pertinenciis in Suttona que fuit de suo libero maritagio et que est in loco qui vocatur Gildehusdale ratam et firmam habere. In huius rei testimonium huic scripto sigillum meum apposui. Hiis testibus domino Willelmo de Lasceles milite, Waltero filio Stephani de Turkilby, Willelmo de Karletona, Galfrido de Hupsale, Willelmo Arundel, Roberto tinctore de Trech', Radulfo de ballio eiusdem ville, Ricardo clerico, Galfrido serviente, Guidone de ballio eiusdem ville, Roberto de barra, Willelmo le surrays, Willelmo de Paris, Rogero de Welle clerico archidiaconi, et aliis.

SOURCE: VC 3/Vv 86 (154 mm. × 99 mm.)
ENDORSEMENT: *Carta Rob' Ridel de Gildehusedale*; *capitulo Ebor'.*
SEAL: round (30 mm. dia.), green, impression of a pilgrim shell, legend + SIGILL' RO[.] RIDEL

DATE: Presumably at the same time as 108.
NOTE: 107.

111. Notification by mag. Roger de Insula dean of York that he has granted to his fellow canon William de Laneham, archdeacon of Durham, or to whom he wishes to assign, whether a religious house or a hospital, the half carucate of land in the fields of Sutton which Eleanor daughter of Adam Fossard gave in her widowhood, in free alms, to God, blessed Peter, and Roger, lying in a place near Thirsk called Gildusdale; the land is from the carucate which Adam Fossard gave Eleanor as her marriage portion; paying Roger and his successors 2s. a year, half at Martinmas and half at Pentecost. If William or his assigns lose the half carucate by force or by a formal agreement, Roger will not give them an exchange. [1220–1]

Magister Rogerus de Insula decanus Ebor' universis sancte matris ecclesie filiis salutem in Domino. Noverit universitas vestra nos dedisse et concessisse et hac presenti carta nostra confirmasse dilecto fratri et concanonico nostro Willelmo de Lanum archidiacono Dunelm' vel cui assignare voluerit sive domui religiose cuiuscunque, sit religionis sive hospitali, sive cuicunque alii dimidiam carucatam terre in campis de Sutton cum omnibus pertinenciis infra villam et extra sine aliquo retenemento quam scilicet Alienor filia Ade Fossard in sua viduitate existens et sua libera potestate constituta Deo et beato Petro et nobis in puram et liberam contulit elemosinam, quequidem dimidia carucata terre iacet in loco qui vocatur Gildusdale et que est propinquior ville de Tresch; que etiam dimidia carucata terre est de carucata terre quam Adam Fossard pater ipsius Alienor dedit ei in liberum maritagium; tenendam et habendam de Deo et beato Petro et nobis et successoribus nostris sibi et suis assignatis ita libere sicuti aliqua terra liberius teneri et haberi potest quiete, pacifice, et solute ab omni servicio et exactione seculari; reddendo inde nobis et successoribus nostris annuatim pro omni servicio duos solidos, medietatem in festo sancti Martini in hyeme et aliam medietatem in festo Pentecostes. Si vero dictus Willelmus archidiaconus vel sui assignati dictam dimidiam carucatam terre vi vel ratione amiserint, non dabimus eis escambium. His testibus magistro Nicholao, Serlone de Stainegate capellano, Jacobo capellano magistri Thome de Lichesfeld, Thoma capellano de Bolum, Hugo de Selebi maiore Ebor', Alexandro de Hil, Ricardo Fossard, Willelmo de Donewiz, Galfrido de

Ottelei, Waltero de Roma, Rogero Page, Gocelino de Armtorp, Roberto scriptore, et multis aliis.

SOURCE: VC 3/Vv 88 (189 mm. × 93 mm.)
ENDORSEMENT: *Gildhusdal'*; *capituli Ebor' facta Willelmo Lanum archidiacono dunellemensis.*
SEAL: seal of the chapter of York, vesica (65 mm. × 53 mm.), red wax.

DATE: When Roger de Insula was dean of York and before Thomas de Lichfield became a canon of York.
NOTE: See 107. The suggested date supplies evidence for William de Laneham as archdeacon of Durham (earlier than in *Fasti, York*) and for another of Hugh de Selby's mayoralties (cf. *Chs. Vicars Choral*, i, dating note to no. 21).

112.   Letter of Robert Ridel knight notifying that William archdeacon of Durham has paid him each year since the death of his mother Eleanor 1 lb. of cummin for a half carucate of land in Sutton which was part of her marriage portion and which Eleanor in her widowhood leased by cirograph to the archdeacon.   [probably early 1220s]

Omnibus has litteras visuris vel audituris Robertus Ridel miles salutem in Domino. Noverit universitas vestra quod Willelmus archidiaconus Dunolm' singulis annis post mortem Alienor matris mee solvit michi unam libram cymini pro dimidia carucata terre in Suttona que fuit de suo libero maritagio et quam dicta Alienor mater mea in sua viduitate existens concessit prefato archidiacono ad terminum per cyrografphum. In huius rei testimonium huic scripto sigillum meum apposui. Valete.

SOURCE: VC 3/Vv 87 (171 mm. × 44 mm.)
ENDORSEMENT: *Gildusdale.*
SEAL: sealed close, with seal of Robert Ridel (as on 109) on a tongue and a wrapping-tie beneath the tongue.

DATE: Probably about the same time as 111.
NOTE: See 107.

113.   Grant by Henry abbot of Byland and the convent, at the urging of William de Laneham archdeacon of Durham, to God and the church of St. Peter of York and the vicars serving God there of half a carucate in Sutton in a place called Gildehusdale, as is contained in a charter of the archdeacon which the vicars have. The abbot and convent wish that the vicars shall possess everything in peace, and that they and Robert Ridel knight and his successors shall be exempt from anything which appertains to the abbey as regards the land.   [1241 × 1243−4]

Omnibus hanc cartam visuris vel audituris Henricus abbas de Bella Landa et eiusdem loci conventus salutem in Domino. Noveritis nos divine pietatis intuitu ad instanciam domini Willelmi de Lanum archidiaconi Dunolm' concessisse et hac carta sigillo nostro roborata confirmasse Deo et ecclesie sancti Petri Ebor' et vicariis in dicta ecclesia Deo servientibus dimidiam carucatam terre in Suttona in loco qui dicitur Gildehusdale cum bosco et cum omnibus aliis pertinenciis, libertatibus, et aysiamentis sine aliquo retinemento, secundum quod continetur in carta predicti archidiaconi quam inde dicti vicarii habent. Et ideo volumus et concedimus quod dicti vicarii et successores sui omnia predicta in pace possideant. Et quod ipsi et Robertus Ridel miles et successores eius sint liberi et inmunes ab omnibus que nos et successores nostros occasione predicte terre contingunt vel contingere poterunt in perpetuum.

Hiis testibus domino Laurencio archidiacono Ebor', magistro J. Blundo cancellario, domino Serlone archidiacono Cliveland', magistris Nicolao et Johanne de Tyve, canonicis Ebor', Willelmo Arundel, Willelmo de Karletona, Rogero de Welle, et Galfrido de Karletona, clericis, Rogero filio Roberti de Stretton', et aliis.

SOURCE: VC 3/Vv 89 (2045 mm. × 95 mm.)

ENDORSEMENT: *Carta abbatis de bella landa de Gildehusedale.*

SEAL: vesica (48 mm. × 28 mm.), green, standing figure of abbot, legend SIGILLVM ABBATIS DE BELLA LANDA

DATE: When Laurence de Lincoln was archdeacon of York and before 114.

NOTE: See 107. As Laurence de Lincoln was still alive on 24 June 1245 but died later that year, the death of William de Laneham, which is given in *Chs. Vicars Choral*, i, no. 158 note as 17 April 1245 × 1249, must be revised as 17 April 1246 × 1249.

114.   Grant, in the form of a cirograph, by the vicars of the church of St. Peter of York to Roger de Stretton of a carucate of land in Sutton in a place called Gildusdale with the whole wood of Gildusdale and the common of Sutton, which land mag. William de Laneham archdeacon of Durham gave to the vicars in free alms; paying the vicars at York 3½ marks [£2 6s. 8d.] of silver a year, half at Pentecost and half at Martinmas.   [1241 × 1243–4]

Omnibus Christi fidelibus hanc cartam visuris vel audituris vicarii ecclesie sancti Petri Ebor' salutem eternam in Domino. Noveritis nos communi assensu dedisse, concessisse, et hac presenti carta nostra confirmasse Rogero de Stretona unam carucatam terre in Suttona in loco qui vocatur Gildusdale cum toto bosco de Gildusdale et cum communa de Suttona et omnibus aliis pertinenciis, aisiamentis, et libertatibus suis ubique et sine omni retenemento; quam quidem terram cum pertinenciis magister Willelmus de Lanum archidiaconus Dunolm' nobis caritative et divine pietatis intuitu in liberam, puram, et perpetuam elemosinam contulit; tenendam et habendam eidem Rogero et heredibus et assignatis suis et eorum heredibus tanquam assignatis nostris de nobis et successoribus nostris in feodo et hereditate inperpetuum; reddendo inde nobis et successoribus nostris annuatim tres marcas et dimidiam argenti, videlicet medietatem ad Pentecostem et medietatem ad festum sancti Martini in hyeme apud Ebor' pro omni servicio, consuetudine, et demanda. Et nos vicarii et successores nostri predictam terram cum omnibus pertinenciis suis eidem Rogero et heredibus et assignatis suis et eorum heredibus warantizabimus et defendemus contra omnes homines et de omnibus sectis, serviciis, consuetudinibus, et demandis debitis et non debitis adquietabimus inperpetuum per predictum servicium. In cuius rei testimonium tam nos vicarii quam ipse Rogerus sigilla nostra presenti carte cyrographate huic inde appossuimus. Hiis testibus domino F. Basseth tunc decano Ebor', magistris S. precentore, L. archidiacono Ebor', J. archidiacono Richemund', W. de Lanum archidiacono Dunolm', canonicis Ebor', Roberto parsona de Kilwingtona, dominis Nicholao de Bolteby, Waltero de Menil', Galfrido de Hupsale, militibus, Radulfo de ballio de Tresch, W. de Buthu' clerico, et aliis.

SOURCE: VC 3/Vv 90 (215 mm. × 189 mm.). CARTA CYROGRAPHATA, written at top (not indented).

ENDORSEMENT: *Carta vicariorum ecclesie beati Petri Ebor' de terris de Gildusdal'.*

SEAL: remains of vicars' common seal (for a description see *Chs. Vicars Choral*, i, p. xxii).

DATE: When Fulk Basset was dean of York and Laurence de Lincoln archdeacon of York.

NOTE: See 107.

115. Counterpart of 114 (reading Strettona for Stretona, apposuimus for appossuimus, Kilvingtona for Kilwingtona, Willelmo de Buthum for W. de Buthu', and adding domino before Roberto parsona de Kilvingtona).

SOURCE: VC 3/Vv 91 (215 mm. × 194 mm.)

ENDORSEMENT: *Gildusdale*; *per vicarios*; *Dimissio de toto Gyldhusdall' Rogero de Strettona et suis assignatis redd' vicariis ecclesie Ebor' in libera firma tres marcas et dimidiam.*

SEAL: slit.

116. Grant by Thomas son of Robert de Strettona, rector of the church of Santona, to Henry son of Walter Cook (*Coci*) de Tresk' clerk of a carucate of land in Suttona sub Wystayn in a place called Gyldusdale with Thomas's wood of Gyldusdale and with the common of Sutton', which land mag. William de Lanum archdeacon of Durham (*Dunolm'*), moved by charity and divine piety, conveyed (*contulit*) in pure and perpetual alms to the vicars of the church of blessed Peter of York; paying the vicars and their successors at York 3½ marks [£2 6s. 8d.] of silver, half at Pentecost and half at Martinmas. Warranty. Seal.

Witnesses: John Maunsel de Bruddeford, Thomas Maunsel de Heton', Ralph de Thorneton', Baldwin (*Bildewyno*) de Skyptona, Nicholas the hunter (*venatore*) de Catton', Henry de Carleton', Hugh Ke de Dalton', Robert son of Robert de Thorp', Roger de Kirkeby in Sutton', William son of Gamel of the same place, Adam de Aynderby in Tresk', Ranulph de Seleby, William de Aynderby, and others.

Santon', on the feast of the apostles Peter and Paul [29 June] 1273.

SOURCE: VC 3/Vv 92 (203 mm. × 166 mm.)

ENDORSEMENT: *Carta Thom' de Stretton' facta Henrico coco de terra de Gildusdal'*; *pro libera firma vicariis xlvj s. viiij d.*

SEAL: vesica (30 mm. × 18 mm.), red, impression of a fleur-de-lys, legend.

NOTE: See 107.

117. Grant by William Cook (*Cocus*) de Thresk to Peter de Kilvington' of the whole moiety of a carucate of land in the field of Gildusdale in the territory of Sutton' sub Wystaynclyf, and with all William's wood of Gildusdale; to be held of the chief lord of the fee for the service owed; paying the vicars of the church of blessed Peter 23s. 4d. a year. Warranty. Seal.

Witnesses: Robert de Foxoles, William Wysebarn, Robert Oliver, William de Sutton', John le Baker, William de Scheffeld, Walter the tailor (*cissore*), William Taleva(? c), and others.

Thresk, Tuesday after the feast of St. Peter in cathedra 1307, 1 Edward son of king Edward [27 February 1307/8].

SOURCE: VC 3/Vv 93 (217 mm. × 163 mm.)

ENDORSEMENT: *Cart' Willelmi Coci de terra de Gildusdale facta Petr' de Kilvington*; *pro libera firma vicariis xlvj s. viij d.*

SEAL: round (12 mm. dia.), plain, face rubbed.

NOTE: See 107.

118.   Plea at Westminster before R[oger] Hillary and his fellow justices of the king's
bench 3 weeks from Easter 16 Edward [III] [22 April 1342].
     Robert Swetemouth, warden of the house of vicars of the church of blessed Peter
of York, through Walter de Askham his attorney, claims against Tessanta de
Derlington 4 bovates of land and 4 a. of wood in Sutton under Whitestancliff,
which Tessanta holds of him by service and which ought to revert to the warden
according to statute because Tessanta has ceased the service for two years etc. The
warden says that Tessanta holds of him as of the right of his house [i.e. of the vicars]
for fealty (*per fidelitatem*) and the service of 23s. 4d. a year, of which John de Burton,
his predecessor as warden, was seised by the hand of Tessanta as of the right of his
house in peacetime in the time of the present king. For two years before the issue of a
writ on 6 February 16 Edward [III] [1341/2] Tessanta ceased the service etc., and
Robert proceeds with the suit etc. Tessanta through Thomas de Grantham her
attorney came and did not deny that she holds the land of the warden for the said
service and that she has ceased etc. as the warden has stated. It is judged that the
warden should recover the land etc. Tessanta is in mercy etc. The warden waives
damages etc. But because there is suspicion of collusion between them the sheriff is
ordered to make [a jury of] 12 men come here 15 days from Michaelmas [14 October]
or come before W[illiam] Basset, king's justice, if he should come to York before
Thursday after the feast of St. Laurence [8 August] etc.; meanwhile the process is
stayed etc.

SOURCE: VC 3/1/1, fo. 36v.

NOTE: See 107.

119.   Jury [sworn in the case] between Robert Swetemouth and Tessanta de
Derlington.
     Afterwards on the day and at the place required the warden came before William
Basset and his associate William Playce knight. The sheriff reported that the mandate
from Adam Mulgreve, bailiff of the liberty of the abbot of Byland (*Bella Landa*), had
stated that he had taken the land mentioned in the writ into the king's hands and that
he had informed the abbot, as mesne lord of the fee, and Thomas Wake de Lidell', as
the immediate lord of the fee, that they should be here on the day noted in the writ
[delivered] by William Wakeman and John Barker; [although] solemnly summoned,
the two lords did not come. The jurors chosen with the consent of the warden came,
and said on oath that the vicars of the church of blessed Peter of York were seised of a
carucate of land in Sutton under Whitestancliff and of 8 a. of wood in the same vill in
a place called Gildhousdal in the time of King H[enry] the great-grandfather of the
present king. The vicars had enfeoffed Roger de Stretton for a rent of 3½ marks
[£2 6s. 8d.] a year payable at York, half at Pentecost and half at Martinmas; Roger
died seised of the land, which came after his death into the hands of a certain William
Cok of Thresk. Afterwards William gave the moiety of the land now sought to John
de Derlingon in free marriage with his daughter Tessanta, to be held of the vicars for
half of the said rent, namely 23s. 4d. a year, of which the warden in the time of king
H[enry] and his successors as warden were seised up to the time of John de Burton,
the predecessor of the present warden. In the present king's reign John [de Burton]
received the rent from John [de Derlington] and Tessanta or from their tenants. John

de Derlington died and Tessanta continued seised of the land after his death; she paid the rent to John de Burton until she ceased 2 years before the issue of the writ, allowing the land to lie uncultivated. The present warden could not find distress in the land and still cannot. The jurors were asked if there was any fraud or collusion between the parties, and they said that the warden claimed arrears of rent from Tessanta at the stated time. Tessanta said that she wished to surrender the land to the warden because it was not worth the rent, but the warden refused to accept the surrender because he was a religious; he said that he wished to sue a writ against Tessanta, and she agreed to come on the first day of the plea; in order to determine the warden's legal standing, Tessanta came and pleaded as is shown in the record. Therefore it is decided etc.

SOURCE: VC 3/1/1, fos. 38r.–v.

NOTE: See 107.

120.   Record of the [decision of the king's] bench before W[illiam] Basset in the county [court] of York on behalf of Robert Swetemouth.
   Thomas de Rokeby sheriff of York to the bailiff of the liberty of the abbot of Byland (*Bella Landa*) has received a royal writ in these words:
   Writ ordering the sheriff of York to deliver seisin to Robert Swetemouth, warden of the house of vicars of the church of blessed Peter of York, of 4 bovates of land and 4 a. of wood in Sutton under Whitestancliff, which Robert has recovered from Tessanta de Derlington in the royal court at Westm[inster] because of her default, with no collusion or fraud, as is shown by the jury before William Basset at York. Witnessed by J. de Stonor at Westm[inster] on 26 October 16 Edward [III] [1342].
Wherefore the sheriff of York orders the bailiff to execute the writ.

SOURCE: VC 3/1/1, fos. 36v.–37r.

NOTE: See 107.

121.   Appointment by Robert Swetemouth, warden of the house of vicars of the church of blessed Peter of York, of Walter de Derlington, vicar of the said church, as his attorney to receive the seisin of 4 bovates of land and 4 a. of wood in Sutton under Whitestancliff, which he has recovered from Tessanta de Derlington. Seal.
York, 6 Kalends February 1342 [27 January 1342/3].

SOURCE: VC 3/1/1, fo. 37r.

NOTE: See 107.

122.   Memorandum that Robert [Swetemouth] was seised of the land by Adam de Molgreve bailiff of the liberty of the abbot of Byland (*Bella Landa*) on Monday on the morrow of the purification of the blessed Mary 1342 [3 February 1342/3], through his attorney Walter de Derlington vicar of York and in the presence of Robert Marschal' de Thresk, Thomas del Trend of Dalton', John de Baggeby, William Walsch' de Felicekirk, Thomas del Chaumbr' of Thresk, John Chace de Tresk, and others.

SOURCE: VC 3/1/1, fo. 37r.

NOTE: See **107**.

123. [Plea heard at] York Michaelmas term 16 [Edward III] [1342].

Robert Swetemouth, warden of the house of vicars of the church of blessed Peter of York, through his attorney Walter de Askham, claims against William son of John de Kylvyngton 4 bovates of land and 4 a. of wood in Sutton under Whitestanclyff, to which William has no right unless through John de Kilvyngton, who demised them to him and who held them of the warden for a set rent; the land ought to revert to the warden according to statute because William has now withheld the rent for the last 2 years etc. Robert says that William holds the land of him as of right of his house [of the vicars] for fealty and the service of 23s. 4d. a year, which John de Burton, his predecessor as warden, received from John de Kilvyngton in the time of the present king; William ceased the service for 2 years before the issue of a writ on 8 May 16 [Edward III] [1342], and Robert proceeded with the suit etc. William came and defended his right etc.; he readily acknowledged that he holds the land of the warden for the stated rent, but says that on the day of the issue of the writ nothing was owed to the warden as arrears and so he puts himself on the country and Robert likewise. The sheriff is ordered to summon [a jury of] 12 men to come here a month from Easter [12 May 1343] etc.

SOURCE: VC 3/1/1, fo. 37v.

NOTE: See **107**.

124. Memorandum that on that day [i.e. 12 May 1343; see **123**] the jury [to be sworn in the case] between Robert Swetemouth, warden of the house of vicars of the church of blessed Peter of York, plaintiff, and William son of John de Kilvyngton, defendant, was postponed until 3 weeks after Michaelmas [20 October] unless W[illiam] Basset, king's justice, should first come to York on Friday after the feast of blessed Mary Magdalene [24 July]; [the postponement is] because of the default of the jurors, none of whom came [on 12 May]; the sheriff 'has the bodies'.

SOURCE: VC 3/1/1, fo. 37v.

NOTE: See **107**.

125. Jury [sworn in the case] between Robert Swetemouth and William son of John de Kylvyngton.

Afterwards on the day and at the place required the parties came through their attorneys before William Basset and his associate Thomas de Fencotes, and before the jurors chosen with the consent of the parties; the jurors say on oath that William de Lanum formerly archdeacon of Durham (*Dunelm*) was seised of the said land in the time of the present king's great-grandfather and gave it to the vicars of the church of blessed Peter of York; in the same time the vicars enfeoffed Roger de Stretton and his heirs to hold [the land] for 23s. 4d. a year, and that by virtue of that enfeoffment Roger and all the tenants of the said land paid the rent to the vicars up to the time of John de Kylvyngton, who refused to pay the rent to John de Burton. Asked if William ceased to pay the rent for 2 years before issue of the writ or not, the jurors say that he did withhold the rent in that period; and asked if there is any fraud or collusion between the parties, the jurors say there is none. It is therefore judged that Robert

Swetemouth warden etc. should recover his seisin of the land as of the right of his house [of the vicars] and that William son of John is in mercy etc.

SOURCE: VC 3/1/1, fos. 37v.–38r.

NOTE: See 107.

126. Writ of Edward III to the sheriff of Yorkshire to deliver seisin to Robert Swetemouth, warden of the house of vicars of the church of blessed Peter of York, of 4 bovates of land and 4 a. of wood in Sutton under Whitestancliff', which Robert has recovered against William son of John de Kylvynton.
Westminster, 22 October 17 Edward [III] [1343].

SOURCE: VC 3/1/1, fo. 37r.

NOTE: See 107.

127. Indenture witnessing that Nicholas de Holm', warden of the house of vicars of the cathedral church of blessed Peter of York, and all the vicars of the same college have demised at farm to Richard de Kyrekby of Thresk for 12 years from Martinmas 1408 a carucate of land in Suttona in a place called Gildusdale with all the wood of Gildusdale, the common of Sutton, and all easements as regards growing trees (*grossis arboribus*), except oak (*ak'*), holly (*holin*), maple (*mapill'*), and crab apple (*crabtre*); paying the vicars 24s. of sterling a year, in equal portions at Pentecost and Martinmas. If the rent is in arrears 40 days after the terms, the warden and vicars may distrain the carucate with the wood and common and take distress until they are satisfied. If the rent is still in arrears 40 days later, the warden and vicars may enter and retain the property and dispose of it as they wish. Warranty. Seal.
Witnesses: Thomas Simson' de Thresk, John Bradelay of the same place, and William Bageby of the same place.
Thresk, on Martinmas [11 November] the year aforesaid, 10 Henry IV [1408].

SOURCE: VC 3/Vv 94 (303 mm. × 204 mm.; torn, in two parts). Indented at top with letters.
ENDORSEMENT: *Indentura de Gildusdale anno domini m^l cccc octavo; Eodem tempore solut' erat xxiiij s.*
SEAL: slit.

NOTE: See 107.

128. Indenture witnessing that William Hutton, warden of the college of vicars in the choir of the cathedral church of blessed Peter of York, and the vicars of the same place have demised at farm to Robert Hubberd, rector of the parish church of Flixburgh, diocese of Lincoln, for 39 years from last Martinmas [11 November 1467], land next to Thresk in a place called Gillesdalefeld; paying the warden and vicars 13s. 4d. of sterling a year, in equal portions at Pentecost and Martinmas ¹or within 10 weeks after either term.¹ If the rent is in arrears and there is insufficient distress to be found there, the warden and vicars may re-enter and hold the land. The warden and vicars allow (*concedunt*) Robert and his assigns to take a reasonable parcel of land (*racionabilem garcellum*) next to the land as a close and take herbage there for his cattle.

Robert or his assigns may not cut down any trees or wood growing in the virgate. Warranty. Seal.

York, 5 March 1467, 8 Edward IV [1467/8].

SOURCE: VC 3/Vv 95 (278 mm. × 105 mm.). Indented at top.
ENDORSEMENT: *Thryske.*
SEAL: tag.

1–1 Text interlineated in a different hand.

NOTE: See **107**.

129.   Indenture [in English] made on 6 February 24 Henry VIII [1531/2] between Master Thomas Marsar, succentor (*subchauntor*) of the vicars choral of the church of York, and the vicars and James Robinson of Thriske husbandman, by which the vicars have demised at farm to Robinson for 15 years from next Martinmas land near Thriske in a dale called in Gildhousdale; paying the vicars 20s. a year, in equal portions at Pentecost and Martinmas, the first term of payment to begin at Pentecost 1534 and payments to be made within the Bethern' [i.e. the Bedern] at Yorke. If the farm is unpaid in part or in whole 20 days after any term, the vicars may re-enter the premises and let them to anyone else. James binds himself to leave all the land, both arable and meadows, in sufficient manuring and tillage at the end of the 15 years. For the performance of this agreement James is bound with Thomas Whipp' and Richard Pagett of the town of Thriske, husbandmen, by deed of obligation in the sum of £10. Seal.

Given in the Bethern' at Yorke the day and year abovesaid.

SOURCE: VC 3/Vv 96 (369 mm. × 168 mm.). Indented at top.
ENDORSEMENT: *Indentura Jacobi Robynson pro Gyldhouse daill' iuxta Thirske.*
SEAL: round (20 mm. dia.), red, impression rubbed, legend.

NOTE: See **107**.

THORNBOROUGH
(in Allerton Mauleverer parish, Claro wapentake WR)

130.   Grant, in free alms, by Richard del Kenne for the salvation of his soul and the souls of his ancestors and successors to God, the church of St. Peter of York, and the vicars serving God in the same church of 1½ bovates of land without toft in Thornborough, lying next to the land of Aldelin le Vessaie on the east; also, of 2 tofts with crofts, a third toft without croft, and 4 a. in the same vill, namely: one toft with croft lying next to the toft of Stephen son of Amfrey on the west; the other toft with croft lying between the toft of Henry de Hopperton and the pool; the third toft without croft lying next to the land of Henry de Hopperton on the east; and the acres lying at named places. Warranty.   [earlier 13th century]

Sciant omnes presentes et futuri quod ego Ricardus del Kenne dedi, concessi, et hac carta sigillo meo roborata confirmavi Deo et ecclesie sancti Petri Ebor' et vicariis in eadem ecclesia Deo servientibus pro salute anime mee et animarum antecessorum et successorum meorum unam bovatam et dimidiam terre cum pertinenciis in Thorneburg' sine tofto, videlicet illam bovatam et dimidiam que iacent iuxta terram Aldelini le Vessaie versus orientem; et preterea duos toftos cum croftis et aliis pertinenciis suis in eadem villa; et tercium toftum cum pertinenciis excepto crofto in eadem villa; et preterea quatuor acras terre cum pertinenciis in eadem villa; scilicet, unum toftum cum crofto qui iacet iuxta toftum Stephani filii Amfridi versus occidentem; et alium toftum cum crofto qui iacet inter toftum Henrici de Hoperton' et stangnum; et tercium toftum sine crofto qui iacet iuxta terram Henrici de Hoperton versus orientem; et ad Sleteb'gh' et ad Whetelandes et ad Wandalepit unam acram terre de prenominatis quatuor acris; et ad strete furlanges et ad brakenehille aliam acram terre; et ad Harthegripes terciam acram terre; et ad Wandale et ad Heselrane quartam acram terre; habendam et tenendam dictis vicariis in perpetuum in liberam, puram, et perpetuam elemosinam cum omnibus pertinenciis et aisiamentis suis ubique sine omni retenemento. Et ego Ricardus del Kenne et heredes mei warantizabimus et defendemus dictis vicariis predictam bovatam et dimidiam terre cum pertinenciis et predictos tres toftos cum pertinenciis et predictas quatuor acras terre cum pertinenciis sicut liberam, puram, et perpetuam elemosinam contra omnes homines in perpetuum et de omnimodis sectis, consuetudinibus, et demandis adquietabimus. Hiis testibus Henrico de Hamerton', Roberto Luvel, Waltero de vestiario, Stephano sacrista, Galfrido de Ottelaie, David' de Useburn', Radulfo filio Gamelli, Ricardo filio Johannis, Radulfo de Hoperton', Waltero de Hoperton', Johanne fratre suo, Luca Revel, Roberto filio Hugonis de Hoperton', Ricardo fratre Hugonis, Petro de Gailestorp, Henrico fratre suo, et aliis.

SOURCE: Hailstone collection, in folder Box 3.24 (162 mm. × 130 mm.)
ENDORSEMENT: *Carta Ricardi del Kenne de Thorneburgh.*
SEAL: tag.

WARTHILL

(in Gate Helmsley parish, Bulmer wapentake NR)

131. Grant by Walter son of [Richard][1] Richeman de Warthill' to mag. John le Cras, canon of York, and his heirs of two tofts and crofts in the vill of Warthill', lying between the land of Richard de Tang' on the south and that of Thomas Norays on the north; paying for them and for the two bovates of land which John has of Walter's gift in the same vill 2*d*. a year, namely 1*d*. at Christmas and 1*d*. at the feast of the nativity of St. John the Baptist. Warranty. Seal.
Witnesses: [names not entered into cartulary]. [1266 × 1279]

SOURCE: VC 3/1/1, fo. 31v.

[1] The name, which is omitted in MS., is supplied from 132.

DATE: When John le Cras (or Gras) was canon of York.
NOTE: This and the next four charters relate to land in Warthill which John le Cras gave to the vicars to support his obit. Cras died in 1279, possibly on 6 November,

the day stipulated for the payment of the rent from the land (**135**). The application of the rent in support of the obit was noted in the rental for 1309 (VC 4/1/1).

132. Quitclaim by Walter son of Richard Richeman de Warthill' to mag. John le Crase, canon of York, of two bovates of land with one toft and croft in Warthill', lying [dispersed] in the field (*per totum campum*) between Walter's lands and the toft and croft which Henry de Holteby once had between Walter's toft and croft and that of Richard de Tang'; neither Walter nor his heirs may sell or claim [the property]; paying Walter and his heirs 1*d.* a year at Christmas. Warranty. Seal.
Witnesses: [names not entered into cartulary].   [1266 × 1279]

SOURCE: VC 3/1/1, fo. 31v.

DATE: As **131**.
NOTE: See **131**.

133. Grant by John le Gras [*sic*], canon of the church of York, for the salvation of his soul and [the souls] of all his ancestors and successors, to God and the church of blessed Peter of York and to Richard, warden of the house of vicars, and the vicars of the same church of two bovates of arable land with two tofts and two crofts in the vill and territory of Warthil, lying in the fee of the prior and convent of St. Andrew of York, order of Semp[r]ingham; John has the two bovates and the two tofts and crofts of the gift of Walter Richeman de Warthil'. Each year the vicars shall pay on the day of John's obit 2 marks [£1 6s. 8d.] of silver to the vicars, clerks, and boys who shall be present at his exequies, namely 20s. to the vicars and ½ mark [6s. 8d.] to the clerks and boys. Warranty. Seal.
Witnesses: dom. Stephen de Sutthona, mag. Thomas de Heduna, canons of the church of York, Peter de Santona citizen of York, John de Gartona, Bego Fayrfax, Roger Trossebuth, and others.   [probably 1279]

SOURCE: VC 3/3/3 (194 mm. × 117 mm.)
ENDORSEMENT: *Donacio magistri Johannis le Gras de terra de Warthil; custodi domus vicariorum; sine data.*
SEAL: tag.
COPY: VC 3/1/1, fos. 31v.–32r.

DATE: Thomas de Hedon occurs as a canon of York in 1279, the year in which John le Cras died.
NOTE: See **131**.

134. Quitclaim by Emma widow of Walter Richeman de Warthill to Richard, warden of the vicars of the church of blessed Peter of York, and the vicars of two bovates of land with tofts and crofts in the vill of Warthill, which mag. John le Cras, formerly canon of York, bought from her husband (*viro*) Walter and gave to the vicars. Seal.
Witnesses: [names not entered into the cartulary].   [after 1279]

SOURCE: VC 3/1/1, fo. 32r.

DATE: John le Cras died in 1279.
NOTE: See **131**.

135. Grant, in the form of a cirograph, by Richard, warden of the house of vicars of the church of blessed Peter of York, and the vicars of the same church, by their common agreement and consent, to the prior and convent of St. Andrew in York, order of Sempringham, of two bovates of arable land and two tofts and two crofts in the vill and territory of Warthil, which the vicars were given by mag. John le Cras, canon of the church of York; paying the vicars and their successors in the great church of York 2 marks [£1 6s. 8d.] on St. Leonard's day [6 November] each year. The prior and convent agree that, provided the 2 marks are paid on that day, the vicars may enter and distrain the property and also the tenement which William Wither holds of the prior and convent in Warthil for a rent of 32d. Warranty. Sealed with the vicars' common seal and with the common seal of the chapter of the prior and convent. Witnesses: [names not entered into the cartulary].   [1279 or shortly afterwards]

SOURCE: VC 3/1/1, fos. 32r.–v.

DATE: Probably shortly after the death of John le Cras.
NOTE: See **131**.

WHELDALE

(in Ferry Fryston parish, Osgoldcross wapentake WR)

136. Quitclaim by Everard the glover (*cirotecarius*), son of Henry de Queldall', to Thomas de Queldall', for a sum of money, of a toft in the vill of Queldall', lying between the land of the church on the south and that of Adam son of Pain on the north, one end abutting on the way which leads through the middle of the vill and the other end on the croft; paying to Everard a rosebud (*flosculum rose*) at the feast of St. John the Baptist [24 June] each year. Seal.
Witnesses: Richard son of Hugh de Queldall', Hugh de Castilfort, John the chamberlain de Pontefract, William of the cellar (*de celario*), William son of Ellis, Walter the Scot (*Scotico*), Adam de Batalyy, Adam de Layrthorp, Thomas Beverley (*Beverlaco*), and many others.   [probably second half of 13th century]

SOURCE: VC 3/1/1, fo. 23r.

NOTE: The form of the charter suggests a date before the vicars acquired the appropriation of the parish church of Fryston in 1332. A note in the margin of the cartulary text reads 'This charter is in the hand of Edmund Smith (*Fabr'*) in Fristun, and this copy is written on account of the house and croft and toft in Queldall''.

Out-county

ASBY (Westmorland)

137. Grant and demise at farm in perpetuity by William son of Robert son of Colman and his heirs to God and the hospital of blessed Peter of York and its brethren of 160 a. in Asby and common pasture for their men, namely for the beasts of those who live on the land, for a rent of 10s. 8d. [a year], half at Pentecost and the rest at Martinmas. The brethren shall grind corn at William's mill and help make the mill pond; for three days in the autumn they shall help to mow William's corn with 8 men each day; and they shall do forensic service, namely a third of the service which pertains to the moiety which William holds in Asby. Also, William grants to the hospital 2 bovates of land, namely 20 a., and pasture for 400 sheep in the vill, quit of all geld and customs as in free alms. The brethren may erect sheepfolds and hurdles and move them from place to place as suits them. They shall hold their court in free alms, and if by chance any of their men wrongs William or his men, then William shall come to the brethren's court and have justice there; and if any of William's men wrongs the brethren or their men, the brethren shall come to William's court and have justice there.   [1177–81]

Willelmus filius Roberti filii Colemanni et heredes eius omnibus videntibus et audientibus has litteras salutem. Sciatis nos concessisse et dimississe Deo et hospitali beati Petri Ebor' et fratribus eiusdem domus Dei octies viginti acras terre in Askebi ad firmam in perpetuum et communem pasturam hominibus suis, scilicet pecuniis eorum qui habitabunt in predicta terra libere et quiete ab omnibus serviciis quae ad nos pertinent, excepto quod reddent nobis et heredibus nostris decem solidos et viii denarios, scilicet v solidos et iiij denarios ad Pentecosten et totidem ad festum sancti Martini; et molent ad molendinum meum et adiuvabunt facere stagnum molendini; et tribus diebus adiuvabunt nos in autumpno ad metendum bladum nostrum unaquaque die cum octo hominibus; et facient forense servitium, scilicet terciam partem forensis servicii quod pertinet ad illam medietatem quam nos tenemus in Askebi. Preterea vero sciendum est nos concessisse et dedisse prefato hospitali duas bovatas terre, videlicet xx acras in se continentes, et quadringentis ovibus propriis pasturam in prefata villa liberam et solutam et quietam ab omnibus geldis et consuetudinibus et exactionibus et auxiliis et ab omni humano et seculari servicio sicut puram et perpetuam elemosinam. Licebit autem predictis fratribus facere ovile suum et caulas in prefata elemosina[1] et movere de loco ad locum quocumque sicut placuerit sine contradictione. In qua vero elemosina fratres predicti hospitalis facient curiam suam, et si forte quispiam[2] de hominibus eorum forefecerit nobis vel hominibus nostris, veniemus in curiam eorum et ibi habebimus rectum; et si aliquis de nostris sibi vel suis forefecerit, venient in curiam nostram et ibi habebunt rectum. Hii sunt testes Robertus decanus Ebor', Hamo cantor, Radulphus archidiaconus, magist[ri] Guido, Hugo Murdac, Alanus, Stephanus, Jeroldus, Thomas filius Paulini, Adam de Thorn', Reginaldus Arundel, canonici beati Petri, et totum capitulum, Murdac decanus de Apelbi, Adam de Overtunia, Robert de Bamt', Willelmus de Kirkebi, Walterus de Milnebrunne, et capitulum de Westmer', Robertus filius Petri, Ricardus Anglicus, Willelmus le Bret, Hervicus niger, Gilbertus dengame, Robertus de Sanfort, Thomas de Musegrave, et multis aliis.

SOURCE: VC 3/Vv 7 (232 mm. × 141 mm.)

ENDORSEMENT: *Will' Robert fil' Colemanni de occies viginti acris in Askebi*; [bundle mark] *vij*; (in a 17th-cent. hand) *A grant of eight score acres of land in Askeby by William son of Robert son of Coleman to the Hospital of St. Peter in Yorke.*

SEAL: tag.

¹ MS. has a mark of abbreviation at the end of *elemosina'*.
² MS. has *quisopiam*, with apparently a point under the *o* to indicate deletion.

DATE: Hamo the precentor and some of the canons who appear as witnesses are all first recorded 1177 × 1181; Robert Butevilain died as dean of York in 1186.

NOTE: Although a stray, the charter was probably in the archive by the later 17th century, as the endorsement of that date is in the hand of Anthony Wright, a vicar choral who annotated many documents in the post-Restoration period.

St. Peter's hospital originated as a pre-Conquest foundation. It was given a new site in York in the late 11th century, and King Stephen authorised the construction of a hospital chapel dedicated to St. Leonard, whose name later replaced St. Peter's (*VCH Yorks.* iii. 336–7).

CAXTON (Cambridgeshire)

138. Appointment by John de Bretton' of John Wodeward chaplain and Roger Toynton' as assigns to deliver in John's name to dom. Thomas Darundell', archbishop of York and primate of England, William Pappeworthe knight (*chivaler*), Richard de Treton' clerk, John Woderone, John Harlyngton', William Notton', Henry Oundell', clerk of the estreats in Common Pleas (*de extractis in communi banco*), Richard Forster chaplain, Henry Conquest de Chefierton', William Cothurstoke, John Weldon', and Roger Barker seisin of all his lands and tenements, rents, reversions, and services in the vill of Caxton', according to the charter made by him.
Wermyngton', 20 April 17 Richard II [1394].

SOURCE: VC 3/Vv 23 (294 mm. × 77 mm.)
ENDORSEMENT: *Feffament' . . . in Caxton*; *Caxton*.
SEAL: round (17 mm. dia.), red, impression of a cross formed by four roundels, legend.

NOTE: The charter is a stray in the archive.

KIBBLESWORTH (Co. Durham)

139. Grant by Geoffrey de Kibbelesworth' to Thomas Scrotevyle de Kibbelesworth of 1 a. of land in the vill and in the field of Kibbelesworth, lying on (*super*) Brerilawe. Warranty. Seal.
Witnesses: William de Kibbelesworth, John de Farneacres, Gilbert de Merley, Richard de Ravenesworth, and Robert son of Adam de Ravenesworth, and others.

Kibbelesworth, Thursday on the feast of the annunciation of the blessed Virgin Mary [25 March] 1333.

SOURCE: VC 3/Vv 54 (223 mm. × 82 mm.)
ENDORSEMENT: none.
SEAL: tag.

NOTE: The two Kibblesworth charters are strays in the archive.

140.	Grant by Geoffrey de Spenithurne to William Batte del Ryding of 14 a. of arable land in the field of Kiblesworth, namely: 8 a. in a place called le Overfeld, of which 5 a. abut on (*super*) Elnelawe, 2 a. on Auldton'lawe, and 1 a. on Derlyng; and 6 a. in a place called le Southfeld, of which 3½ a. abut on le Louynges, 1 a. on le Shouelbrades, and 1½ a. lie in Shipwas. Warranty. Seal.
Witnesses: William de Kiblesworth, Thomas de Scroteville, Richard de Ravenesworth, and many others.
Kiblesworth, 12 December 1342.

SOURCE: VC 3/Vv 55 (252 mm. × 114 mm.)
ENDORSEMENT: none.
SEAL: tag.

NOTE: See **139**.

Miscellaneous

141.	Quitclaim by Thomas son of Oliver de Gunneby made before the abbot of Peterborough (*de burgo sancti Petri*) and Roger de Thurkilby, royal justices on eyre in full assize at York, as is written and witnessed in their rolls, to the dean and chapter of blessed Peter of York of Philip son of Henry le Palmer de Dunington with all his offspring (*sequela*) and chattels. Neither Thomas nor his heirs may exact anything from Philip or sell him by reason of neifty or any other pretext, but Philip and all his offspring shall be free tenants of the dean and chapter. For [which the dean and chapter shall pay Thomas] 12*d*. a year, half at Pentecost and half at Martinmas. Seal.
Witnesses: dom. Gerard Salvayn, Robert the constable de Holum, Peter de la Hay, knights, Richard de la Hay, Roger Russel, Walter Bacheler, James Bataille, Peter Batail', Richard de Herilthorp, Henry de Herelthorp, Richard de Gunneby, Roger de Wresil, Richard of the same place, Alan the clerk, and others.	[possibly 1257]

SOURCE: VC 3/1/1, fo. 52v.

DATE: Both justices were at York in 1257: *Yorkshire Deeds*, ed. C. T. Clay, vii (YASRS, lxxxiii, 1932), p. 148.
NOTE: A marginal note against the cartulary copy of **141** reads 'Bubbewith', which suggests a connexion with the grant made 1262 × 1269–71 by Simon de Evesham, archdeacon of Richmond, to the dean and chapter of York of land in Bubwith,

together with the homage and service of one free man in Laytham (*Chs. Vicars Choral*, i, no. 413). Gunby is in Bubwith parish.

142. Quitclaim by Thomas son of Thomas de Gunneby to the dean and chapter of blessed Peter of York of Philip son of Henry le Palmer de Dynington with all his offspring and chattels. Thomas's parents Thomas and Elizabeth gave and quitclaimed Philip to the chapter of York before the abbot of Peterborough (*de burgo sancti Petri*) and Roger de Thurkilby, royal justices on eyre then at York. Neither Thomas [the present grantor] nor his heirs may demand anything from or sell Philip or his offspring by reason of neifty or any other manner. Seal.

Witnesses: dom. Thomas de Gunneby, German Hay de Aukton', Gilbert de Cokeryngton, Roger de Lynton', Roger de Hugat', James Batail, Roger de Cave, Richard de Gunneby, William son of Walter de Bubbewith', Richard ad Flet' of the same place, Richard son of Thomas de Herlethorp, Henry son of Peter of the same place, William the fisherman of the same place, Richard de Gunneby clerk, and others.   [later 13th century]

SOURCE: VC 3/1/1, fo. 53r.

DATE: After **141**.
NOTE: See **141**.

Appropriated Churches

COTTINGHAM

143. Grant by Richard III to the warden of the house of vicars and the vicars of the cathedral church of blessed Peter of York of the advowson of the parish church of Cotyngham in the county and diocese of York, to be held in free alms.
Westminster, 15 December [anno] 2 [1484].

SOURCE: Rehearsed in **145**.
CALENDARED: *Cal. Pat. R.* 1476–85, p. 507.

NOTE: Although Archbishop Rotherham allowed the appropriation and ordained a vicarage (**145**), the vicars did not acquire seisin.

144. Confirmation by Richard III of **143**, together with a licence to appropriate the church; the king wishes that the vicar of the church shall be sufficiently endowed, and that a competent sum of money from the fruits and income of the church shall be distributed among poor parishioners of the church by the diocesan.
Westminster, 18 December anno 2 [1484].

SOURCE: Rehearsed in **145**.
CALENDARED: *Cal. Pat. R.* 1476–85, p. 507.

145. [*Appropriation of Cottingham church and ordination of vicarage.*]

Notarial instrument of John Deyce, clerk of the diocese of Coventry and Lichfield and apostolic notary, rehearsing a letter of Thomas [Rotherham], archbishop of York [as follows]:

The dean and chapter of the cathedral church of blessed Peter of York and the warden of the house of vicars choral (*vicariorum choralium*) and the vicars have shown the archbishop that the vicars, on account of the impoverishment and diminution of their fruits, possessions, and income, which consist mostly of the rents of buildings and tenements in the city of York, are unable to maintain their usual number (*numerum solitum habere non possunt*). Whereas at the foundation [of the house] the rents supported 36 vicars, now they are so diminished that they can scarcely support 26 vicars; as a result of which divine service is not a little reduced (*non modicum extat imminutus*). Wherefore King Richard, wishing to restore the number [of vicars], has granted to the warden and vicars the advowson of the parish church of Cotyngham, in York diocese, with a licence for obtaining the church to their own uses, so that it should be appropriated to them; the tenor of the grant and licence is given below.

The archbishop ordains the appropriation of the said church, saving the portion of the vicar and saving the payment of 40s. a year to himself and his successors, 10s. a year to the dean and chapter and their successors, and 20d. a year to the archdeacon of the Estridding and his successors, payable in the church of York at Martinmas and Pentecost, together with the distribution of 2 barrels (*barellos*) and 2 casks (*cados*) of eels and 2 quarters of corn baked in loaves (*in panes pist'*), taken from the fruits and income of the church of Cotyngham, among poor parishioners there each year in Lent.

Also, the archbishop ordains that when the church of Cotyngham next becomes vacant, there is to be a perpetual vicarage to which, whenever it is vacant, the chancellor of the university of Cambridge or his deputy and the regents and non-regents of the university or the greater part of them, with the assent and consent of the greater part of the doctors there, shall present to the archbishop and his successors, or in the case of a vacancy [in the see] to the dean and chapter [of York], a doctor of divinity or a doctor of decretals or of laws, or at least a bachelor in divinity, within a month of the notification of the vacancy of the said vicarage. The vacancy is to be certified to the chancellor of the university or the vice-chancellor by a messenger of the house of vicars [sent] at their own costs within a month after it [has occurred]. The archbishop ordains that if the regents and non-regents, or the greater part of them, neglect to make the presentation within a month [of being notified], then the collation of the vicarage shall devolve on himself and his successors, or on the dean and chapter if the see is vacant.

For the portion and sustenance of the perpetual vicar, the archbishop assigns £40 from the fruits and income of the church of Cotyngham, to be paid by the appropriators each year in equal portions at Martinmas and Pentecost; moreover, the vicar shall have for his dwelling-house (*mansionem*) all the soil and ground (*solum et fundum*) with the buildings of the rectory of the church within the precinct of the rectory [lying] on the west side of a wall, [built] partly of stone and partly of plaster (*lutei*), which runs from the south to the north and divides the dwelling-house of the rectory from the great curtilage, where there are barns, granaries, and other buildings, along with the wall itself. The vicar is to keep the buildings [on the west side of the wall] and the wall [itself] in repair.

Also, the archbishop ordains that whomever has been presented to the vicarage shall be corporally inducted and not seek any dispensation against the constitutions concerning the residency of vicars; and if the vicar shall contravene [the constitutions] by not keeping continual residence in the vicarage, then the appropriators shall pay him only £20 at the said terms and shall pay the other £20 to the dean and chapter of the cathedral church of York for the use in equal portions of the fabric of that church and of the residentiary canons.

If this ordinance is not kept by the warden and vicars as the appropriators, then after a lapse of 40 days the archbishop or his official or the president of the archbishop's court may distrain rents and income to the value of £10 a year from the church. Also, the archbishop ordains that the appropriators shall pay tenths to the king and subsidy to the archbishop and his successors, and do all repairs to the chancel and [bear] all other ordinary and extraordinary burdens.

[*Now follow the texts of the royal grant and licence, **143** and **144**.*]

The ordinance and notarial instrument was made before (*coram*) Archbishop Thomas in his chapel in his manor of Scroby on 28 June 1485, in the presence of mag. William Sheffeld, doctor of decretals and the archbishop's chancellor, John Kirkhall, master in arts, Robert Welyngton, public notary, and William Alynson, chaplain of the dioceses of Lincoln, Coventry and Lichfield, and York.

SOURCE: [i] VC 3/4/Cot/1a (509 mm. × 534 mm.); [ii] VC 3/4/Cot/1b (554 mm. × 525 mm.).

ENDORSEMENT: [i] (too faded to read); [ii] *Appropriacio ecclesie de Cotyngham cum licenciis regis.*

SEAL: [i] remains of archiepiscopal seal in green wax on a parchment tag; [ii] slit.

SIGN: [i] and [ii] notarial sign of John Deyce, notary.

COPY: The ordinance is partly entered in Rotherham's register, ending in the middle of the section dealing with the presentation to the vicarage, at which point the bottom half of the folio has been cut away: BIHR, Reg. 23, ff. 283v.–284.

FRYSTON

146. Agreement [in French], in the form of an indenture, between Henry le Vavasour and the warden of the house of vicars of the church of St. Peter of York, whereby Henry grants to the vicars in pure and perpetual alms the advowson of the church of St. Andrew of Friston on the water (*sur leawe*) next to Pountefract, on the condition that the warden and vicars shall maintain in perpetuity three chaplains celebrating (*chauntauntz*) for the souls of Henry, his wife (*sa compaigne*), and his ancestors, namely two celebrating in the church of St. Peter of York and one in the chapel of Heselwod' or in the church of Friston, being chosen by Henry. The warden and vicars shall also celebrate in perpetuity obits for Henry and his wife each year after their deaths, sharing 36s. at each obit. Moreover, the vicars shall celebrate an obit each year for William le Vavasour and his wife Dame Nichole during Henry's life, when nothing shall be shared out among the vicars unless Henry wishes to give it from his own funds. Henry shall maintain the three chaplains at his own costs during the lifetime of the present incumbent (*vivaunt la parsoun q'ore eist*), and will give the vicars £10 a year for the chaplains' support. He will also be responsible for all the costs payable to the king and other lords concerning the mortization (*mortissement*) of the

advowson of the church of St. Andrew of Friston; the vicars will be responsible for all the costs payable to the archbishop of York, the dean and chapter, and all other clergy of the church of St. Peter of York concerning the appropriation of the church of Friston to themselves and their successors for ever. That part of the indenture remaining with the warden and vicars is sealed with Henry's seal, and the other part remaining with Henry with the common seal of the warden and vicars.
York, 1 March 5 Edward III [1330/1].

SOURCE: VC 3/1/1, fo. 54.

NOTE: The requirement to celebrate obits for Henry and his wife was repeated in 1332 (**170**).

147. Licence of Edward III, after an inquisition ad quod damnum held by John de Houton, royal escheator beyond the Trent, for Henry le Vavasour to assign the advowson of the church of Friston on the water (*super aquam*) next to Pontefract (*iuxta Pontem fractum*), which Queen Philippa holds in chief as of the castle and honor of Pontefract, to the . . [gemipuncti] warden of the house of vicars of the church of blessed Peter of York and the vicars. The vicars shall provide three chaplains celebrating every day for the well-being (*pro saluti statu*) of Henry and his wife Constance while they live, and for their souls after death, and for the souls of Henry's father and mother, and his ancestors and heirs, namely two in the church of St. Peter [of York] and one in the chapel of Heselwode or in the church of Friston, according to Henry's ordinance. The vicars shall also celebrate anniversaries for Henry's father William le Vavasour and his mother Nichole in the church of St. Peter during Henry's life, and anniversaries for Henry and Constance after their deaths in the same church. If Henry dies with his heir under age, the queen or whoever is lord of the said castle and honor shall waive claims (*amitterent*) to the right of presentation to the church when it is vacant.
Dovorr', 22 April 5 Edward III [1331].
By a fine of 20 marks [£13 6s. 8d.]; York.

SOURCE: VC 3/4/FF/1 (314 mm. × 217 mm.).
ENDORSEMENT: *Carta domini regis super advocacionem ecclesie de Friston*; [bundle mark] *A xv.*
SEAL: slit.
COPY: VC 3/1/1, fos. 54r.–v.
CALENDARED: *Cal. Pat. R.* 1330–4, p. 103.

148. Grant by Henry le Vavasour knight, son and heir of William le Vavasour knight, to John de Burton, warden of the house of vicars of the church of blessed Peter of York, and the vicars of the advowson of the church of St. Andrew of Friston on the water next to Pontefr', with glebe, dwelling-house, meadow, and all other rights, to be held according to the king's charter granted to Henry conferring the advowson on the warden and vicars. Warranty. Seal.
Stubbis, 15 Kalends August [18 July] 1332, 6 Edward III.
Witnesses: dom. Geoffrey le Scrop', justiciar of the king, Thomas de Eyvill', Adam de Hoperton, Ellis de Smetton, Wigard de Stubbis, Thomas Ode, and others.

SOURCE: VC 3/1/1, fos. 54v.–55.

149. Draft petition to the archbishop of York from his chaplains, the vicars of the choir of the church of blessed Peter of York, noting that the rents and income from outside the city by which the vicars are accustomed to live have been diminished by the hostile incursion of the Scots, burnings (*incedia*), plunderings (*predas*), the desertion of their estates, the impoverishment of their tenants, and the expense (*apposicionem*) of the heavy costs concerning their houses and estates both inside and outside the city, so that they are seriously burdened by debt; the vicars beseech the archbishop to allow them to acquire the church of Friston granted to them by Henry le Vavasour. [A variant ending, associating the dean and chapter with the archbishop, follows in the same hand, running into the margin.]

SOURCE: VC 3/1/1, fo. 55v.

NOTE: The petition was rehearsed in Archbishop Melton's appropriation of Friston church to the vicars (**174**).

150. Outline of petition as **149** but addressed to the dean and chapter of York.

SOURCE: VC 3/1/1, fo. 55v.

151. Letter of Archbishop William [Melton] to the official of the court of York or his commissary. The vicars of the church of blessed Peter of York have shown by their petition that they are occupied day and night in divine obsequies in the said church; that the rents and income by which they live have been much diminished outside the city by the hostile incursion of the Scots, burnings, plunderings, the desertion of their estates, the impoverishment of their tenants, and the expense of the heavy costs concerning their houses and estates both inside and outside the city; that from these and other necessary causes they are heavily burdened with debt; that for many of them their stipends are insufficient for a suitable living (*ad congruam eorum sustentacionem*); and that out of the benevolence (*ex largicione caritativa*) of Henry le Vavasour knight [and] by the grant of the king, the vicars will have the patronage of the church of Friston [in return] for maintaining two chantries in the church of York and a third in the church of Friston, if and when the church [of Friston] is appropriated to them. The vicars have asked the archbishop to grant them the church of Friston to their own uses and to annex and unite it in perpetuity to their college.

The archbishop, wishing to make the appropriation, orders the commissary general to seek through sworn witnesses the truth of what the vicars say and to report back what he has found.

Thorp next to York, 8 Ides August 1332 [6 August], and in the 5th year of his pontificate.

SOURCE: Rehearsed in **154**.

152. Letter of Henry le Vavasour, son and heir of William le Vavasour knight deceased, appointing William de Craven as his attorney to deliver seisin of the advowson of the church of Friston on the water to John de Burton, warden of the house of vicars of the church of blessed Peter of York, and the vicars. Seal.
Stubbis, 18 Kalends September [15 August] 1332.

SOURCE: VC 3/1/1, fo. 55.

153. Draft letter of the official of the court of York to the [rural] dean of Pontefr' recording the receipt of letters of the archbishop of York and ordering the dean to cite all those concerned to appear before the official or his commissary.

SOURCE: VC 3/1/1, fos. 55v.–56.

DATE: Before 20 August 1332: see **154**.

154. Certificate of the commissary general of the official of the court of York to Archbishop William [Melton], rehearsing the archbishop's commission and mandate (as **151**).

The commissary general replies that he interviewed 13 witnesses on behalf of the vicars in the church of York on Thursday after the feast of the assumption of blessed Mary [20 August], and he submits a copy of their depositions, with the originals. York, 11 Kalends September [22 August] 1332.

SOURCE: This certificate and the following list of articles and depositions (**155–68**), as well as **176**, are taken from a notarial exemplification of an inspeximus of Archbishop William de la Zouche dated at Spofforth on 5 October 1343. The exemplification was drawn up by the archbishop's registrar, William [son of] Alfred de Thorplond called de Fakenham, clerk of Norwich diocese and apostolic notary. The original survives as VC 3/4/FF/7 (629 mm. × 791 mm.); remains of red wax on tag; notarial sign. It was copied into the cartulary and covers VC 3/1/1, fos. 62r.–68r.

NOTE: According to a note that immediately precedes the notarial eschatocol the witnesses were in fact questioned on Thursday and Friday after the feast of the assumption of the blessed Mary [20 and 21 August].

155. Articles that the warden of the house of vicars of the church of blessed Peter of York and the vicars intend to prove concerning the case for granting them the appropriation of the church of Friston.

Firstly, that there are in the said college 36 vicars and priests maintaining (*intendentes*) divine office in the church by day and night, at suitable and canonical hours, and serving in it most assiduously (*altissimo in eadem famulantes*).

Item, that they live together in a place which is called the Bedern (*Bederna*), wearing the habit of vicars in cathedral churches.

Item, that they have the right to sue as a body (*conveniunt*), support many burdens, and have a common seal.

Item, that their commons amount to only 7*d.* a week [for each vicar].

Item, that the rents and income which faithful Christian people, considering the vicars' devotion and burdens, have given them in diverse places [are]:

[a] in Gildhousdale next to Thresk 46*s.* 8*d.* a year, of which 6*s.* 8*d.* a year has been lost through the incursion and burning of the Scots and the impoverishment of the tenants;

[b] in Warthill 26*s.* 8*d.*, of which 14*s.* 8*d.* has been lost and the cause is as above;

[c] in Grymeston next to Malton 30*s.*, of which 40*d.* has been lost and the cause is as above;

[d] in Bubwith 6*s.*, from which they receive nothing because the rent is withheld unjustly by powerful men (*per magnos*), and the vicars' resources (*facultates*) are insufficient to induce the men to pay by bringing them to court (*per placitum*);

[e] in Oustgate Sutton 12d.; in Ercewik 12d.; from land next to the church of St. John beyond the Ouse (*ultra Usam*) 4s.; and from houses once of Adam Bukk 2s.; from all of which [rents] they receive nothing and the cause is as in the case of Bubwith;

[f] in Bouthum in the suburb of York 5s., from which they receive nothing on account of the impoverishment of the tenants;

[g] from land next to the church of St. Edward 4s., where they now receive 20d.;

[h] from the great hall opposite the Bedern 66s. 8d., where they receive nothing;

[i] in the houses of Hustwayt 50s., of which 15s. has been lost;

[j] in the land of John the illuminator (*illuminatoris*) 2s. and from the houses once of Agnes Buk 3s., where they receive nothing and the cause is as in the case of Bubwith;

thus, without fault on their part, the vicars' rents are greatly lost, diminished, and destroyed through war and other chance happenings.

Item, that their burdens, labours, and expenses necessarily increase daily, because of the cost of repairing estates (*predia*) and houses and other necessaries.

Item, that their resources are insufficient for their full and sufficient maintenance and support without some other assistance.

Item, that they are manifoldly burdened by debt, as it appears.

Item, that in consideration of these things (*pensatis premissis*) Henry le Vavasour knight, wishing out of charity to help them, has given them the patronage or advowson of the church of Friston on the water, intending that they should appropriate the church with the agreement of the king and of those others whose concurrence is required.

Item, that these things are well-known in the city and diocese of York, and are moreover widely talked about (*super eis laborat puplica vox et fama*) so that there is grave scandal in the province and diocese of York, both among the clergy and the people; that the rents and income and resources are meagre and insufficient for such a college and in such a church; and that these abuses and scandals cannot be hidden.

The vicars intend to prove these things jointly and individually.

SOURCE: See **154** note.

COPY: VC 3/1/1, fos. 63r.–v.

NOTE: A draft list of these articles was also entered into the cartulary: VC 3/1/1, fo. 56.

156. Deposition of John de Brotherton chaplain sworn, examined, and questioned on the matters contained in the commission of Archbishop William [Melton] (**151**) and on the articles (**155**) appended to this roll.

[i] Asked how many vicars there are in the choir of the cathedral church of York, he says that there are 36; that each of them receives or ought to receive each year 40s. from his prebendary for his stipend and 13s. 4d. from the church of Pidseburton; that they maintain the canonical hours in the church day and night in the choir; that they live together in the Bedern, wearing the habit of vicars in a cathedral church; and that they have a common seal and have had it more than 50 years ago by licence of the king of England.

[ii] Asked the extent of the annual rents and income by which the vicars now live and are accustomed to live, he says that before the incursion and depredation of the Scots they used to amount both inside and outside the city of York to £83 3s. 7d.

[iii] Asked how he knows this, he says that he was the once vicars' chamberlain before the burning and incursion of the Scots; he rendered his account and audited (*reddiaudivit*) the accounts of others, and knows well the said rents and income; and he says that after the incursion, depredation, and burning of the Scots the rents and income were diminished by £9 9s. 6d. inside and outside the city.

[iv] Asked how and in what manner the rents and income were diminished and by whose fault, he says that it was not the vicars' fault but by an accidental and unexpected cause (*set casu fortuito et inopinato*), both through the incursion, depredation, and burning of the Scots outside the city and the impoverishment of their tenants both inside and outside the city: outside the city, namely at Gildhousdale, Warthill, Grymeston, Bubwith, Gaythill, Oustgate Sutton, and Ercewik, and at some places outside the city which he does not recollect at present, as he says; inside the city and its suburbs, namely in Bouthum, Munkegate, Walmegate, the land next to the church of St. Edward, and in the great hall opposite the Bedern, in Staynegate and Aldewerk, and the land next to the church of St. John beyond the Ouse (*ultra Usam*), and in the houses once of Adam Bok, in the houses of Hustweit, in the land of John the illuminator, and in the houses once of Agnes Buck, [all] on account of the devastation of many tenements, the impoverishment of the tenants, and the want (*defectum*) of tenants, whom the vicars could not find to inhabit the tenements. So from the said sum of £83 3s. 7d. there remains £73 14s. 1d., out of which the vicars have to pay £15 9s. a year in various rents and to various chantry priests in the church [of York]; and after that deduction there remains £58 4s. 7d., from which it was and is necessary to set aside £20 each year for the repair of the vicars' tenements inside and outside the city.

[v] The witness says that each year the vicars pay deacons, choristers, and the sacrists who ring the bells for obits (*pro pulsacione obituum*) 32s. 4d.; their janitor 19s. 4d.; and their two chamberlains 13s. 4d. [each]; [so that] there remains only £35 5s. 7d. to be distributed among the vicars for all their necessary expenses, victuals, and other things, apart from the stipends [from their prebendaries and Pidseburton] concerning which he deposed earlier; and the rents and income are so meagre that they are insufficient for half the vicars' necessary costs and expenses. On that account many vicars, up to a third of them, find work (*locant operas suas*) celebrating for the faithful departed [in churches] in the city, outside the cathedral, and that has caused great scandal and obloquy among both the clergy and the people.

[vi] The witness says that because of all this the vicars are manifoldly burdened by debt, from which it is impossible to believe that they can be freed unless for charity's sake unless they are helped and supported from elsewhere (*nisi caritatis intuitu provideatur et subveniatur eis aliunde*). He says that these things are widely talked about in the city of York and neighbouring places.

SOURCE: See **154** note.
COPY: VC 3/1/1, fos. 63v.–64.

157.   Deposition of mag. William de Stocking. Answers as **156** [i–v] (with minor variations, and referring in [v] to parish churches in the city). He further states that he himself celebrated for 10d. a week after he was admitted as a vicar and before he obtained a chantry in the cathedral. He also says that in the year when he was the vicars' chamberlain he set aside £10 for a palisade (*circa brectagia*) and 100s. and more in law suits (*in litibus*). Concludes as **156** [vi].

SOURCE: See **154** note.
COPY: VC 3/1/1, fos. 64r.–65r.

158. Deposition of William de Wyverthorp chaplain. Answers as **156** [i–v] (referring in [v] to parish churches in the city). He further states that he himself celebrated in the belfry (*in Berefrido*) for the soul of Hugh de Nassington, because he was not able live honourably according to the state of a vicar in such a church [i.e. the cathedral] only from his portion (*si ex porcione sua*). He also says that as the chamberlain in one half-year he set aside £17 in the repair of tenements and buildings and the laying down of pavements (*factura pavimentorum*). Concludes as **156** [vi].

SOURCE: See **154** note.
COPY: VC 3/1/1, fos. 65r.–v.

NOTE: The 'belfry' was the cathedral bell-tower, which stood close to the Minster on its south side near the present site of the the church of St. Michael-le-Belfry: C. Norton, 'The Anglo-Saxon Cathedral at York and the Topography of the Anglian City', *Journal of the British Archaeological Association*, cli (1998), 1–42 (at 5–9).

159. Deposition of William de Cotyngham chaplain. Answers as **156** [i–v]. He further states that not long ago he heard some vicars say that to support themselves (*pro sustentacione sua*) they had put their robes up for sale (*exposuerunt robas suas vendicioni*). Concludes as **156** [vi].

SOURCE: See **154** note.
COPY: VC 3/1/1, fos. 65v.–66v.

160. Deposition of William le Wayder chaplain.
He says that there are 36 vicars, who wear habits in the cathedral church of York and maintain the canonical hours day and night; they live together in the Bedern; and they have a common seal and have had it for 50 years or more. Each vicar receives 40s. a year from his prebendary for his stipend and one mark [13s. 4d.] from the church of Pidseburton'.

Asked the extent of the vicars' annual rents and income before the incursion and burning of the Scots, he says that at the one term of the year [they amounted to] £41 11s. 9½d. and to the same sum at the other term. He knows this because he was the vicars' chamberlain for a long time (*per magnum tempus*), and he rendered his own account and audited the accounts of other chamberlains.

Asked the extent to which the rents are now diminished, he says that it was by at least £8 19s. a year: outside the city of York by the incursion and burning of the Scots; and both inside and outside the city on account of the impoverishment and loss of tenants, whom the vicars were unable to find to inhabit houses, and on account of the vicars' inability (*impotenciam*) to repair and restore ruined houses. He says that for the repair of tenements the vicars set aside (*apponunt*) £20 or a little more (*parum circiter*) every year, and sometimes £30, and that was besides the £35 9s. 6d. which they spend each year on fixed rents (*pro sicco redditu exeunte*) [i.e. rent charges] on tenements and on other requirements. Asked the extent of the annual portion of each vicar, apart from the 40s. and one mark already noted, he says that it amounts to 16s. 7d. and no more.

SOURCE: See 154 note.
COPY: VC 3/1/1, fo. 66v.

161.   Deposition of Thomas de Ludham, vicar of the church of St. Martin in Conyngestrete.

He says that the vicars' rents and income, both inside and outside the city of York, amounted to at least £83 before the incursion and burning of the Scots, when he was the vicars' chamberlain.

Asked by how much the rents and income were diminished after the incursion and burning, he says that in his opinion (iudicio suo) by £10 a year, because their lands and property at Warthill, Gildhousdale, Cornburgh, Gaithill, and Oustgate Sutton, and at other places which at present he does not remember, were burnt and wasted by the Scots. He knows well the vicars' houses in the city of York, namely Cambehalle opposite the Bederne from which they used to receive most years (communibus annis) 6 marks [£4], and the houses once of Roger de Cawode from which they use to receive 40s.; also, [he knows] other houses from which they now receive nothing at all on account of the lack of tenants and the decay of the houses; and they have for many years received nothing because the houses are inhabited by the lowest sort of people and paupers (viles persone et pauperes), from whom they receive or have received nothing or only a little (modicum), and that is because the vicars' resources are insufficient to repair the houses.

Asked what are the vicars' annual expenses, he says that they pay £15 and more a year to diverse people for fixed rents on the tenements and to certain persons ministering in the cathedral, namely mag. John de Tynewell, dom. William Wayder, and dom. Richard de Cave, vicars, each of whom [receives] 5 marks [£3 6s. 8d.]; he says that 20 marks [£13 6s. 8d.] and more have to be set aside each year for the repair of the vicars' houses and tenements inside and outside the city, if they are to be adequately kept in repair (si sufficienter debeant reparavi); and that the portion of each vicar is scarcely worth 6½ marks [£4 6s. 8d.] each year, and that on account of the meagreness (exilitatem) of their portion, 10 or 12 vicars celebrate for the souls of the dead [in churches] in the city, outside the cathedral.

SOURCE: See 154 note.
COPY: VC 3/1/1, fos. 66v.–67r.

162.   Deposition of Adam de Gerford chaplain.

He says that there are 36 vicars in the choir, who maintain divine service and the canonical hours and who wear a habit; they have a common seal and have had it for a long time.

Asked the extent of the vicars' rents and income, he says that they amounted to £80 and a little more (parum ultra), and he knows this because he was the vicars' chamberlain for almost two years before the quinquennium now ended [i.e. 1327–32]. Also, he says that at Grymeston the vicars used to receive 30s. [a year], which sum is now diminished by 40d., and from Gildhousdale and Warthill 26s. 8d. but by how much that is diminished he does not know; nor does he know the sum of the shortfall of rents [caused] by the incursion and burning of the Scots or by the impoverishment and want of tenants and buildings inside and outside the city.

He says he is unable to depose further, and was not questioned on other matters.

SOURCE: See **154** note.
COPY: VC 3/1/1, fo. 67r.

163. Deposition of William de Welleton chaplain.

He says that the vicars of the church of York used to receive a rent of 20s. [a year] at Gildhousdale but they [now] receive only 10s., and at Bubwith [they received] 10s. a year, where they now receive nothing; he knows this from the report of others. He was unable to depose further.

SOURCE: See **154** note.
COPY: VC 3/1/1, fo. 67r.

164. Deposition of Thomas son of Adam de Warthill.

He says that the vicars have two bovates of land in Warthill with a plot of land (*placea*), and that two houses were built there, one of which is totally destroyed and the other ruinous; from these two bovates and houses the vicars at first used to receive 20s. a year and then 26s. 8d. up to the incursion of the Scots and from that time less than (*citra*) 12s.

Asked how he knows this, he says that first his father and then he himself lived in the said houses before the incursion of the Scots and that afterwards they were so impoverished by them (*per Scotos fuerunt adeo depauperati et depredati*) that they abandoned the wasted tenements (*tenementa devastata dimiserunt*) and were unable to hold them any longer and lived elsewhere in the vill of Warthill; and the two bovates and houses which beforehand used to render 20s. or 26s. 8d. now render 12s.

He is unable to depose further.

SOURCE: See **154** note.
COPY: VC 3/1/1, fo. 67r.

165. Deposition of John de Cave, janitor of the Bedern.

He says that the vicars' rents and income have been reduced by £9 9s. 7d. [a year]; he knows this because it is his duty (*pertinet ad officium suum*) to be present at the reckoning of every account roll (*in reddicione singulorum compotorum*) by the chamberlain, and he was thus present for two years and saw and heard as he says.

Although carefully questioned, he is unable to depose further.

SOURCE: See **154** note.
COPY: VC 3/1/1, fos. 67r.–v.

166. Deposition of William de Aynderby clerk.

He says that the vicars' rents and income in the city of York are greatly depleted because of the lack and impoverishment of the tenants; that some tenements are destroyed (*diruta*), being either on the verge of ruin or in fact ruined (*aliqua minantur ruinam et aliqua ruinosa existunt*), and tenants cannot be found for them; and that the rents are insufficient for half the vicars' needs, and so they find work celebrating for the souls of the departed in parish churches in the city, outside the cathedral.

SOURCE: See **154** note.
COPY: VC 3/1/1, fo. 67v.

167.   Deposition of mag. William de Jafford, warden of the altar of the blessed Mary
Magdalene in the church of York.

He says that there are 36 vicars and that they live together in the Bedern. He knows
their tenements in the city of York from which they used to receive a not
inconsiderable sum of money (*non modicam summam*): namely, the great hall opposite
the Bedern called Romaynhalle, which in the old days (*antiquitus*) used normally to
render to the vicars 5 marks [£3 6s. 8d.] or sometimes 40s. [a year], depending on
whether it was inhabited or not, but for the most part it was uninhabited; likewise, [he
knows] their hall called Hustweythalle in Ogleford, which is frequently uninhabited
and [even] when it is inhabited does not render as it used to. Also, he says he knows
that many of the vicars' buildings in the city are so ruined that the vicars cannot find
inhabitants for them, and that they are unable to repair the defects because their
resources are so meagre, being scarcely sufficient for half their necessary sustenance;
on this account, therefore, many of them celebrate in the parish churches in the city,
outside the cathedral, to their great shame (*in magnam verecundiam eorum*) and that of
the mother church. He also says that he himself has the altar of the blessed Mary
Magdalene in the same church, whose rents used to be worth 100s. a year but have
now fallen by 14s. a year.

SOURCE: See **154** note.
COPY: VC 3/1/1, fo. 67v.

NOTE: The name 'Romaynhalle' for the great hall opposite the Bedern was altered in
    the cartulary copy to 'Cambhall', the name given in **161**.

168.   Deposition of John de Coyngesburgh clerk.

He says that he does not know what the vicars' rents amount to, but he believes that
they have been reduced both inside the city and outside by £10 a year; and he knows
that many of the vicars' buildings in the city have been uninhabited for some time, and
that they used to receive great profit (*magnum comodum*) [from the property]; that some
buildings are destroyed (*diruta*) and others ruined, and the vicars cannot find inhabitants
for them; and that they are unable to rebuild and repair them because what they do
receive [in rent] is insufficient for their necessary expenses, so that a third of them
celebrate for the departed in parish churches in the city, outside the mother church.

He was the vicars' janitor for four years, for which he was paid 16s. 4d. a year, like
the janitors before and after him and the present janitor.

SOURCE: See **154** note.
COPY: VC 3/1/1, fos. 67v.–68r.

169.   [*Letter to Archbishop William Melton recording the findings of an inquisition into the
value of Fryston church.*]

The inquisition states that the tithe of wool and of lambs is worth 6½ marks
[£4 6s. 8d.], the tithe of corn (*garbarum*) and of hay 44 marks [£29 6s. 8d.], and
oblations and other lesser tithes pertaining to the altar (*ad ipsum alteragium*) 5 marks
[£3 6s. 8d.]; that in the territory of Friston there are 36 a. of land pertaining to the
church worth more than (*preter*) 24s. [a year] and in the field of Queldal' 28 a. of land
worth more than 28s. [a year]; thus, altogether the church is worth 60 marks 5s. 4d.
[£40 5s. 4d.], but not net (*non de claro*) because it is burdened with ordinary and
extraordinary payments which [the jurors] cannot estimate.

SOURCE: VC 3/1/1, fo. 55v.

170.   Grant in free alms, in the form of a quadripartite cirograph, by Henry le Vavasour, son and heir of William le Vavasour knight, to John de Burton, warden of the house of vicars of the church of blessed Peter of York, and the vicars of the advowson of the church of St. Andrew of Friston on the Aire (*super Eyr*), [in return] for finding three chaplains, namely two in the church of St. Peter of York and one in the chapel of St. Leonard of Heselwod, to celebrate in perpetuity for the souls of Henry, his wife Constance, and his free heirs and ancestors, and also for maintaining each year an obit for Henry and one for his wife Constance solemnly in the choir of the church of blessed Peter of York after their deaths; on the day of his obit the 36 vicars are to be paid 36s., namely 12d. to each vicar of the choir, and on the day of Constance's obit the same amount. The warden and vicars agree to maintain the chantries and obits, and if they default the . . [gemipuncti] archbishop, or during a vacancy in the see the . . dean and . . chapter [of York], may distrain them and compel them to maintain the chantries and obits. The warden and vicars also agree that after Friston church is appropriated to them, and the [parochial] vicar's stipend there has been agreed by the archbishop, they will admit at Henry's nomination a worthy parson to the vicarage; afterwards the vicars [themselves] are to present to the church. Warranty. The four parts of this charter are to be held by the archbishop of York, the dean and chapter, Henry, and the warden and vicars. Sealed with the seals of Henry and of the warden and vicars.
Witnesses: Roger de Novomercato, James de Bosvyl, knights, William de Scargil, John de Everyngham de Birkyn, John de Rotherfeld, Ellis de Smytheton, John de Lascy, Robert his brother, Roger de Farburn, Robert de Sancto Paulo, and others.
York, Tuesday on the eve of the [feast of the] apostles Simon and Jude, 6 Edward III [27 October 1332].

SOURCE: VC 3/4/FF/2 (225 mm. × 209 mm.). Indented and CYROGRAPHATA written along the top and right-hand sides.
ENDORSEMENT: *Capellano de Esylwod*; [bundle mark] *xv*.
SEAL: tag; slit.
COPY: VC 3/1/1, fos. 56r.–v.

NOTE: On the same day Vavasour bound himself to the vicars for £400: *Cal. Close R.* 1330–33, p. 607. The requirement to celebrate the obits repeats that made in 1331 (**146**).

171.   Letter of the college and community (*cetus et communitas*) of the vicars of the church of blessed Peter of York appointing William de Wirthorp, fellow vicar, as their attorney to receive seisin of the advowson of the church of blessed Andrew of Friston on Air next to Pontefr'.
York, Wednesday on the feast of the apostles St. Simon and St. Jude [28 October] 1332.

SOURCE: VC 3/1/1, fo. 55v.

172.   Notarial instrument of William Pedefer, clerk of York diocese and apostolic notary. On 29 October 1332, in the dwelling-house of the rectory of the church of St. Andrew of Fryston on the water of Ayre, William de Craven, servant (*vadlectus*) of Henry le Vavasour knight and his attorney, showed a royal charter under the great seal and another charter under Henry's seal. As Henry's attorney William had full power to deliver seisin of the advowson of the church of St. Andrew to the warden of the house of vicars of the church of blessed Peter of York and the vicars, and he duly delivered it to John de Burton, warden of the house of vicars, and to William de Wyrethorp, the vicars' attorney, in the presence of Roger de Fryshton chaplain, Simon son of Robert de Fryshton, Robert Bateman, Robert Atte Water, Henry called Pieresknave, Roger del Lane, Matthew Gymp, and many other witnesses specially summoned. Immediately afterwards William de Craven, John de Burton, and William de Wyrethorp went off (*divertebant*) to the church of St. Andrew, and repeated the process of granting seisin in the church and at its door, showing the royal charter and the letters of attorney and explaining them in English to the parishioners and other people present there.

Witnesses [to the notarial instrument]: John called Laverok, William Maweson, William the clerk of Frishton, Richard son of Hugh, John Bate, Alan the smith, William Bateson, and Adam son of Thomas de Fery.

SOURCE: CCA, DCc/Charta Antiqua Y 58 (257 mm. × 278 mm.)
ENDORSEMENT: *Instrumentum de seisina ecclesie de Friston.*
SIGN: notarial sign of William Pedefer.
COPY: VC 3/1/1, fos. 55r.–v.

NOTE: The charters referred to are presumably **147** and **148**, and the letters of attorney **152** and **171**.

173. Letter of John de Burton, warden of the house of vicars of the church of blessed Peter of York, and the vicars. Since Henry le Vavasour knight is bound to them for £40 by a recognisance made in the royal chancery on 27 October 6 Edward III [1332], the vicars grant that if Henry, his heirs, and assigns pay them £10 a year during the lifetime of Roger de Gunnerthwayt, rector of the church of blessed Andrew of Friston on the water next to Pontefract, half at Pentecost and half at Martinmas, for the support of three chaplains celebrating for the well-being (*pro salubri statu*) of Henry and his wife Constance while they live and for their souls after they have died, as well as for the souls of Henry's parents, ancestors, and heirs, and of all the faithful departed, namely in the church of blessed Peter of York and in the chapel of Heselwod, as is more fully contained in an indenture between Henry and the vicars, then the execution of the recognisance shall be wholly void. If, however, they fail to pay the £10, then the vicars may prosecute the recognisance. Seal.
York, 31 October 6 Edward III [1332].

SOURCE: LDA, Vavasour deeds, no. 470 (239 mm. × 126 mm.)
ENDORSEMENT: *Ec' Petr' Ebor'; defeancio super recogn' pro x li. durante vite rectoris Friston etc; a° vj° E. iij.*
SEAL: tag.

NOTE: The £10 was duly paid in two instalments in 1333 (**177**, **178**).

174. [*Appropriation of Friston church and ordination of vicarage.*]
Letter of Archbishop William [Melton] rehearsing the vicars' petition [which stated] that the rents and income which faithful Christians had assigned to them for

their support had been much reduced, not by the vicars' negligence or blame, but by the hostile incursion of the Scots, burnings, spoils and plunders, the well-known desertion of their estates, the impoverishment and needs of their tenants who fled leaving every thing (*qui dimissis omnibus abierunt*), and the heavy cost of repairing buildings and cultivating estates, both inside and outside the city of York; [that rents] had been detained unjustly by great men, nobles, and magnates (*per potentes, proceres, et magnates*), whom it is impossible to coerce by law to pay because of the insufficiency of the vicars' resources; and that their burdens and labours increase daily, so that their income is insufficient for a suitable living (*ad congruam vite sustentacionem*), unless it is helped (*succuretur*) by the parish church of Fryston, given by the benevolence of Henry le Vavasour knight, with the assent of the king and others.

Witnesses having been questioned, the archbishop has found the petition to be true, and with the consent of the dean and chapter of the church of York he has granted the church of Fyston to the vicars' community and college, so that they may freely take possession on the resignation or death of the present rector, Roger de Gunnerthwayt, saving the appointment of a perpetual vicar to reside personally and have the cure of souls and serve the church.

The archbishop decrees that the endowment of the vicarage should consist of the following: a third part of the dwelling-house of the rectory of the church of Fryston, consisting of the hall of the rectory with a chamber behind it, the hall site (*sedem . . . aule*), another fine chamber (*camera formosa*) with stone walls in the lower part of it, the granary, the kitchen, and the bake-house and brew-house under the same roof; a large and suitable garden on the south side of the hall, [measuring] 60 feet in breadth next to the house of Robert son of Thomas and stretching in length from the royal street to land called Lynelandes, with free entry and exit from the north side of the rectory barn (*grangia*); 18 a. of land in the vill of Fryston with a moiety of the meadow there belonging to the church and 14 a. in the vill of Queldale with a moiety of the meadow there belonging to the church; mortuaries, both living and dead, and tithes of lambs, cows, calves, piglets, colts, geese, hens, ducks, doves, mills, flax, hemp, herbs (*olerum*), and leeks; oblations, Easter offerings, and all altar dues; and 5½ marks [£3 13s. 4d.] to be paid by the vicars of the church of York to the vicar of Fryston in equal portions four times a year.

Not assigned to the vicar are the tithes of corn (*garbarum*), hay, and wool, and two thirds of the dwelling-house of the rectory of the church of Fryston, the rectory barn with 4 feet beyond it on its south side, the cow-house and stable, and [the remaining] lands and meadows. These are to be held by the vicars [of the church of York].

The vicar of Fryston is to pay the vicars a tithe only from the lands and meadows which constitute his vicarage or from his animals or whatever else, and the vicars, in turn, are to pay the vicar a tithe from the lands and meadows assigned to them in this ordination or from their cattle (*pecoribus*), pastures, or whatever else.

The vicar shall find at his own costs a chaplain to celebrate three times a week in the chapel of Queldale and shall maintain that chantry in future, as the rector of the church of Fryston used to do or ought to have done before this time; and he shall bear all ordinary debts and customs in their entirety (*insolidum*) and ¼ of the extraordinary burdens, and the vicars ¾ of the extraordinary burdens.

There shall be two perpetual chantries in the cathedral church of York and one in the chapel of Heselwode, to be maintained by the vicars from the time that they take peaceful possession of the church of Fryston by virtue of this appropriation, the three chantry chaplains celebrating for the souls of Henry le Vavasour, who lately conveyed the patronage of the church of Fryston to the vicars, his wife Constance, his ancestors and benefactors, and the faithful departed. The collation and provision of a parson (*personis*) in priest's orders to each of the two chantries in the church of York, whenever vacant through death, retirement, deprivation, or removal, is vested in the vicars and their community if they wish to take responsibility for the chantries, otherwise it is to fall to the . . [gemipuncti] dean and chapter of York according to present usage. The presentation of chaplains to the chantry in the chapel of Heselwode is vested in the vicars, and their admission and institution in the archbishop or, in the case of a vacancy in the see, in the . . dean and chapter. All the chaplains are to be bound by oath (*iuramenti vinculo astringantur*) at their admission to say daily the commendation and offices of the dead and to maintain their chantries.

The vicars are to pay each of the three chaplains 5 marks [£3 6s. 8d.] a year in equal portions at Martinmas and Pentecost, and the chaplains are to celebrate each year an obit or anniversary for Henry and one for Constance in the choir of the church of York, when each vicar present shall receive 12d. from the revenues of the church of Fryston.

In recompense for the loss to the church of York, which has customarily received the income of the church of Friston during a vacancy, the vicars are to pay the archbishop and his successors 6s. 8d. a year at Pentecost. Seal.

Thorp next to York, 10 Kalends March 1332 and in the 16th year of his archbishopric [20 February 1332/3].

SOURCE: VC 3/4/FF/3 (622 mm. × 714 mm.).
ENDORSEMENT: *Appropriacio ecclesie de Friston, Ordinacio . . . . . . et cantariarum ij in monasterio, j in Heselwod, et omnium aliorum ad dictam ecclesiam spectantium.*
SEAL: fragments of archiepiscopal seal hung on green cord.
COPIES: VC 3/1/1, fos. 56v.–59; BIHR, Reg. 9a, fos. 237–9.

NOTE: For a draft version of the vicars' petition see **149**.

175.   Inspeximus and confirmation of **174** by the dean and chapter of York.
York, 7 Kalends March 1332 [23 February 1332/3].

SOURCE: [i] VC 3/4/FF/4a (554 mm. × 603 mm.); [ii] VC 3/4/FF/4b (584 mm. × 692 mm.).
ENDORSEMENT: [i] *Appropriacio ecclesie de Fryston*; [ii] *Proventus ecclesie de Fryston*.
SEAL: [i] holes for cord; [ii] holes for cord.
COPY: VC 3/1/1, fo. 59.

176.   Certificate of the [rural] dean of Pontefract (*Pontisfracti*) that in obedience to a mandate of Archbishop William [Melton] he went on Wednesday on the feast of St. Mathias the apostle [24 February] to the dwelling-house of the rectory of Friston together with William Waider and Walter de Derlyngton, vicars of the church of blessed Peter of York, Thomas the chaplain de Brotherton, and many other worthy people from the vill of Friston, both clergy and lay, and measured the dwelling-house, garden, and other rectory buildings and garden (described as in **174**) and divided them according to the archbishop's mandate. The new vicar is to make a wall between his part and the vicars' part at his own expense.

Friston, on the day given above 1332 [24 February 1332/3].

SOURCE: Rehearsed in the inspeximus of Archbishop William de la Zouche discussed in 154 note on source.
COPY: VC 3/1/1, fo. 62.

177.   Letter of John de Burton, warden of the house of vicars of the church of blessed Peter of York, and the vicars. Henry le Vavasour knight is bound to them for £40 by a recognisance made in the king's chancery to pay them £10 a year, in equal portions at Pentecost and Martinmas, and so from year to year until the £40 is fully paid; the £10 is to be paid during the lifetime of Roger de Gunnerset, rector of the church of blessed Andrew of Fryston on the water next to Pontefract, for the support of three chaplains celebrating throughout the year in the church of blessed Peter of York and in the chapel of Heselwode for the souls of Henry and his wife Constance and for the souls of his ancestors and heirs, as is more fully contained in a royal charter issued (*edita*) to the vicars, and after Roger's death the recognisance should be void. By virtue of that grant the vicars have received from Henry 100s. for the Pentecost term 7 Edward III [1333], in part payment of the £40, and so Henry is quit.
York, Thursday after Holy Trinity in the year above [10 June 1333]. Seal.

SOURCE: LDA, Vavasour deeds, no. 482 (238 mm. × 164 mm.)
ENDORSEMENT: none medieval.
SEAL: tags.

NOTE: For the recognisance see 173.

178.   As 177, acknowledging the receipt of 100s. from Henry for Martinmas term 7 Edward III [1333].
York, Thursday after feast of St. Andrew the apostle in the year above [2 December 1333].

SOURCE: LDA, Vavasour deeds, no. 485 (238 mm. × 91 mm.)
ENDORSEMENT: medieval text illegible because written over in a later hand.
SEAL: tag.

179.   Recognition by Henry le Vavasour knight that he owes the warden of the house of vicars of the church of blessed Peter of York and the vicars £2,000, to be paid in instalments of £10 a year at Pentecost and Martinmas, or otherwise to be levied in default of payment on his lands and chattels in the county of York and elsewhere.
Perth (*villam de Sancto Johanne*), 25 August 9 Edward III [1335].

SOURCE: VC 3/1/1, fo. 59.
CALENDARED: *Cal. Close R.* 1333–7, p. 520.

180.   Agreement, in the form of a cirograph, recording that whereas Henry le Vavasour knight is bound by a recognisance (179) made in the royal chancery at York [*sic*] on 25 August 9 Edward III [1335] to pay the warden of the house of vicars of the church of blessed Peter of York and the vicars £2,000, John de Burton, now warden of the house of vicars, and the vicars promise to bring no action against Henry or his successors provided he or they pay £10 a year during the lifetime of Roger de

Gunnerset, lately rector of the church of Friston on the water of Aire, after whose death Henry, his heirs, and executors shall be quit. The warden and vicars shall take no action against Henry, his heirs, or executors to seek or recover the debt, and after Roger's death the recognisance in chancery shall be void, but if Henry, his heirs, or executors default in the payment of the £10 during Roger's lifetime, then it shall remain in force. Seal.

York, 26 August 1335.

SOURCE: VC 3/1/1, fos. 59r.–v.

NOTE: For payments of instalments in 1336 and 1337 see **191** and **192**.

181. Letter of John de Burton, warden of the vicars of the church of blessed Peter of York, and the vicars appointing Walter de Derlington, fellow vicar, as their proctor with power of being inducted into any ecclesiastical benefice, with or without cure, and of receiving, holding, and retaining possession of the same.

York, 26 August 1335.

SOURCE: Rehearsed in **184**.

182. Notarial instrument of William de Carleton, clerk of York diocese and apostolic notary. On 27 August 1335, in the manor of Archbishop William [Melton] at Cawod and in the presence of Walter de Derlyngton, proctor of John de Burton, warden of the house of vicars of the church of blessed Peter of York, and the college (*cetus*) of vicars, Roger de Gunnerset, clerk and rector of the church of St. Andrew de Friston on Ayre, resigned the church of Friston before the archbishop in the following manner:

I, Roger de Gunnerset, rector of the church of St. Andrew of Friston on Ayre, believing myself to be serving that church less than adequately (*reputans me regimini dicte parochialis ecclesie minus sufficientem*) and wishing to be relieved of the burden of such a cure (*et affectans exui ab onere tante cure*), resign the church into your [i.e. the archbishop's] hands, beseeching that you allow the resignation.

The resignation having been read out, the archbishop allowed it.

Witnesses [to the notarial instrument]: mag. Hamund de Cessay, John de Barneby, public notary, and William de Popelton, the archbishop's steward, clerks of York diocese.

SOURCE: CCA, DCc/Charta Antiqua Y 60 (247 mm. × 259 mm.)
ENDORSEMENT: *Instrumentum super resignacionem ecclesie de Friston.*
SIGN: notarial sign of William de Carleton.
COPIES: VC 3/1/1, fos. 59v. (resignation), 60v.–61r. (notarial instrument); BIHR, Reg. 9a, f. 248v. (memo. and text of resignation).

NOTE: The notarial instrument as copied into the cartulary does not repeat the text of the resignation, which is entered elsewhere in the cartulary.

183. Letter of Archbishop William [Melton] to the archdeacon of York or his official. Roger de Gunnerset, lately rector of the church of St. Andrew of Fryston super Ayre, has resigned that church, lately appropriated to the vicars of the church of blessed Peter of York and their community and college (*cetui et collegio*). The archbishop orders the archdeacon to induct the vicars into corporal possession of the church.

Cawode, 5 Kalends September [28 August] 1335, and in the 18th year of his pontificate.

SOURCE: Rehearsed in **187**.
COPY: BIHR, Reg. 9a, f. 248v.

184. Notarial instrument of John Thomas de Barneby on Done, clerk of York diocese and apostolic and imperial notary, rehearsing an ordinance of Archbishop William [Melton].

The archbishop has accepted the resignation of Roger de Gunnerset as rector of the church of St. Andrew [of Friston] on Aire, and also the appointment of Walter de Derlington as proctor of the warden and vicars. Derlington agrees that Gunnerset should receive a pension, and the archbishop ordains that one of 20 marks [£13 6s. 8d.] a year shall be paid from the income of the church of Friston, in equal portions on the feasts of the nativity of St. John the Baptist (24 June) and St. Nicholas (6 December); the first payment is to be on the next feast of St. John.

Ordination and instrument sealed with the archbishop's seal and the sign of mag. John de Barneby, apostolic and imperial notary, in the archbishop's manor of Cawod, 29 August 1335, and in the 18th year of his pontificate, in the presence of William de Wrelleton' public notary and of William de Welleton and John de Gunnerset, clerks of York diocese.

SOURCE: VC 3/1/1, fos. 59v.–60v.
COPY: BIHR, Reg. 9a, fos. 249–49v.

185. Letter of the warden of the house of vicars of the church of blessed Peter of York and the vicars approving and ratifying the ordinance of Archbishop William [Melton] establishing an annual pension of 20 marks. [No dating clause.]

SOURCE: VC 3/1/1, fo. 61.

NOTE: For the ordinance see **184**.

186. Letter of the warden of the house of vicars of the church of blessed Peter of York and the vicars granting to Roger de Gunnerset clerk for his lifetime a pension of 20 marks [£13 6s. 8d.] a year to be paid to Roger or his attorney in the cathedral church at York by the warden. Dates and commencement of payments as in **184**. In default of payment the dean and chapter of York shall compel the vicars to make satisfaction for arrears. Seal. [No dating clause.]

SOURCE: VC 3/1/1, fos. 61r.–v.

187. Letter of the official of the archdeacon of York rehearsing **183**, and stating that he inducted Walter de Derlington, the vicars' proctor, on 3 Kalends September [30 August].

Pontefr', Kalends September [1 September] 1335.

SOURCE: VC 3/4/FF/5 (256 mm. × 75 mm.)
ENDORSEMENT: *Resignacio ecclesie de Friston; dominus Walterus de Derlyngton procurator in nomine . . . ..*
SEAL: tag.
COPY: VC 3/1/1, fo. 61v.

188.   Pro forma of letter of the warden of the house of vicars and the vicars of the church of blessed Peter of York to Archbishop William [Melton] presenting N. de B. chaplain to the vacant vicarage of Friston. Sealed with their common seal.

SOURCE: VC 3/1/1, fo. 61v.

189.   Abbreviated pro forma of letter of presentation [by the vicars] of N. de B. chaplain to the chantry in the chapel of Heselwod'.

SOURCE: VC 3/1/1, fo. 61v.

190.   Memorandum recording that on 11 October 1335 William de Wirthorp and Walter de Derlington divided the lands and meadows of the vills of Friston and Queldal' between the vicars of the church of blessed Peter of York and the vicar of the church of Friston. According to the ordination of Archbishop William [Melton], 18 a. of land and 1 a. of meadow in the field land of Friston appertains to the rectory of the church and all the rest to the vicar; and as there are two bovates of land appertaining to the church, the rectory shall have one and the vicar the other. And these are the names of the acres of both parts.

In the south field of Friston: in the upper field del Skynnedamme 1 a.; in the lower part [*sic*] of Skynnedamme 1 a.; at le castelbrigg' 1 a.; at Robert Sitfast 1 a.; at le ald milne 1 a.; at le claylandis 1 a.; at le sandlandis 1 a.; at le gate end and at Sweyn hill 1 a.; on the north side of the church 1 a.; at le skiterthornis, upper and lower, 1 a.; at Hennedritt' Flatt' and between the ways (*inter vias*) 1 a.; next to the mill 1 a.; at le Wendhill next to [the lands of] Hugh son of Ralph and Hugh son of Malyn, in two places, 1 a.; at the small cross ½ a.

In the west field: from the south part of the mill ½ a.; from the north part of the mill 1 a.; at Crossedal' 1 a.; at langris and le breche 1 a.; at Branthill 1 a.; at Wilmerhow 1 a.; at le toun end and in Ceddal' 1 a.; at le croft endis 1 a.; in Ceddal' 1 a.; at Hullesterlandis 1 a.; at south Hullesterlandis 1 a.

In the north field: in Havercroft 1 a.; over Queldale sti 1 a.; at Crokhill and Queldal' croft endis 1 a.; in le yondir dale 1 a.; in Riggeway 1 a.; in pese croft and Pynkesforthmouth 1 a.; at le dalebank and blakelandis 1 a.; at le stane and le ox was dede 1 a.; at le Brakenraw 1 a.; at brokholis and brade eng' 1 a.; at fischyard and le toftis under the way (*subtus viam*) 1 a.; at le Wranglandis and at their end (*ad finem earundem*) 1 a.; at le toftis over the way (*supra viam*) ½ a.

The rectory portion shall always have the nearest part of the land (*a parte viciniori soli*), whether divided into selions or not, and the vicarage portion shall have the remoter part (*a parte remociori a sole*).

In the field of Queldal' there are 2 bovates of land with 1 a. 1 r. of meadow appertaining to the church of Friston, of which one [bovate] appertains to the rectory and the other to the vicarage, with the meadow equally divided between them. Each bovate contains 14 a., of which the rectory portion is to be the nearest part of the land

and the vicarage portion the remoter part, as is the case in the field of Friston above. And these are the names of the acres.

SOURCE: VC 3/1/1, fo. 53v.

NOTE: There follows in the cartulary enough space on the remainder of the folio for the addition of the Wheldale field names, as was evidently intended.

191. Letter of John de Burton, warden of the house of vicars of the church of blessed Peter of York, and the vicars as **177** (reading £2,000 for £40). The vicars have received from Henry 100s. for Pentecost term 10 Edward III [1336] in part payment of the £2,000, and so Henry is quit. Seal.
York, on the feast of Holy Trinity [26 May] 1336.

SOURCE: LDA, Vavasour deeds, no. 478 (248 mm. × 114 mm.)
ENDORSEMENT: *Ec' Petr' Ebor'; acquitenc' 5 li. x s.*
SEAL: tag.

192. As **191**, acknowledging the receipt of 100s. from Henry for Pentecost term 11 Edward III [1337].
York, Saturday on the eve of Holy Trinity in the year above [14 June 1337].

SOURCE: LDA, Vavasour deeds, nos. 477 (245 mm. × 187 mm.)
ENDORSEMENT: none medieval.
SEAL: tag.

193. Notarial instrument of Nicholas [son] of John called Smyth of Whiteby, clerk of York diocese and apostolic notary. On 1 July 1343 at York in the Bedern, where the vicars of the cathedral church of blessed Peter live, in the house (*in hospitio habitationis*) of William de Cotyngham, one of the vicars, Thomas de Aberford, vicar and proctor of the warden of the house of vicars of the cathedral church of blessed Peter of York and of the community (*cetus*) of the vicars, recorded the following complaint:
      Although the warden and vicars possess the church of Freston on Aire, together with the Bedern in the city of York in which they live and rents and income both inside and outside the city and in the cathedral church of blessed Peter of York, and various rights and appurtenances, they have heard from many trustworthy people that the canons of the church of blessed Peter of York are threatening to disturb them. Thomas, the proctor, fearing that grave prejudice may arise from such threats, appeals to the apostolic see and to the court of York for protection.
Done in the presence of William de Ampleford, William de Cotyngham, John de Fulford, John de Stowe, Robert de Waghne, chaplains living in the city of York.

SOURCE: VC 3/4/FF/6 (330 mm. × 337 mm.)
ENDORSEMENT: *Pro ecclesia de Freston.*
SIGN: notarial sign of Nicholas de Whiteby.

194. Indenture witnessing that Henry, son and heir of Henry le Vavasour knight, is bound to the warden of the house of vicars of the church of blessed Peter of York and the vicars for £100, payable at York at Martinmas and Pentecost, as is contained in an

obligation made between the parties according to the statute of Acton Burnel, and
also in £2,000 payable according to a recognisance made in the royal chancery at
York. Robert Swetemouth, now warden of the house of vicars, and the vicars grant
that if Henry and his heirs or executors pay the vicars at York £10 a year, namely
100s. at Martinmas and 100s. at Pentecost, during the lifetime of Roger de Gunnerset,
lately rector of the church of Friston on the water (*super aquam*) of Air', and so from
year to year until the £10 is fully paid, then both the obligation and recognisance shall
be void, but if Henry or his heirs fail to pay the £10, then Henry grants that both shall
remain in force. The indenture is sealed alternately with the vicars' common seal and
Henry's seal.
York, Monday on the feast of All Saints [1 November] 1344.

SOURCE: LDA, Vavasour deeds, no. 542 (272 mm. × 165 mm.). Indented at top.
ENDORSEMENT: *Ecclesie beatri Petri Ebor'*; *defesancia super recognicionem prout vicariis Ebor'*.
SEAL: tag.

195.   Indenture, in the form of a cirograph, witnessing an agreement between
Robert Swetemouth, warden of the house of vicars of the church of blessed Peter of
York, and the vicars on the one part and William de Welleton, vicar of the church of
St. Andrew of Friston, on the other. The warden and vicars have granted and demised
at farm to William 32 a. of land with meadow appertaining to the rectory of the
church of Friston in the vills and territory of Friston and Queldal', together with a
house and garden in Queldal'; to be held from Pentecost 1347 for 12 years; paying to
the warden and vicars 30s. a year for the first three years, in equal portions at the feast
of the annunciation and that of the nativity of the blessed Mary [25 March and
8 September], and then 33s. 4d. for the other nine years at the same terms. For the
whole 12 years William shall pay the warden and vicars the tithes of corn (*garbarum*)
and of hay from the land and meadow. If William should die in mid-term (*medio
tempore in fata decedere*), all the land and meadow shall revert to the warden and vicars,
reserving to William and his executors the crop (*vestura*), if he dies at a time when the
land is sown. Warranty. Seal.
York, at Pentecost [20 May] 1347.

SOURCE: VC 3/4/FF/8 (258 mm. × 131 mm.). Indented at top.
ENDORSEMENT: *Vicar' Friston'; de firma*.
SEAL: remains of wax on tag.

196.   Indenture made between Richard, prior of the house of St. John the apostle
and evangelist of Pontefract, and the convent there, rectors of the church of All Saints
in the same vill, appropriated and annexed to them and their monastery, on the one
part and John de Hykelyng, vicar and warden of the college of vicars in the choir of
the cathedral church of blessed Peter of York, and the vicars, rectors of the church of
Fryseton next to Pontefract, appropriated and annexed to them and their college, on
the other part. A controversy has arisen between the two parties concerning the tithes
of corn (*garbarum*), hay, and wool-fells (*veller' lanarum*) within the vill and field of Fery,
which lie within the parishes of the said churches according to the bounds assigned by
Thomas Wynceworth, gentleman (*generosus*), Thomas Williamson of Fery, Robert
Cutteller of the same place, Robert Hugeonson, and John Kylnesay [who say that the
bounds are as follows]:

Beginning from Spitelrawe, le nethertathes on the east side, up to a plot of land (*placeam*) of John Bubwyth next to it, and from there up to a cross called Wyotcrosse, and from the cross to another cross called Whytecrosse, and from Whytecrosse up to a place (*locum*) called Monjoy, and from there by a stream (*rivosum*) called Northbek up to the south side of the church of Fryseton, and from there descending to the water of Ayre up to the point (*princtum*) of Fordales, the brothers' (*fratrum*) meadow of Foulesnape on the south side, and from there going (*veniendo*) along the Southbek up to the baulk (*ad liram*) which divides the land of the abbot of Pountfreyt lying on the west side and the field of Knottynglay lying on the east side, and from there ascending by the same baulk between the land of St. Leonard of York lying on the west side called Penyhill and the field of Knottyngley lying on the east side, abutting on a plot of land called Crombehaugh, and thus ascending by the bank (*per ripam*) called Puttall bank at its headlands (*per capita*) up to Douferode along the headlands of Puttall Wro between the field of Pountfreyt on the south side, turning there by the side (*per latus*) of Puttall Wro, the field of Pountfreyt on the west side, and so from there back (*sursum*) by 'le rawe' of John Wakefeld up to the headlands of the 'fflattes' of the same John Wakefeld, and so diverting up to the headland of Bulhill by the side of Cheker there, and then there is the field of Fery by its ends, le Cheker on the west side, and then by the ends of 'longdales' up to the 'duo Henelandes' of Shortdales in the same field of Fery, and taking the headlands up to le Spitelbalk and so shooting up to le Spitelrawe.

Mag. John Wodham, chancellor of the archbishop of York, Thomas Percour, residentiary canon of the cathedral church of blessed Peter of York, mag. John Selowe, canon of the same and registrar of the archbishop of York, and others have reconciled the dispute, in the following manner: the prior and convent and their successors shall have a moiety of all the tithes of corn, hay, and wool (*lane ovium*) within the vill and field of Fery as described by the said bounds, and the warden and vicars and their successors shall have the other moiety, to come just as well from the lands of the priory within the boundaries as from Shepcotes, whether the land and Shepecotes [*sic*] are in the hands of the prior and convent or their farmers [i.e. lessees]. Pontefract, in the chapter house of the prior and convent, 3 October 1422.

SOURCE: VC 3/4/FF/9 (462 mm. × 190 mm.) Indented at top.
ENDORSEMENT: *Indentura facta inter priorem Pontisfract' et vicariorum de garbis, feni, et lane.*
SEAL: tag.
PRINTED: A partial translation is given in *Pontefract Archaeological Journal* (1969), 15–16.

197. Letter of the warden of the house and college of vicars of the cathedral church of York and the vicars to Archbishop Henry [Bowet], presenting John Dalton chaplain to be admitted to the chantry in the chapel of Heselwod.
York, 3 July 1419.

SOURCE: VC 1/1, p. 49 (ink pagination).

198. Draft indenture made 25 April 1514, 6 Henry VIII, between Christopher [Sele],[1] warden of the house of vicars of the cathedral church of St. Peter of York, and the vicars, appropriators of the parish church of Waterfryston, on the one part, and William Grene gentleman (*gent'*) and . . . . .[2] chaplain, on the other part. The warden and vicars have granted and demised at farm to William Grene and . . . . . . chaplain the parish church of Waterfryston with all the houses appertaining to the church, and all tithes, fruits, rents, profits, and emoluments coming from two bovates of arable land lying in the fields of Waterfryston, with all meadows and pastures appertaining to the bovates and the church; reserving to the warden and vicars the vicarage house there and the endowment (*dotacio*) or portion of the vicarage and the advowson and presentation of the vicarage; to hold from the feast of St. Mark the evangelist [25 April] next for a term of [*blank*]; paying the vicars £18 13s. 4d. a year, in equal portions at the feasts of the purification of the blessed Virgin Mary [2 February] and St. Peter ad vincula [1 August]. If the rent is behind in part or in whole at any term and remains unpaid after 40 days, then the warden and vicars may re-enter and retain the church. Grene is to maintain and repair at his own costs the walls, plaster (*luteis*), and thatched roofs (*tecturis straminium*) of the houses and buildings belonging to the church. The warden and vicars will pay all the ordinary and extraordinary burdens of the church. Seal.

In the college of the Bederne, day and year given above.

SOURCE: [i] VC 3/4/FF/10a (457 mm. × 213 mm.) [ii] VC 3/4/FF/10b (448 mm. × 194 mm.). Both indented at top.

ENDORSEMENT: [i] and [ii] none.

SEAL: [i] and [ii] no evidence of sealing.

[1] MS. rubbed.
[2] The chaplain's name has been rubbed out.

HUNTINGTON

199. Licence of Edward III for the abbot of Whiteby to assign the advowson of the church of Huntington next to York to the warden of the house of vicars and the vicars of the church of blessed Peter of York, and for the warden and vicars to receive the church to hold to their own uses.

Westminster, 15 March 25 Edward III [1350/1].

SOURCE: VC 3/2/8 (283 mm. × 165 mm.).

ENDORSEMENT: *Hontyngton*; *Confirmacio regis Edwardi tercii de advocacione ecclesie.*

SEAL: great seal in green wax hung on green and pink cord.

COPY: VC 3/1/1, fo. 118v.

CALENDARED: *Cal. Pat. R.* 1350–54, p. 53; *Cartulary of Whitby Abbey*, ed. J. C. Atkinson, ii (Surtees Society lxxii, 1879), p. 478.

200. Grant, in the form of a cirograph, by Thomas, the abbot, and the convent of Whiteby to Ellis de Walkington, warden of the house of vicars of the cathedral church of blessed Peter of York, and the vicars, of the advowson of the church of Huntington next to York with glebe, dwelling-house, meadow, commons, and all rights and appurtenances, saving a pension of 13s. 4d. a year to the abbot and convent, payable at Martinmas. Warranty. Seal.

Whiteby, in the chapter [house], 17 Kalends August [16 July] 1351, 25 [Edward III].

SOURCE: VC 3/4/Hun/1 (363 mm. × 217 mm.). Indented at top, CARTA CYROGRAPHATA.
ENDORSEMENT: *Concessio advocacionis ecclesie de Huntington vicariis per abbatem de Wy[t]by.*
SEAL: tag.
COPY: VC 3/1/1, fos. 118v.–119.
CALENDARED: *Cartulary of Whitby Abbey*, ed. Atkinson, ii, p. 479.

201. Letter of Thomas, the abbot, and the convent of Whiteby appointing mag. Geoffrey de Langeton, clerk and advocate of the court of York, and John Giffun, parson (*personam*) in the choir of the cathedral church of blessed Peter of York, as their attorneys to deliver seisin of the church of Huntington to Ellis de Walkington, warden of the house of vicars of the church of blessed Peter of York, and the vicars, or to their proctor.
Whiteby, 20 July 1351, 25 [Edward III].

SOURCE: VC 3/4/Hun/2 (226 mm. × 121 mm.).
ENDORSEMENT: *Concessio advocacionis ecclesie de Huntington vicariis.*
SEAL: two tags.
COPY: VC 3/1/1, fo. 119.

202. Letter of the warden and the community of vicars of the church of blessed Peter of York appointing Richard de Greyngham, fellow vicar, as their attorney to receive seisin of the church of All Saints, Huntington.
York, Monday 8 August 1351.

SOURCE: Rehearsed in **203**.

203. Notarial exemplification of John [son] of Robert de Hakthorp, clerk of Carlisle diocese and apostolic notary. After the ninth hour on 8 August 1351, in the churchyard of the parish church of Huntington next to York, Ellis de Walkyngton, warden of the house of vicars, showed four letters patent sealed with different seals, namely: **199–202**.

After the charters and letters had been read out, John Giffun, the attorney of the abbot and convent, went to each corner (*singula angulos sive corneria*) of the church on the outside and to the church's two doors on the south side, together with Richard de Greyngham, the attorney of the warden and vicars for receiving the advowson of the church, and handed over and delivered to Greyngham each corner of the church, the chancel door (*hostium chori*) by means of its iron ring (*per anulum ferreum*), the main door (*magnum hostium*) of the church by means of its iron bar (*per barram ferream*), and afterwards the gate of the manor or dwelling-house of the rectory of the church by means of a wooden bar fixed on the door with keys (*per quoddam lignum in dicta porta cum clavis fixum*), and then the croft on the west, lying behind the rectory barn (*grangiam*), and the land appertaining to the croft; and Greyngham took seisin for the use of his lords (*ad opus dominorum suorum*).
Done in the presence of Simon de Munkton, John de Coppegrave, William de Murton, Robert de Housum, William Carter, John de Keysmaby, William de Flathwath of Huntington, John de Skidbrok of Munkgat', and John de Hundemanby.

SOURCE: VC 3/1/1, fos. 118v.–119v.

204. Draft petition of the vicars of the choir of the church of blessed Peter of York to [the archbishop of York] noting that the rents and income from which they live have been diminished by the recent pestilence (*pestilenciam hominum*), by the desertion and loss (*irrecuperabilem*) of their estates and buildings, and by the waste (*consumpcionem*) of their houses and estates; and that the burdens imposed on what little remains, especially the 25 marks [£16 13s. 4d.] which they have to spend on the celebration of divine service in the church of York, means that they have incurred such debts that they cannot free themselves without outside assistance. They beseech the archbishop to allow them to appropriate the church of Huntington.

SOURCE: VC 3/1/1, fo. 119v.

NOTE: The petition was made possibly as late as December 1351: see **206**.

205. Shortened version of **204**, addressed to the chapter of York.

SOURCE: VC 3/1/1, fo. 120r.

206. Certificate of the official of Cleveland (*Clifland'*) to Archbishop William [de la Zouche]. He has received the archbishop's commission and mandate given at Cawod' on 13 December 1352 [*recte* 1351], which rehearsed the archbishop's receipt of the vicars' petition (**204**) and ordered the official to hold an inquisition. The official summoned witnesses who appeared before him in the church of York on Wednesday before the feast of the nativity of Our Lord [21 December], the vicars producing twelve witnesses to depose on the truth of their petition; each witness was interviewed by the official in secret and their depositions under his seal have been sent to the archbishop.   12 January [1351/2].

SOURCE: VC 3/1/1, fos. 120r.–v.

DATE: The MS. has the archbishop's mandate dated as '1352 and in the 10th year of his pontificate', but Zouche died in July 1352 and so the correct date should be '1351'.
NOTE: The depositions are **208–19**. A note on VC 3/1/1, fo. 123r. records that witnesses **208–14** were examined on Wednesday, Thursday, and Saturday before Christmas [21, 22, and 24 December] and a note on fo. 124v. that the remaining witnesses **215–19** were examined on Tuesday and Wednesday after Christmas [27 and 28 December].

207. Articles that the warden of the house of vicars of the church of blessed Peter of York and the vicars intend to prove concerning their plea to appropriate the church of Huntington next to York.

Firstly, that there are in the said college 36 vicars and priests, who maintain (*intendentes*) divine office in the church by day and night, at suitable and canonical hours, and serve in it most assiduously (*altissimo in eadem continue famulantes*).

Item, that they live together in a place called the Bedern (*Bederna*), wearing the habit of vicars as is customary in other cathedral churches, support many burdens, and have a common seal and other marks of a recognized college (*alia insignia collegii approbati*).

Item, that their commons amount to only 7d. a week [for each vicar].

Item, that the rents and income of the 35 [*sic*] vicars which faithful Christian people, considering their devotion and burdens, have given them in diverse places [are]:

[a] in Gildusdal next to Thresk 46s. 8d. [a year], which is diminished by (*usque ad*) 14s. a year through the recent pestilence of men and the impoverishment of the tenants;

[b] in Warthill 26s. 8d., which is diminished by 14s. as a result of the causes given above;

[c] in Grimston next to Malton 30s., which is diminished by 15s., as above;

[d] in the houses of mag. Simon de Evesham in Stayngat in York £8 9s., which is diminished by 100s. 4d., as above;

[e] in the houses of Richard de Wreshill of York in Petergat 40s., which is diminished by 30s., as above;

[f] in the houses of Robert the potter (*ollarii*) in Godorumgate 36s. 8d., which is diminished by 22s., as above;

[g] in the houses of John the cook in Godorumgat 65s. 4d., which is diminished by 20s. 8d., as above;

[h] in the houses of Thomas de Kyllum in Godorumgat 35s., which is diminished by 26s., as above;

[i] in the houses of Robert the cook in Godorumgat 40s., which is diminished by 28s., as above;

[j] in the houses of Thomas Sarcerin 46s. 8d., which is diminished by 30s., as above;

[k] in the houses of John Caperon in Godorumgat 26s. 8d., which is diminished by 16s., as above;

[l] from the great hall opposite the Bederne 66s. 8d., from which they now receive nothing, for the causes as given above;

[m] and in many other places, as in Petergate 25s., [*struck through*: Mungate], Sceldergate 7s., Mickelgate 4s., and Bowthum 5s., from which they receive nothing because the rents are withheld unjustly by powerful men (*per magnos et potentes*) and the vicars' resources (*facultates*) are insufficient to compel the malefactors to pay by bringing them to court (*eos per litem et placitum ad solucionem compellendi*); thus, without fault on the vicars' part, their rents are lost, diminished, and destroyed through wars and the recent pestilence and other chance happenings.

Item, that the vicars' burdens, labours, and necessary expenses are increasing daily because of the cost of repairing their estates and houses and other necessities.

Item, that the vicars are so overburdened by debt that their resouces are inadequate to maintain them unless they receive help from elsewhere.

Item, that taking these things into consideration, the abbot and convent of the monastery of Whiteby, wishing to help the vicars, have given them the patronage or advowson of the church of Huntington next to York, with the intention that the vicars should appropriate the church with the agreement of the king and of all those whose concurrence is required.

Item, that these things are well-known in the city and diocese of York and are widely talked about (*super eis laborat publica vox et fama*), and that the vicars will prove them.

SOURCE: VC 3/1/1, fos. 120v.–121.

208. Deposition of Richard de Scrayngham chaplain sworn, examined, and questioned on the contents of the commission of Archbishop William [de la Zouche] and on the articles (i.e. 207) appended to this roll.

[i] Asked how many vicars there are in the choir of the cathedral church of blessed Peter of York, he says that there are 36; that each of them receives or ought to receive 40s. each year from his prebendary for his stipend and all but one of them receives 13s. 4d. from the church of Pideceburton; that the vicars attend the canonical hours, wearing the habit of vicars as is customary in other cathedral churches; that they live together in a place called the Bedern; that they have a common seal and other marks of a recognized college by the express consent of the king; and that they have had these things for a long time (*per multa tempora elapsa*).

Examined on each of the articles appended to the roll, he says on oath that they are all true, as far as he knows.

[ii] Asked how he knows this, he says that the vicars' annual rents and income before the pestilence that lately affected both the city of York and elsewhere amounted to £93 14s.; he was the chamberlain who rendered the account of the income before the pestilence and audited [the accounts] rendered by other chamberlains. Moreover, he says that the income now amounts scarcely to £69 6s. 6d. a year.

[iii] Asked why the rents have been diminished, he says that it is not by the vicars' fault but by misfortune and by the pestilence and the impoverishment of their tenants, both inside and outside the city: outside the city, namely in Gildusdall', Warthill, Grimston, Bubwith, and Ercewik, and at other places which at present he cannot recollect; and in the city of York and its suburb, namely in Bowthum, Stayngate, Goterumgate, Petergat, and in the great hall opposite the Bedern. The vicars' tenements are in decay, and moreover the vicars cannot find reliable tenants (*tenentes sufficientes*) for them.

[iv] Asked about the vicars' expenses, he says on oath that they have to spend £18 5s. 1d. a year on paying various rents (*firma*) and chantry chaplains in the cathedral, and they have to set aside (*apponere*) £15 each year for the repair of their tenements, both inside and outside the city. Moreover, he says that each year the vicars pay deacons, choristers, and the sacrists who ring the bells for obits (*pro pulsacione obituum*) 32s. 4d.; their janitor 24s. 4d.; and their two chamberlains 26s. 8d. Thus, there remains only £32 3s. 1d. to be distributed among the vicars in respect of (*propter*) their stipends.

[v] He says that the rents and income are so meagre that they are insufficient for half the vicars' necessary expenses, and on that account many vicars celebrate for the faithful departed [in churches] in the city of York, outside the cathedral, to the grave scandal and obloquy of both clergy and people.

[vi] He says that because of all this the vicars are increasingly burdened by debt, from which it is impossible to believe that they can be freed unless they are helped for charity's sake from elsewhere (*nisi caritatis intuitu eisdem provideatur et subveniatur aliunde*).

[vii] Finally, he says that these things are widely talked about, both in the city and in neighbouring places.

SOURCE: VC 3/1/1, fo. 121r.–v.

209. Deposition of Roger de Everton, vicar in the choir of the cathedral church of blessed Peter of York. Answers as 208 (with minor variations and omissions; and in

HUNTINGTON

[ii] stating that he was often present when the vicars' chamberlains rendered their accounts and giving £69 6s. for £69 6s. 6d.; and in [iv] giving the janitor's stipend as at least 24s.).

SOURCE: VC 3/1/1, fo. 121v.–122r.

210.   Deposition of Richard de Grayngham, vicar in the choir of the cathedral church of blessed Peter of York. Answers as **208** (with minor variations and omissions; and in [ii] stating that before the pestilence he saw the old rolls (*rotulos antiquos*) of the vicars' chamberlains when they rendered their accounts and giving £69 6s. for £69 6s. 6d.; in [iv] giving the janitor's stipend as 24s.; and in [vi] adding that the annual net value of the parish church of Huntington is 24 marks [£16]).

SOURCE: VC 3/1/1, fo. 122r.–v.

211.   Deposition of John de Thorne, vicar in the choir of the cathedral church of blessed Peter of York. Answers as **208** (with minor variations and omissions; and in [ii] stating that before the pestilence he was present when the vicars' chamberlains rendered their accounts and that after the pestilence he himself was chamberlain and knows that the vicars' income never amounted to its earlier level; and in [iv] giving the janitor's stipend as 24s.).

SOURCE: VC 3/1/1, fos. 122v.–123r.

212.   Deposition of William de Gerthorp, vicar in the choir of the said church.
     He says that there are 36 vicars in the cathedral church of blessed Peter, attending divine service; that each vicar receives 40s. a year for his stipend, and each vicar except one receives one mark [13s. 4d.] a year from the church of Pydceburton; that they live in the Bedern, and have a common seal and other marks of a recognized college.
     The vicars' annual rents and income before the pestilence amounted to £93 14s., the witness being the vicars' chamberlain in the year of the pestilence and having audited other chamberlains' accounts before the pestilence. The income now amounts to £69 6s. 6d., and it has been diminished not by the vicars' fault but by misfortune and by the pestilence and the impoverishment of their tenants. The vicars have to spend £18 5s. 1d. a year on paying various rents and chantry chaplains in the cathedral; 32s. 8d. a year [sic] on deacons, choristers, and sacrists; and 24s. a year on their janitor. The [remaining] income is insufficient for their necessary expenses, unless they are helped from elsewhere. Each year the vicars also set aside £15 for the repair of their tenements in the city of York and outside.

SOURCE: VC 3/1/1, fo. 123r.

213.   Deposition of mag. Roger de Sutton, vicar in the choir of the cathedral church of blessed Peter of York.
     He says that there are 36 vicars in the cathedral church, attending divine service and the canonical hours; that each vicar receives from his prebendary 40s. a year for his stipend, and that all but one receives one mark [13s. 4d.] a year from the church of Pydceburton.

The vicars' annual rents and income before the pestilence amounted to £93 14s., the witness often auditing the chamberlains' accounts. Now they are so meagre because of the pestilence and the impoverishment of tenants and other misfortunes that they scarcely amount to £69 6s. 6d. Each year the vicars are obliged to pay £18 5s. 1d. on various rents and chantry chaplains in the cathedral; 32s. 4d. on deacons, choristers, and sacrists; 24s. a year on their janitor; and 26s. 8d. a year on their two chamberlains. Each year the vicars also set aside £15 for the repair of their tenements in the city of York and outside.

SOURCE: VC 3/1/1, fo. 123r.–v.

214.   Deposition of Hugh Attewatt' of Ercewyk, layman.

He says that the vicars' rents in the vill of Ersewyk and in the city of York have been greatly diminished by the pestilence and by the impoverishment of the vicars' tenants.

He also says that he has generally heard it said that from the rents which the vicars now receive they cannot bear the charges imposed on them, nor continue the celebration of divine office in the cathedral in the customary manner, unless they are helped from elsewhere.

The net annual value of the parish church of Huntington is 24 marks [£16].

SOURCE: VC 3/1/1, fo. 123v.

215.   Deposition of Thomas de Kyllum of York, layman.

He says that the vicars' rents and income are worth £24 a year less than before the pestilence. He knows this because both before and after the pestilence he lived in one of the vicars' houses in Goderumgat, for which he used to pay 46s. 8d. a year before the pestilence and now only 26s. 8d.; and the vicars' rents elsewhere inside and outside the city have been diminished proportionately. This is because of misfortune and the recent pestilence, and especially because the vicars cannot find tenants to inhabit their tenements. The vicars cannot maintain themselves from the present rents, nor bear their charges, unless they are helped from elsewhere, and many of them find work celebrating for the faithful departed in various churches in York.

He also says that the net annual value of the church of Huntington is 24 marks [£16].

SOURCE: VC 3/1/1, fos. 123r.–124v.

NOTE: For Kilham's house see Chs. Vicars Choral, i, no. 144.

216.   Deposition of John de Caperoun of York, layman.

He says that as a result of misfortune and the recent pestilence the vicars' rents have been diminished by 38 marks [£25 6s. 8d.] a year; he knows that some of their arable land lies sterile and uncultivated and that many tenements in the city of York and outside are empty because the vicars cannot find tenants for them. The vicars cannot maintain themselves from their present rents, nor bear their charges, unless they are helped from elsewhere, and by necessity (propter indigenciam) they find work in the city of York celebrating for the faithful departed.

Although he was questioned on the articles in English (in lingua materna), he was unable to depose further.

SOURCE: VC 3/1/1, fo. 124r.

217. Deposition of Richard de Helay of Huntington, layman.

He says that he has generally heard from others that the vicars' rents have been greatly diminished because of the recent pestilence, and that the vicars cannot find tenants for their property.

He also says that the net annual value of the parish church of Huntington is 24 marks [£16], and he knows this because for 4 years immediately before the pestilence he was the servant (*serviens*) of mag. Richard de Snaweshill, formerly rector of the same church.

SOURCE: VC 3/1/1, fo. 124r.–v.

218. Deposition of William de Huntington, citizen of York.

He says that the vicars' rents have been diminished by a third because of the recent pestilence and the impoverishment of their tenants. He also says that the net annual value of the parish church of Huntington is 20 marks [£13 6s. 8d.].

Although questioned in English, he was unable to depose further.

SOURCE: VC 3/1/1, fo. 124v.

219. Deposition of Simon de Munkton of York.

He says that the vicars' rents [now] amount scarcely to half the sum received before the recent pestilence, and the vicars cannot find tenants for their property either inside the city of York or outside. The vicars' present rents are insufficient for their necessary expenses and other charges, unless they are helped from elsewhere, and by necessity many vicars find work celebrating for the dead in various churches in York.

He also says that the annual net value of the parish church of Huntington is 20 marks [£13 6s. 8d.], and he knows this because he is a parishioner of that church.

SOURCE: VC 3/1/1, fo. 124v.

220. [*Appropriation of Huntington church.*]

Letter of Archbishop John [Thoresby] to the vicars of the church of blessed Peter of York. He has received a petition from the vicars to his immediate predecessor, William la Zouche, for the appropriation of the church of Huntyngton next to York, to help relieve their poverty, caused by the pestilence (*epidimeam*) lately happening in this as in other parts of the world, by the diminution of their houses, fruits, income, and rents and the heavy costs of repairing buildings and estates, beside the unjust detention of certain rents and pensions, and by the various payments they have to make to clergy. The archbishop's predecessor laboured so that the vicars should benefit by the appropriation of the church of Huntynton, according to the tenor of their petition, but he was prevented by death from completing what was required.

The archbishop [i.e. Thoresby] has found the contents [of the petition] to be true and has annexed and united the church to the uses of the vicars' community and college on the resignation or death of the present rector, John de Cotyngham; reserving an annual pension of 6s. 8d. payable by the vicars to the archbishop and his successors at Pentecost each year, in recompense for the loss of that appropriation, and reserving episcopal and archidiaconal rights and the dignity of the church of York.

Moreover, the archbishop reserves to himself the ordination of a vicarage in the church of Huntyngton. Seal.

York, 9 September 1353, and in first year of his translation.

SOURCE: [i] VC 3/4/Hun/3a (492 mm. × 194 mm.); [ii] VC 3/4/Hun/3b (411 mm. × 236 mm.)

ENDORSEMENT: [i] *Confirmacio appropriacionis ecclesie de Huntington*; [ii] *De Hontyngton ecclesie; Ratificatio.*

SEAL: [i] archiepiscopal seal of John Thoresby, vesica (84 mm. × 55 mm.), hung on blue and yellow cord; [ii] remains of archiepiscopal seal, green wax, hung on parchment tag.

COPIES: VC 3/1/1, fo. 125r.–v.; BIHR, Reg. 11, fo. 12v.

NOTE: Archbishop Zouche died in July 1352 before he could complete the appropriation of Huntington church, although one of his last acts was to order (on 6 July 1352) the institution of John de Cottingham to Huntington rectory at the vicars' presentation (BIHR, Reg. 10, fo. 173v.). The vicars petitioned his successor, John Thoresby, to complete the process, and in August 1353 he instructed the chapter of York to meet with his commissary to discuss the matter (BIHR, Reg. 11, fos. 21, 22v.). The appropriation was made a few days later.

221.   Notarial exemplification of Hugh de Fletham, clerk of York diocese and apostolic notary, rehearsing an inspeximus and confirmation by the chapter of the church of blessed Peter of York, in the absence of the dean, of a letter of Archbishop John [Thoresby] (as 220).

The confirmation was dated in the chapter house of York on 6 December 1353, in the presence of mag. William de Langeton, advocate of the court of York (*iurisperito curie Eboracen' advocato*), William de Burton'annays, rector of the church of Esyngton' in York diocese, John de Synythwayt and Peter de Sutton, clerks of York diocese.

SOURCE: [i] VC 3/4/Hun/4a (519 mm. × 473 mm.); [ii] VC 3/4/Hun/4b (574 mm. × 431 mm.)

ENDORSEMENT: [i] *Appropriacio ecclesie de Huntyngton*; [ii] *Appropriacio ecclesie de Huntington; Appropriacio de Huntyngton.*

SEAL: [i] seal of chapter of York, vesica (80 mm. × 52 mm.), brown wax, hung on green and pink cord, only part of legend survives; [ii] slit

SIGN: [i] and [ii] notarial sign of Hugh de Fletham.

222.   Letter of Ellis de Walkynton, warden of the house of vicars of the church of blessed Peter of York, and the community (*cetus*) of vicars appointing William de Feriby, canon of that church, as their proctor, and granting him general power and special mandate to have and to hold all their goods and especially the church of Huntington, appropriated to them by Archbishop John [Thoresby]. Sealed with their common seal.

York, 1 May 1354.

SOURCE: Rehearsed in 223.

223.   Letter of Archbishop John [Thoresby]. Since John de Cotyngham, lately rector of the church of Huntington, has resigned the church, which the archbishop has appropriated to the vicars of the cathedral church of York through their proctor, William de Feriby, appointed by a letter of 1 May 1354 (as **222**), the archbishop orders that the vicars shall pay Cotyngham a pension of £10 a year, and that after his death they shall celebrate a mass for his soul on the day of his burial and then celebrate each year on the day of his anniversary.

In the archbishop's manor next to Westminster, 15 May 1354.

SOURCE: BIHR, Reg. 11, fo. 31v.

224.   [*Ordination of vicarage of Huntington.*]

Letter of Archbishop John [Thoresby]. Having approved the appropriation of the church of Huntington to the vicars of the cathedral church for their support, the archbishop has reserved the ordination of a perpetual vicarage and suitable portion from the income of the church for the maintenance of a perpetual vicar, with the consent of William de Feryby, canon of the cathedral church and proctor of the vicars, as constituted in **222**.

The vicar of the church [of Huntington], instituted at the presentation of the vicars [of the church of York] by the archbishop, or during a vacancy in the see by the chapter of the cathedral, shall have the rectory house with its buildings on the east side of the church, its garden, and two bovates of arable land on the west side of the Fosse, with the meadows, pastures, and pasture rights appertaining to the two bovates; and also, all the lesser tithes, oblations, and mortuaries, alive and dead, tithes of mills, offerings to the altar and the whole altarage itself (*obventiones de altaragio provenientes qualitercumque et in ipso alteragio toto*). The tithes of corn, hay, and wool, land called Angrum with buildings and croft on the west side of the church, and two bovates of land on the east side of the water of Fosse, with meadows, pastures, and pasture rights appertaining to the church, not being assigned to the vicarage, shall remain in the hands of the vicars [of the church of York].

The vicar of Huntington church is to pay to the vicars [of the church of York] a tithe from the lands of his vicarage, as well as from animals pastured in the parish, and the vicars are bound similarly to pay to the [parochial] vicar tithe from the lands here assigned to them and from beasts pastured on those lands. The [parochial] vicar shall pay a quarter of all the ordinary and extraordinary dues and customary payments and the vicars of the church of York three-quarters of them. The vicars shall also pay an annual pension of 6s. 8d. to the archbishop and his successors. Seal.

In the archbishop's manor next to Westminster, 16 May 1354, and in the 2nd year of his translation.

SOURCE: VC 3/4/Hun/5 (396 mm. × 275 mm.)

ENDORSEMENT: *In Hontyngton; Ordinacio perpetue vicarie per archiepiscopum vicariis; Nota de quatuor bovatis terre ibidem.*

SEAL: remains of green wax on tag.

COPIES: VC 3/1/1, fos. 125v.–126v.; BIHR, Reg. 11, fo. 32.

NOTE: The tithe barn at Angrum was rethatched in the late 1380s (VC 4/2/FF and Hun/8).

225.   Letter of the official of York recording that he has ordered the induction by the dean of Christianity of York of the warden of the house of vicars and the vicars of the choir of the cathedral church of blessed Peter of York, in the person of their proctor Richard de Graingham, fellow vicar, into corporal possession of the church of Huntington next to York, vacant through the resignation of the last rector, John de Cotingham.

York, 14 June 1354.

SOURCE: VC 3/1/1, fo. 126v.

NOTE: Archbishop Thoresby's mandate to the official ordering the induction was issued at Westminster on 15 May 1354: BIHR, Reg. 11, fo. 31v.

226.   Notarial instrument of William Driffeld, clerk of York diocese and apostolic notary. On 10 December 1415 in the churchyard of the parish church of Huntyngton, William Forest chaplain received on behalf of the vicars of the cathedral church of York letters from the commissary general of the official of the court of York under the commissary's seal, and showed them to mag. Roger Esyngwald, pretending himself to be the official of mag. William Pelson, archdeacon of Clyveland, and by their authority he inhibited Roger from attempting to prejudice an appeal pending in the court between the archdeacon and the vicars and so prevent the vicars, as the appellants, from having freedom of appeal or prosecution. Immediately Roger ordered Walter Aresom, vicar of the parish church of Huntyngton, to hand over the key of the church door or to open the door so that he might be able to enter into the church. Walter said that he did not have the key and was not able to open the door.

Roger then held in his hand a letter of the official of the court of York, itself containing, he claimed, the text of letters of the king and the archbishop of York. John Hiklyng, succentor of the vicars, in his own name and . . . . . .[4 or 5 words illegible because of rubbing], and also Robert Appilton, William Wath, Thomas Swanland, and Thomas Wylton, vicars of the church of York, protested before Roger and others that they wished to obey the letters of King Henry, Henry [Bowet], archbishop of York, and the official of the court of York and also to obey the orders of their canons, and that they did not wish to impede Roger in executing the letters, but that they refused to concede (*consentire*) in any way that the archdeacon and his pretended official should exercise any jurisdiction over the parishioners or over the church of Huntyngton, which was canonically appropriated, as they assert, to the succentor and vicars.

This having been said, Roger replied that he did not wish to execute any letters of the king or archbishop, but only letters and mandates of his master, the archdeacon of Clyveland.

This was done in the presence of mag. John Carlton, rector of the parish church of Escryk, William Darell of Huntyngton . . . [one word illegible because of rubbing], Thomas Seteryngton otherwise called Magh', John Brantyngham clerk, and many others of the diocese of York.

SOURCE: VC 3/4/Hun/6 (415 mm. × 372 mm.)
ENDORSEMENT: none medieval.
SIGN: notarial sign of William Driffeld.

227. Letter of the succentor and vicars of the college of vicars in the choir of the church of York to Archbishop Henry [Bowet], presenting Richard Couper chaplain to be instituted to the perpetual vicarage of the parish church of Huntyngton, vacant as a result of the resignation of Walter Areshom.
In the chapel of the vicars' college in York, 25 April 1422.

SOURCE: VC I/I, pp. 72–3 (ink pagination).

NOTE: Areshom had moved to York, where earlier in April 1422 he was instituted, at the vicars' presentation, to a chantry in St. Sampson's church (**257**).

228. Letter of Archbishop Henry [Bowet] to Richard Couper priest, instituting him to the perpetual vicarage of the parish church of Huntyngton, vacant as a result of the resignation of Walter Areshom; Couper is presented by the succentor and vicars of the college of vicars in the choir of the cathedral church of York.
Thorp next to York, 26 April 1422, and in the 15th year of his translation.

SOURCE: VC I/I, p. 73 (ink pagination).

229. Notarial instrument recording that on 16 May 1422 in the cathedral church of York, Richard Couper, perpetual vicar of the parish church of H[untington], resigned his vicarage. [Text of resignation follows.]
Witnesses: P[eter] M[oreby], succentor of the vicars in the choir of the cathedral church and Thomas Garwardby, fellow vicar.

SOURCE: [two versions of same text] VC I/I, pp. 73–4 and 82–3 (ink pagination).

230. Award of John [Kempe], archbishop of York, as arbiter, to mag. William Duffeld, archdeacon of Clyveland, and the vicars of the church [of York] in a dispute between the two parties concerning the right of visitation to the church of Huntyngton in the said archdeaconry. The archbishop declares that it is unlawful for the vicars to prohibit the archdeacon from visiting the church or deny him entry into the churchyard or the church at legitimate times; and he prohibits the vicars from doing so in future under pain of excommunication.

Moreover, as the archbishop has learnt not only from the complaint of mag. William [Duffeld] but also from public report, that in the course of denying mag. William, the archdeacon, and his retinue (*suis familiaribus*), access (*transitum et progressum*) by a path next to or near the churchyard of the church of Huntyngton, various wounds and blows (*varia plage et vulnera*) were rained on several of mag. William's retinue, and especially on a man called William Gilson, who as a result of those wounds or blows, or at least one of them, died not long afterwards.

Considering that such an unfortunate event would not have occurred if the vicars had refrained (*se continuissent*) from denying access and had not gone out so heedlessly (*improvide et inconsulte fuissent egressi*), the archbishop ordains that each year for 7 years from the time of this arbitration or award the vicars shall on the day immediately preceding William Gilson's anniversary, sing for his soul solemnly and with note in the chapel of the blessed Virgin in the church of York, namely that beyond (*supra*) the high altar towards the east, where the mass of the blessed Virgin, Placebo, and Dirige are sung daily, solemnly and with note, and that they shall on the morrow sing similarly with note a requiem, with a special collect for William's soul as the first and principal [collect]. On Monday each week throughout the 7-year period, one of the vicars shall celebrate a requiem mass for William's soul at the said altar, with the special collect that was read beforehand in the mass.

As for the injuries or offences that were committed by the vicars, or at least by their negligence or blame, against mag. William the archdeacon, the archbishop condemns them and regards them as worthy of compensation. Considering, however, the tenuous state of the vicars and their meagre resources (*pusillam exiguamque sub-stanciam*), from which they are unable to support themselves comfortably, and the burden of making a monetary compensation, and considering that mag. William is not moved by avarice or cupidity but rather by more important values, the archbishop ordains that at his next arrival in the city of York, or if that happens to be delayed beyond a year from the date of this award then before the dean of the church of York, the vicars shall appear before mag. William in a suitable place appointed by the archbishop or the dean, and through their leader apologise as follows:

> Venerable and distinguished lord, archdeacon of Clyveland and canon and prebendary of the church of York, of which we are the vicars and ministers: your lordship knows the grave offence committed by us, or by others acting for us, in opposing the exercise of your archidiaconal visitation of the parish church of Huntyngton, appropriated to us. We declare that it was not and shall never be our intention or desire to do anything to offend or injure your authority, and if anything was done heedlessly by us against you we humbly beseech you to pardon us, and that hereafter we shall be acceptable to you.

In so far, however, as the archbishop is not yet fully informed about the other injuries alleged by others of mag. William's retinue, and as he wishes to learn something certain, he ordains that a suitable compensation for those men should be set by the arbitration of two worthy men, chosen if possible by mag. William and the vicars jointly (*concorditer*), or otherwise by one nominated by William and the other by the vicars. If the men cannot agree, then the archbishop orders that the assessment should devolve on Robert Rolleston, canon of York.

Regarding the main business of the visitation, the archbishop has been informed: firstly, that both according to the letter of appropriation of Huntyngton church to the vicars by Archbishop John Thuresby, and the evidence of worthy men, the church at the time of its appropriation was fully subject to ordinary jurisdiction, without any exemption or other privilege of freedom; and that before the appropriation, the induction of a person into corporal and canonical possession of the church, after having been admitted by the archbishop, belonged to the archdeacon of Clyveland, and that after the appropriation, with the admission then being by the vicars, it still belonged to the archdeacon; and, secondly, that mag. William Pelson, the immediate past archdeacon of Clyveland, obtained protection in an appeal in the court of York for the exercise of his archidiaconal authority in opposition to the vicars, and that afterwards the present archdeacon, mag. William Duffeld, visited the church. Wherefore, the archbishop ordains that Duffeld and his successors may freely exercise the right of visitation in the church of Huntyngton, provided that, if within five years of this award the vicars can prove that the church should be exempted from visitation, then the archbishop or his successors shall declare the church free of the archdeacon. Dated on the eve of Pentecost, which was the last day of May [31 May] 1438.

SOURCE: VC 3/4/Hun/7 (569 mm. × 335 mm.) Indented at top.
ENDORSEMENT: *Sentencia archiepiscopi contra visitacionem de Huntington.*
SEAL: slit.

COPY: BIHR, Reg. 19, fos. 199v.–201.

NOTE: After Duffeld's death early in 1453, his executors gave the vicars £40 to celebrate his obit (VC 6/1/9).

ST. SAMPSON'S, YORK

231. Letter of Godfrey [de Ludham], archbishop of York and primate of England. Noting (*attendentes*) that the revenues of the church of St. Benet in York are meagre and indeed almost nothing (*proventus . . . exiles sunt immo verius fere nulli*), and that those of the church of St. Sampson in the same city are slender and meagre (*tenues sunt et exiles*), so that both incomes are scarcely sufficient for the stipend of a priest, the archbishop with the consent of the archdeacon of Richemund, the patron of both churches, has united (*duximus*) the livings, so that both parishes shall have the church of St. Sampson as a mother church (*tanquam ad matricem*) and that its rector shall have the rule (*regimen*) of both. Seal.
Beverley, 12 Kalends October [20 September] 1263.

SOURCE: Rehearsed in **234**.

232. Mandate of R[obert Pickering], the dean, and the chapter of blessed Peter of York, . . [gemipuncti] keepers of the spiritualities, . . the archbishopric then being vacant, ordering the dean of Christianity to go personally to the church of St. Sampson in York, having summoned some senior parishioners who have good knowledge of the parish, being long-term inhabitants, [to meet him there,] and to take them to the place where the church of St. Benet once stood. He is to ask the men on oath whether the church of St. Benet or its churchyard had been consecrated and whether a feast of that dedication was celebrated as in other churches, and if so by whom and when the church or churchyard was consecrated; also, whether any bodies were buried in the church or churchyard and if there are tombs (*sarcophoga mortuorum*), and if so how long it has been since the last burial (*quantum tempus postmodum est effluxum*). He is to report the findings of the inquiry.
York, 6 Ides of March [10 March] 1316 [*sic*].

SOURCE: Rehearsed in **233**.

DATE: 10 March '1316' should by modern reckoning be 1316/17, but '1316' is probably in error for '1315' as a result of assimilation with the date of **233**. The mandate, therefore, should probably be dated 10 March 1315/16.

233. Certificate of the dean of Christianity of York to R[obert Pickering], the dean, and the chapter of blessed Peter of York. In accordance with their mandate (**232**), he reports that he went personally to the church of St. Sampson, and diligently inquired through worthy sworn men, who say that neither the church [of St. Benet] nor its churchyard was ever consecrated, as they firmly believe. William de Hamelton, once . . [gemipuncti] dean of the church of York, inquired about this because he had heard for certain that the church had not been consecrated, nor its churchyard, and if it had at any time been consecrated then he would never have permitted its walls to have been demolished. The men also say that tombs (*sarcophoga mortuorum*) have been found there, but that they have not seen anyone being buried in the church or churchyard. Seal.

York, 12 Kalends June [21 May] 1316.

SOURCE: VC 3/4/Sam/1 (259 mm. × 239 mm.)

ENDORSEMENT: *Reverendis viris et discretis dominis decano et capitulo ecclesie Ebor'.*

SEAL: seals were affixed to several tags, of which only a few remain with traces of wax.

234.   Inspeximus of John Broun, rector of the church of St. Sampson, York, of a letter of Archbishop Godfrey (as **231**).

Authorized by this letter John has granted to Roger de Buggethorp' carpenter the site of the church of St. Benet with its churchyard in Patrikpol in York, to hold of the chief lords of the fee for the service due; paying 5s. a year to the chantry of the blessed Virgin Mary in the church of St. Sampson, at Martinmas and Pentecost. Seal.

Witnesses: Nicholas le Flemang, then mayor of the city of York, Thomas de Alwarthorp', Nicholas de Colonia, Richard le Toller, bailiffs of the same city, Roger Basy, John Gra, Thomas le Nedler, Richard Tunnok, John de Leycestr', Thomas Durant, John de Sexdecim Vallibus, William de Apelby clerk, and others.

York, the day of St. Andrew the apostle [30 November] 1316, 10 Edward son of King Edward.

SOURCE: Rehearsed in **235**.

235.   Inspeximus of Roger de Northburgh, archdeacon of Richemund and patron of the church of St. Sampson in York, of letters patent of John Broun, rector of the said church (as **234**), in no way altered (*non cancellatas, non abolitas, nec in aliqua sui parte viciatas*). Seal.

York, Wednesday before Michaelmas [28 September], 1317, 11 Edward son of King Edward.

SOURCE: VC 3/4/Sam/2 (396 mm. × 187 mm.)

ENDORSEMENT: *Unio ecclesiarum sanctorum Sampsonis et Benedicti per Godfredum archie-piscopum Ebor'.*

SEAL: remains of red wax on tag.

236.   Inquisition held at York on Monday after the feast of St. Peter ad vincula 13 Edward III [2 August 1339] before Richard de Aldeburgh and William Basset, appointed with Robert Parnyng by the king, to inquire what right Robert de Wodehouse, archdeacon of Richemund, has to the advowson of the church of St. Sampson in York.

William de Hothum, Thomas de Bilham, Thomas de Askham, John de Housum, Abell' de Hesill, John de Eskerig nailer (*nailler*), John de Cathale, John de Bugthorp', John de Coupmanthorp', Robert de Sallay, Peter le Pulter, and William Fox, chapman, say on oath that the present archdeacon has the right of advowson of the said church and that all his predecessors as archdeacons of Richemund had that right and were seised of the advowson; they also say that Francis de Luco, archdeacon of Richemund and the present archdeacon's predecessor, presented John Broun, his

clerk, to the church and he was admitted and instituted in the time of Edward [II]. Before [that] mag. Henry de Newerk, archdeacon of Richemund, presented Ralph de Skurveton', who was admitted and instituted in the time of Edward [I], and before [that] mag. John de Craucumbe, commissary of the archdeacon of Richemund, on behalf of the archdeacon presented mag. William de Ocham, who was admitted and instituted in the time of Edward [I]. They say that the present archdeacon was arraigned in the king's court on an assize of last presentation against the prior of Pontefract concerning the advowson, and that afterwards because the archdeacon did not prosecute the assize the prior recovered the presentation to the church, but that because it was suspected that the archdeacon and the prior had colluded fraudulently against the king, the advowson was seized and taken into the king's hand. They also say that the advowson appurtains to the archdeaconry, and that 'they do not know from whom the advowson is held nor by what service' [*text in inverted commas written over:* no service is owed for it to any lord, *struck through*]; and they say that the church is worth £10 a year. Seal. [*Followed by a sentence that has been struck through:* And know that this inquisition was stitched to the writ of the king that came to the said Richard, William, and Robert].
York, day and year given above.

SOURCE: VC 3/4/Sam/3 (223 mm. × 150 mm.)
ENDORSEMENT: *Informacio pro archidiacono Richem' pro patronatu ecclesie sancti Sampsonis Ebor'.* [Also text of **237.**]

NOTE: Luco was in fact the archdeacon's chaplain: **237.**

237. Letter of William [Melton], archbishop of York and primate of England. Having inspected the registers of his predecessors, Walter Giffard, William Wykwane, and William de Grenefeld, the archbishop records the following memoranda:
[i] On the Ides of January 1275 [13 January 1275/6] mag. John de Craucumbe, commissary of the archdeacon of Richem', presented mag. William de Ocham to the vacant church of St. Sampson, York, and an inquiry was held in the customary manner, [thus]:
Letter of Walter [Giffard], archbishop of York and primate of England, to mag. William de Ocham, clerk, ordering his admittance and institution to the church of St. Sampson on the presentation of the archdeacon of Richem'. Cawode, 14 Kalends March 1275 [16 February 1275/6].
[ii] On the presentation of mag. Henry de Neuwerk, archdeacon of Richem', Ralph de Thornton, priest, was admitted and instituted to the church of St. Sampson at Cawode on 10 Kalends December [22 November], 1281, and in the 3rd year of the pontificate of William Wykwane.
[iii] On 16 Kalends June [17 May] 1312 Robert de Pykering, canon of York and vicar general of Archbishop William [de Grenefeld], admitted John Broun of York, deacon, to the church of St. Sampson on the presentation of Francis de Luco, chaplain of Francis Gaytani, cardinal, archdeacon of Richem', and vicar general. Broun was corporally inducted into the church of St. Sampson on the same day.
Thorp next to York, 4 Nones August [2 August] 1339, and in the 22nd year of his pontificate.

SOURCE: Endorsement on **236.**

NOTE: The relevant entries in the archbishops' registers are: *Register of Walter Giffard,* ed. W. Brown (Surtees Society, cix, 1904), 255 (Ocham); *Register of William*

Wickwane, ed. W. Brown (Surtees Society, cxiv, 1907), p. 42 (Thornton): *Register of William Greenfield*, ed. W. Brown and A. H. Thompson (Surtees Society, cxlix, 1934), p. 116 note (Broun).

238.   Licence of Richard II to mag. John de Waltham clerk and William Lovell clerk to assign a messuage in York to a chaplain celebrating daily in St. Sampson's church for the soul of Nicholas de Burton clerk.
8 May 2 Richard II [1379].

SOURCE: VC 3/2/16 (360 mm. × 180 mm.)
ENDORSEMENT: *Waltham*; *licencia pro canteria in ecclesiam sancti Sampsonis*.
SEAL: great seal in green wax hung on red and green cord.
CALENDARED: *Cal. Pat. R.* 1377–81, p. 345.

239.   Ordinance of Archbishop Alexander [de Neville]. Certain tenements were given for the foundation of a chantry of one perpetual chaplain to be celebrated at the altar of the blessed Virgin Mary in the parish church of St. Sampson in York, namely four messuages in Patrikpole and Benetplace with habitable houses for the chaplain in the churchyard of the church. The tenements have so declined (*decreverunt*) in value that it is impossible to maintain a suitable chaplain worthily (*congrue*) from the rents; it frequently happens that a chaplain cannot be found to take the chantry, and it will not be possible to find one unless he be provided with additional income.

Having piously considered all this, mag. John de Waltham, canon of the church of York, and William Lovell, rector of the church of Oswaldkirk, in York diocese, having first acquired a licence from the king, have given to the future chaplains of the chantry in augmentation of their income, and for the souls of mag. Nicholas de Burton, whose body rests in St. Sampson's church, and for the souls of his father and mother and of all his benefactors, all that messuage which John de Berden, citizen of York, holds in Jubrettegate; Waltham and Lovell have the messuage by the legacy of the same Nicholas, and the rent of the messuage together with the chantry's old rents will be sufficient for the maintenance of the chaplain.

Since there is no firm evidence of the canonical arrangements made for the chantry (*Verumque de aliqua certa canonica ordinacione ipsius cantarie non habebatur clara noticia*), John de Wirsall, rector of the church of St. Sampson, and the parishioners of the same, on whose ordering (*disposicione*) the chantry has so far depended, as well as mag. John de Waltham and William Lovell, submit the matter to the archbishop, who makes an ordinance for the chantry, [thus]:

Whenever a vacancy occurs the rector of the church of St. Sampson or his proctor and the parishioners, or the greater or more respected (*saniorem*) part of them, being citizens of the said city, shall present [a chaplain] to the archbishop, or during a vacancy in the see to the dean and chapter [of York], within a month of the vacancy being notified. If they do not present a worthy and honest chaplain within the month, the collation shall fall to the archbishop or to the dean and chapter. The chaplain so instituted shall celebrate daily at the altar of the blessed Virgin Mary in the parish church of St. Sampson, and shall celebrate the masses and divine office especially for the first founders of the chantry and for the rector and parishioners of the church and for all the benefactors of the chantry; and he shall say a special collect in each mass for the souls of Nicholas de Burton, his father John de Burton and John's wife Ellen, and the souls of their parents and benefactors, and he shall say the prayers for the dead (*suffragia mortuorum*) every day for the said souls, except on Christmas day and Easter day; if he is prevented (*impeditus fuerit*) by illness or other legitimate cause, he is to make good the omissions (*supplere omissa*) within four days. Moreover, he shall say and sing the canonical hours with the rector, or with other chaplains of the church, in the nave (*in ecclesia*) or in the chancel on Sundays and feast days and on those days when he ought to be present saying high mass at the high altar, and also on those days when a sung mass (*missa cum nota*) is to be celebrated at the Virgin's altar. He shall look after and maintain (*custodiet et sustentabit*) the chantry's books, chalices (*calicos*), vestments, ornaments, and vessels (*vasa*), along with its houses and buildings.

The chaplain shall keep the obit for Nicholas, John de Burton, and Ellen on St. Nicholas's day [6 December] in the church of St. Sampson, paying on that day 2*d.* each to eight priests celebrating in the church for those souls. If there are chaplains who continually celebrate in the church, they shall be given preference in the distribution, but if not then he shall get (*procuret . . . accedere*) up to eight other chaplains to celebrate in the church on the day of the obit. He shall pay 2*d.* to the parish clerk for tolling the bells and for his labour, and 4*d.* to the city bell-ringer (*campanario*) for tolling, as is the custom, a bell throughout the city and calling on people to pray for the said souls (*excitanti populum ad orandum pro animabus predictis*). The chaplain shall provide two candles at each obit, burning on the tomb (*tumulum*) of mag. Nicholas while the masses and prayers for the dead are being sung.

Each chaplain admitted to the said chantry is bound on his admission to swear on the holy gospels that he will faithfully observe this ordinance. Seal.

Cawode, 1 August 1379, and in the 6th year of his consecration.

SOURCE: Rehearsed in 240.

NOTE: The ordinance was not entered into the archbishop's register, but on 2 August 1379 Neville instituted Robert de Folkton to the chantry at the presentation of the proctor of the rector, two wardens of the fabric, and 12 parishioners: BIHR, Reg. 12, fo. 28.

    Waltham and Lovell, as executors of Nicholas de Burton, assigned the Jubbergate land to the chantry chaplain on 27 July 1379: CCA, DCc/Charta Antiqua Y 20. For charters that may relate to the earlier history of the property see *Chs. Vicars Choral*, i, nos. 63–6.

240.   Inspeximus by the chapter of the church of blessed Peter of York, in the dean's absence, of the ordinance of Archbishop Alexander [de Neville] (as **239**).

The chapter of York approve, ratify, and confirm the ordinance. Seal.

York, in the chapter house, 5 August, in the aforesaid year [1379].

SOURCE: VC 3/4/Sam/4 (442 mm. × 365 mm.)
ENDORSEMENT: *Ad altare[m] beate Marie in ecclesia sancti Sampsonis.*
SEAL: seal of chapter of York, vesica (84 mm. × 53 mm.)

241.   Copy letter of Richard II. A college of 36 vicars was established in the cathedral church of blessed Peter of York, and the vicars have a residence (*habitationem*) in which they live in common, next to the churchyard of the church; the king understands that although the vicars have not kept table in that residence continually together as is decent but separately in different places (*non continue insimul et communiter . . . sed divisim in mensa habitaverint vicibus iteratis*), they wish, for greater decency and the increase of charity and the fervour of devotion, to live in their common residence and keep table together in their hall and not separately. The vicars propose to sing an obit for the king and for Anne, his consort, in the cathedral after their deaths, together with an antiphon and a collect of St. John the Baptist at the altar of St. John or before his statue (*ymagine sua*) every day immediately after compline; [in consideration of which] the king grants to them the advowson of the church of St. Sampson, York, in pure alms, with a licence that they may receive the advowson and appropriate the church and hold it to their own uses. Westminster, 1 March 17 [Richard II] [1393/4].

SOURCE: VC 3/4/Sam/5 (298 mm. × 202 mm.)
ENDORSEMENT: *Copia carte regie super advocacionem ecclesie sancti Sampsonis.*
CALENDARED: *Cal. Pat. R.* 1391–6, p. 386.

242.   Letter of Richard II. On 1 March last [1393/4] the king by letters patent gave the college of 36 vicars in the cathedral church of St. Peter, York, the advowson of the church of St. Sampson in the city of York in pure alms, in aid of their sustenance and in support of certain devotions for him and his consort, Queen Anne. He granted a licence to the vicars to appropriate the church and to hold it to their own uses.

A statute made at Westminster in the 15th year [1391] expressly states that in each licence made in chancery for the appropriation of a parish church the diocesan of the place shall set down a suitable sum of money to be paid annually by the appropriators to poor parishioners from the fruits and income of the church, and that a vicar shall likewise be suitably endowed. In consideration, however, of the great number of vicars [choral] and their report that amongst so many clergy there is only a meagre income (*nisi modicum commodum*) from the church of St. Sampson, out of which they could endow a vicar there and provide for the poor according to the statute, the king, wishing to give the vicars a more generous share (*uberiorum . . . graciam*) has granted in the present parliament and by this letter declares that they shall not be bound (*minime teneantur*) to endow a vicar for the church of St. Sampson or pay any sum of money to the parishioners, but that they shall provide a chaplain removable at will (*conducticium ad eorum voluntatem de tempore in tempus remotivum*) for serving and ministering at that place instead of a vicar according to the diocesan's ordinance; and that the vicars and their successors shall be wholly freed (*penitus exonerentur*) from endowing a vicar and from paying and distributing any sum of money to the parishioners. Westminster, 4 March 17 [Richard II] [1393/4].

SOURCE: VC 3/2/17 (426 mm. × 262 mm.)
ENDORSEMENT: *Licencia regia super advocacionem ecclesie sancti Sampsonis infra Ebor'; regis Ricardi ij.*
SEAL: great seal in green wax hung on pink and green cord.
COPIES: [i] VC 3/4/Sam/6a (372 mm. × 211 mm.); [ii] VC 3/4/Sam/6b (296 mm. × 223 mm.)
CALENDARED: *Cal. Pat. R.* 1391–96, p. 386.

NOTE: The 1391 statute is 15 Richard II, c. 6: *Statutes of the Realm*, ii (Record Commission, 1816), 80.

243.   Letter of Archbishop Thomas [Arundel] to mag. John de Neuton, doctor of laws and vicar general in spiritualities. King Richard, having been informed about the vicars in the cathedral church of York and their intention to celebrate an obit and

antiphon (as in 241), wished that the church of St. Sampson should be annexed to the vicars' college, and because the appropriation could not take place without the consent of the cathedral chapter the archbishop secured their permission. On account of the church's poverty, however, the archbishop now grants a licence that the vicars may hold it without having to present or support a perpetual vicar. Nonetheless, the vicars are to carry all the burdens of the church, both of the rector and the [parochial] vicar, and shall maintain out of their own funds a secular chaplain, removable at will, to serve the cure of souls and ministry of sacraments.

In the archbishop's house (*hospicio*) next to Westminster, 10 March 1393 [1393/4], and in the 6th year of his translation.

SOURCE: Rehearsed in 246.

244.   Letter of the prior and convent of the monastery of St. John the evangelist, Pontefract, of the Cluniac order, to Archbishop Thomas [Arundel], or his vicar general in spiritualities, presenting in their full right of presentation mag. William de Horworth, rector of the parish church of Collewell, in Hereford diocese, to the church of St. Sampson in York, vacant by the death of John de Bryn, the last rector, and beeseeching the archbishop to admit and institute him to the said church. Seal.
In the chapter house [at Pontefract], 19 May 1394.

SOURCE: VC 3/4/Sam/7 (271 mm. × 144 mm.)
ENDORSEMENT: *Presentacio Willelmi Horworth ad ecclesiam sancti Sampsonis cassata et (? omnino) adnullata.*
SEAL: priory seal in red wax (damaged).

245.   Letter of Brother Henry, prior of the house of St. John the apostle and evangelist, Pontefract, and the convent of that place. King Richard granted by letters patent to the warden of the house of vicars of the cathedral church of blessed Peter of York and the vicars the advowson or patronage of the church of St. Sampson in York, to be held in perpetuity; at the last vacancy the warden and vicars presented to the church John Braweby, chaplain, who was admitted, instituted, and canonically inducted and who now holds the church by their presentation. The prior and convent release and quitclaim to the warden and vicars all right in the advowson or patronage of the church of St. Sampson. Seal.
The chapter house at Pontefract, on the feast of the conversion of St. Paul, 18 Richard II [25 January 1394/5].

SOURCE: [i] VC 3/4/Sam/8 (309 mm. × 183 mm.); [ii] VC 3/4/Sam/9 (308 mm. × 190 mm.)
ENDORSEMENT: [i] none medieval; [ii] *Irrotulatur in dorso claus' cancellar' regie infrascripti mense Maii anno infrascripto.*
SEAL: [i] priory seal in red wax hung on green and pink cord; [ii] priory seal (damaged) in red wax hung on blue cord.
CALENDARED: *Cal. Close R.* 1392–96, p. 420.

246.   Notarial instrument of John Catryk, clerk of York diocese, apostolic notary, and registrar of mag. John de Neuton, vicar and commissary, drawn up in the presence of mag. Robert de Oxton, official of the court of York and commissary

general, mag. John de Harwodde, advocate of the court of York, mag. Thomas Grenewode, public notary, and others.

Archbishop Thomas [Arundel] has written to Neuton licensing the appropriation of St. Sampson's church in York to the vicars choral (as **243**). The vicars claim that their common income is so meagre that it is insufficient to maintain the 36 that are now in their common residence and at table, to repair their tenements and buildings, or to pay various chantry chaplains and celebrate obits as they are bound to do. They wish, however, to celebrate an obit and antiphon and to continue to live together, as declared in the archbishop's commission. Accordingly, the archbishop orders the appropriation of St. Sampson's church to the vicars.

Neuton, acting as the archbishop's vicar in spiritualities and in this matter as his commissary, has by inquiry found that the vicars' intentions as contained in their petition are true and so declared that the church should be appropriated, the vicars taking possession after the resignation or death of the present rector. Because the church lies a short distance from the vicars' common residence (*a communi vicariorum manso et habitacione modica loci distancia segregatur*), and because it stands in the celebrated and extensive city of York which can easily take in and accommodate a gathered population at will (*in qua quidem civitate populus confluens recipi et hospitari abunde poterit iuxta votum*), and also because the church's income is so meagre and somewhat casual, being constituted from personal tithes, oblations, and people's alms, which are much reduced these days, it is ordained that the vicars shall not be obliged to present or find a perpetual vicar for St. Sampson's, but should nonetheless fully meet the burdens which fall on both rector and vicar and maintain a secular chaplain, removable at will, to serve the cure of souls and ministry of sacraments.

Once the vicars have acquired corporal possession of the church, they are to pay a pension of 6s. 8d. a year to the archbishop and his successors, and in case of a vacancy to the dean and chapter, and also 20d. a year to the chapter, in equal portions at Pentecost and Martinmas.

In the chapter house of York, 29 March 1395.

SOURCE: VC 3/4/Sam/10 (542 mm. × 686 mm.)
ENDORSEMENT: *Pro ecclesia sancti Sampsonis.*
SEAL: cord (but no remains of wax).
SIGN: notarial sign of John Catryk.

247.   Inspeximus of the chapter of the cathedral church of blessed Peter of York, in the absence of the dean, of **246**. Seal.
Chapter house of York, 24 March 1395 [1395/6].

SOURCE: VC 3/4/Sam/11 (405 mm. × 596 mm.)
ENDORSEMENT: none medieval.
SEAL: no evidence of sealing.

248.   Letter of Richard II. Having been granted a licence to acquire the church of St. Sampson (as **241**), the vicars duly appropriated it and now keep their house in common. Some vicars, however, seeking their private advantage, attempt to pocket (*imbursare*) for their own use sums of money derived from the revenues of that church at times when absent from the common table, on such days and times when, by custom of the church of York, they happen of their own choice to be at the table of the residentiary canons or of others. The king orders that in future vicars shall receive

nothing in money or otherwise for such absences, and that the profit arising thereby shall accrue to the vicars' common household expenses.
Westminster, 16 June 19 Richard II [1396].

SOURCE: VC 3/1/2, fos. 11v.–12.
COPY: VC 3/1/2, fos. 16–16v. (addressed to dean and chapter of York).
CALENDARED: *Cal. Pat. R.* 1391–96, p. 725.

249.   Letter of Richard II repeating **248**. Any vicar who contravenes, or attempts to contravene, this order will incur the king's anger.
Westminster, 11 June 20 [Richard II] [1397].

SOURCE: VC 3/2/18 (480 mm. × 288 mm.)
ENDORSEMENT: *Licencia pro incorporacione vicariorum.*
SEAL: great seal in white wax applied to parchment tag.
COPY: VC 3/4/Sam/12 (409 mm. × 249 mm.)

250.   Letter of Richard II to the dean and chapter of the cathedral church of York. The king understands that five vicars no longer live continuously and in common in the vicars' residence but separately, although they wish to live together and keep table in common in the hall of their residence. In order that they should fulfil their intention, the king granted the vicars the advowson of the church of St. Sampson in York, and he also ordained that to avoid dissension amongst the vicars everything should accrue to common expenses. The dean and chapter are now ordered to allow the application of the church's profits to the common expenses of the residence.
20 Richard II [1396–7].

SOURCE: M 2/4d, fo. 6 (abridged text from lost original).

251.   Letter of Richard Clifford, dean, and the chapter of York to the succentor or warden of the vicars of the canons in the choir. Since a question has arisen among the vicars about how the profits of St. Sampson's church in York ought to be applied, and since the vicars submitted the question to the dean and chapter for a decision, the latter ordain as follows:
Each year 10 marks [£6 13s. 4d.] shall be assigned to the common expenses of the vicars' residence or hall; also, each vicar present at the yearly celebration of the obits of Richard [II] after his death and of Anne, his late consort, shall receive 2s. and each vicar present at the daily singing of the antiphon and collect of St. John the Baptist shall receive ¼d. What remains [from the church's income], together with losses (*perdiciones*) from the obits and antiphon, is to go towards the repair of the vicars' tenements and other charges specified in the appropriation of the church. If the church's income declines in the future, the vicars may scale down (*defalcentur*) the payments at the obits and antiphon proportionately.
Sealed with the chapter's seal.
York, in the chapter house, 24 May 1399.
Witnesses: *magistri* Alan de Newerk, John de Harwode, John Hildiard, lawyers (*iuris peritis*), John Feriby, subtreasurer, and Thomas Garton, chamberlain, [all clerks] of York diocese, and others.

Also sealed with the seal of Richard the dean in his house (*in hospicio*) outside Templebarre, London, on 13 November, in the same year.
Witnesses: *magistri* Richard Rouhale, doctor of laws, John de Botekesham, Thomas Weston, licentiates in both laws, William Waltham, Richard Holm, *domini* William Forde, Thomas Feriby, William Noion, John Boor, et William atte Wode, fellow canons of York, and others.

SOURCE: VC 3/4/Sam/13 (360 mm. × 238 mm.)
ENDORSEMENT: none medieval.
SEAL: (left) seal of dean of York in red wax; (right) chapter seal in plain wax.

NOTE: The 'losses' from the obits and antiphon were the sums of money not paid to individual vicars because of unauthorised absences from the services, or because there were fewer vicars in office than the full complement of 36. The 'diverse receipts' section of the chamberlain's account for 1401 records money *de perdicionibus antiphonie* at St. John's altar: VC 6/2/41.

252.   Letter of Richard Clifford, dean of the church of York, to his fellow canons and to their vicars. Since there has lately arisen a dispute between certain vicars and others as to how the income of the church of St. Sampson in York ought to be used or most properly be distributed (*converti debeant vel congruencius distribui possent*), all the vicars submitted the question to the dean and chapter of the church of York, who subsequently ordained as is more fully contained in their ordinance (251). The dean has constituted as his commissaries in this matter his brother canons, mag. John Newton, treasurer of the said church, and mag. Thomas Dalby, archdeacon of Richemond, together with mag. William Cawod, licentiate in canon law and canon of Repon and Suthwell. Seal.
In the dean's house (*hospicio*) outside Templebarr', London, 14 November 1399.

SOURCE: VC 3/4/Sam/14 (373 mm. × 142 mm.)
ENDORSEMENT: none medieval.
SEAL: seal of dean of York in red wax.

253.   Letter of Henry IV inspecting and confirming an ordinance of the dean and chapter of the cathedral church of York (as 251).
Westminster, 1 January 1 Henry IV [1400].

SOURCE: VC 3/4/Sam/15 (502 mm. × 319 mm.)
ENDORSEMENT: *Henricus iiij.*
SEAL: great seal in white wax.
CALENDARED: *Cal. Pat. R.* 1399–1401, p. 172.

254.   [*Draft petition from the vicars to the king.*]
    Richard II, with the consent of parliament, granted the advowson of the church of St. Sampson in York, and a licence to appropriate it, to the vicars in the choir of the church of York and their successors. In return, the vicars promised to sing an obit for the king and for Anne, his consort, and an antiphon and collect each day before the altar of St. John the Baptist in the church of York soon after the end of compline, and to bear other expenses for the souls of the king and Anne; the costs were to be met out of the revenues of St. Sampson's church. The vicars were absolved from the burden of

ordaining or endowing a vicar in the church and of paying any portion to poor parishioners, as is more fully contained in the king's letters patent. The church of St. Sampson was canonically appropriated by the ordinary of the place to the vicars and their successors, and the vicars, by virtue of the royal licence and appropriation, entered into possession of the vacant church, held it to their uses for many years, and fully supported the aforesaid burdens.

The king is humbly petitioned to declare that it was not and is not his intention that the statute 15 Richard II concerning the distribution by [parochial] vicars in every church of a suitable portion of the revenues of their churches to poor parishioners, lately issued in the last parliament at Westminster, should extend to the king's licence or to the appropriation of the church of St. Sampson, and that the licence and appropriation shall be permanent in their effect, the recent statute notwithstanding, especially since the revenue of St. Sampson's church is sufficient scarcely for supporting all the said burdens; if the licence and appropriation were overthrown in whole or in part, the royal obit and all the other aforesaid pious burdens would necessarily cease.

SOURCE: VC 3/4/Sam/16 (323 mm. × 183 mm.)
ENDORSEMENT: none.

255. Letter of Henry IV confirming the estate which the vicars have in the church of St. Sampson in York, which by licence of Richard II they have appropriated in mortmain without the endowment of a vicarage or the payment of any sum to the parishioners, and granting that the vicars may appoint a chaplain removable at their will to serve and minister there in place of a vicar and that they shall not be charged with the endowment of a vicar or of any payment to the parishioners, notwithstanding the ordinance made in parliament at Westminster on the morrow of Michaelmas last [1402].
Westminster, 4 June 1403.

SOURCE: VC 3/2/29 [missing in archive since 1989].
Calendared: *Cal. Pat. R.* 1401–05, p. 235.

NOTE: The 1402 ordinance (or statute) is 4 Henry IV, c. 12: *Statutes of the Realm*, ii (Record Commission, 1816), 136–7. It confirmed a statute of 1391: see **242** note.

256. Letter of the succentor and vicars of the cathedral church of York, appropriators of the parish church of St. Sampson, and Robert Midelton', William Wymondeswald, John Kirkby, and John Gascoigne, the greater and more respected (*sanior*) part of the parishioners of the same church, to Archbishop Henry [Bowet], presenting Thomas Hillory chaplain to be instituted as perpetual chaplain of the chantry at the altar of the blessed Virgin Mary in St. Sampson's church, founded for the souls of mag. Nicholas de Burton and his father and mother; the chantry is vacant as a result of the resignation of T. Martyn.
York, 4 February 1419 [1419/20].

SOURCE: VC 1/1, pp. 49–50 (ink pagination).

257. Letter as **256** (including Henry Preston among the parishioners) presenting Walter Ayrisom chaplain to the chantry, vacant as a result of the resignation of Thomas Hillary.
York, 9 April 1422.

SOURCE: VC 1/1, pp. 70–1 (ink pagination).

NOTE: Ayrisom had recently resigned as parochial vicar of Huntington: (**227**).

258. Letter of Archbishop Henry [Bowet] to Walter Ayrsam priest, instituting him as perpetual chaplain of the chantry at the altar of the blessed Virgin Mary in the St. Sampson's church in York, founded for the souls of mag. Nicholas de Burton and his father and mother; the chantry is vacant as a result of the resignation of Thomas Hilleri. Ayrsam is presented by the succentor of the college of vicars in the choir of the cathedral church, as appropriators of St. Sampson's church, and by Henry Preston, Robert Midelton, William Wymondeswold, John Kirkby, and John Gascoign', parishioners.
Thorp next to York, 23 April 1422, and in the 15th year of his translation.

SOURCE: VC 1/1, pp. 71–2 (ink pagination).

259. Indenture witnessing that John Gaynesburgh, warden of the college of vicars in the choir of the cathedral church of York, and all the vicars have demised at farm to William Barley, citizen and mercer of York, and to William Hoton, one of the vicars of the college, the vicars' church of St. Sampson in York, with the rectory house and all the tenements, rents, tithes, oblations, mortuaries, and profits appertaining to the rectory. They are to hold the property for three years from the feast of St. Parnel the virgin [31 May], 1449, paying 21 marks [£14] a year to the warden and vicars, in equal portions at the feasts of the purification of the blessed Virgin Mary [2 February] and of St. Peter ad vincula [1 August], the first payment being due at the next feast of the purification. Barley and Hoton shall pay all the ordinary and extraordinary charges of the church, except for 12*d.* a year which the warden and vicars shall pay to the cathedral choristers. The warden and vicars as appropriators shall also repair and maintain the rectory house, chancel, and all other tenements of St. Sampson's church. Warranty. One part of the indenture is sealed with the vicars' common seal and the other with the seals of Barley and Hoton.
York, on the feast and year given above, 27 Henry VI [31 May 1449].

SOURCE: VC 3/4/Sam/17 (269 mm. × 124 mm.). Indented at top.
ENDORSEMENT: *Ecclesia sancti Sampsonis.*
SEAL: fragment of vicars' common seal [1421 matrix] in red wax.

NOTE: The payment to the choristers was for lighting candles at St. John's altar: see Introduction: Appropriated Churches (St. Sampson's).

NETHER WALLOP

260. Indenture between John Bernyngham, treasurer of the cathedral church of blessed Peter of York, on the one part, and Hugh Pakenham and John Pakenham, clerks, on the other part, witnessing that the treasurer has demised to Hugh and John all the Hampshire properties that appertain to the treasurership, with perquisites of courts and other profits but excepting all woods, underwoods, and the advowsons of the churches of Overwallop, Broghton, and Mottesfont whenever they should fall vacant. Hugh and John are to hold the properties for 16 years from the feast of Pentecost last [28 May 1447]; paying 20 marks [£13 6s. 8d.] each year in the cathedral church of blessed Peter of York, in equal portions at Martinmas and Pentecost. If the rent is wholly or partly in arrears for three months after one of the rent-days, the treasurer and his assigns may re-enter all the properties. If the rent is four months in arrears, Hugh and John are to pay the treasurer 40s. as a penalty (*nomine pene*), whenever the rent is in arrears on a rent-day, and the treasurer and his assigns may distrain 40s. for that and all the arrears, with the proviso that the 40s. penalty shall not fall as a burden on Hugh and John as clergy (*in oneracionem personarum . . . Hugonis et Johannis*). If John Bernyngham dies within the term of the lease or gives up the treasurership, the lease will terminate. Hugh and John shall pay all the expenses of the property, and the treasurer renounces all actions and suits of court against them. That part of the indenture remaining with Hugh and John Pakenham is sealed with the treasurer's seal, and that part with the treasurer with the seals of Hugh and John. 9 June 25 Henry VI [1447].

SOURCE: VC 3/4/NW/1 (309 mm. × 225 mm.). Indented at top.
ENDORSEMENT: (MS. has been repaired and only 'Montesfont' survives).
SEAL: (right) red wax on tag; (left) red wax, round (15 mm. dia.), impression.
CALENDARED: *The cartulary of the treasurer of York Minster*, ed. Janet E. Burton (Borthwick Texts and Calendars, no. 5, 1978), no. 63 (p. 65).

NOTE: For the significance of the reference to 'Overwallop' (rather than Nether Wallop), see Introduction: Appropriated Churches (Nether Wallop).

261. Indenture between John Bothe, clerk, treasurer of the cathedral church of blessed Peter of York, and Hugh Pakenham witnessing that John has demised to Hugh all properties on the same terms as in **260** (but omitting the conditions about the rent not being paid). Seal. 9 June 35 Henry VI [1457].

SOURCE: VC 3/4/NW/2 (302 mm. × 226 mm.). Indented at top.
ENDORSEMENT: (MS. has been repaired and no text survives).
SEAL: remains of seal (as on **262**).
CALENDARED: *Cartulary of treasurer of York Minster*, ed. Burton, no. 64 (pp. 65–6).

262. Indenture witnessing that mag. John Bothe, treasurer of the cathedral church of St. Peter of York, has granted to Nicholas Byron, Robert Clifton, Richard Bothe, and Seth Worsley, esquires (*armigeris*), and their heirs and assigns the advowson and patronage of the church of Netherwallop, in Hampshire. Warranty. Seal. 1 March 37 Henry VI [1458/9].

SOURCE: VC 3/4/NW/3 (315 mm. × 133 mm.). Indented at top.

ENDORSEMENT: *Irrotulator in dorso claus' regis infrascriptis mense et anno infrascriptis.*
SEAL: red wax, round (15 mm. dia.), impression.
CALENDARED: *Cartulary of treasurer of York Minster*, ed. Burton, no. 65 (p. 66).

NOTE: The four men to whom the advowson was granted were all closely associated
with Archbishop William Booth, and three of them (Clifton, Bothe, and Worsley)
were named as his executors in his will of August 1464: *Testamenta Eboracensis*, ed.
J. Raine, ii (Surtees Society, xxx, 1855), 264–7. A confirmation made by
Archbishop Booth on 10 March 1458/9 was entered into his register, but was
later crossed out: BIHR, Reg. 20, fo. 206v.

263.   Letter of Richard Andrew, dean of the cathedral church of St. Peter of York,
and the chapter rehearsing the grant by mag. John Bothe to Nicholas Byron and
others of the advowson of the church of Netherwallop (as **262**), and ratifying it. Seal.
In the chapter house, 16 April 1459.

SOURCE: [i] VC 3/4/NW/4 (349 mm. × 148 mm.); [ii] VC 3/4/NW/5 (354 mm. ×
    153 mm.)
ENDORSEMENT: [i] and [ii] none medieval.
SEAL: [i] and [ii] chapter seal in plain wax.
CALENDARED: *Cartulary of treasurer of York Minster*, ed. Burton, no. 66 (p. 66).

264.   Licence of Henry VI to Nicholas Byron, Robert Clyfton, Richard Bothe, and
Set[h] Worsley, esquires (*armigeris*), to assign the advowson of the church of
Netherwallop', in Hampshire, to the dean and chapter of the cathedral church of
blessed Peter of York, and for the dean and chapter to appropriate the church for the
support of the clergy (*ministrorum*) in the cathedral.
Coventre, 20 July 37 Henry VI [1459].

SOURCE: VC 3/2/25 (540 mm. × 254 mm.)
ENDORSEMENT: *Carta super Netherwalope.*
SEAL: remains of great seal in dark green wax hung on blue and white cord.
CALENDARED: *Cal. Pat. R.* 1452–61, 512.

265.   Copy letter of Nicholas Byron, Robert Clifton, Richard Bothe, and Seth
Worslaie recording that they have given Richard, the dean, and the chapter of the
cathedral church of blessed Peter of York the advowson and patronage of the church
of Netherwallope. Seal.
20 May 38 Henry VI [1460].
[*At top of MS.*] This release (*relaxatio*) was found in a certain pyx in the treasury of the
cathedral church of York, in chest 'K'.

SOURCE: VC 3/4/NW/6 (261 mm. × 215 mm.)
ENDORSEMENT: none.

266.   Notarial instrument of Thomas Lye, priest of Coventry and Lichfield diocese
and apostolic notary.
     Letter of William [Waynflete], bishop of Winchester. A petition from the dean and
chapter of the cathedral church of York states that the profits and portions by which

the vicars choral of the cathedral church of York are supported are so slender and meagre (*tenues et exiles*) that they are unable to maintain themselves adequately (*nequeant commode sustentari*), nor support their burdens, incumbrances, and debts. The dean and chapter have the advowson of the parish church of Netherwallop, purchased (*adquisitam*) for them at the labour and expense of Archbishop William [Booth], and they requested the bishop [of Winchester] to appropriate the church to the vicars choral. The bishop accepted that the petition was true, and having consulted all whose interests are involved and having examined the royal licence (as **264**), he pronounced the appropriation of the said church to the dean and chapter in support of the vicars choral, in accordance with the statutes and ordinances of the archbishop and following the resignation or death of the present rector, William Fenton.

In recompense for the loss to the cathedral church of Winchester and to the archdeacon of Winchester, the bishop orders that three annual pensions be paid out of the fruits of the church of Netherwallop: 26s. 8d. to him and his successors, 3s. 4d. to the prior and chapter of the church of Winchester, and 3s. 4d. to the archdeacon of Winchester and his successors. Moreover, he orders the dean and chapter of York to pay 6s. 8d. to the poor parishioners of Netherwallop, at Easter each year according to royal statute. Seal and subscription of mag. Thomas Lye, priest and apostolic notary. In a chapel in the bishop's manor of Suthwerk, 8 July 1461, and in the 3rd year of the pontificate of Pope Pius II, and in the presence of mag. William Darsset, doctor of laws, Thomas Gyan', public notary, and Thomas Roose, clerk of the dioceses of Lincoln, Winchester, and Coventry and Lichfield.

Notarial sign and subscription of Thomas Lye.

Ratification and subscription of Robert, prior of the cathedral church of Winchester, and the chapter. In their chapter house, 24 July 1461.

Ratification and subscription of Vincent Clement, archdeacon of Winchester. 24 July 1461.

SOURCE: VC 3/4/NW/7 (556 mm. × 524 mm.)

ENDORSEMENT: *Appropriacio Netherwalope.*

SEALS: (left) seal of Bishop Waynflete in red wax; (middle) seal still in parchment bag, hung on pink and green cord; (right) seal still in parchment bag, hung on pink and green cord.

CALENDARED: *The Register of the Common Seal of the Priory of St. Swithun, Winchester, 1345–1497,* ed. Joan Greatrex (Hampshire ecord Series, ii, 1978), no. 346.

267. Notarial instrument of William Westerdale, clerk of York diocese, apostolic notary, and registrar of the court of York, rehearsing a letter of John Worsley, bachelor in both laws and commissary general of the official of the court of York during a vacancy in the archbishopric.

The commissary general has been informed on behalf of the vicars choral of the cathedral church of York by their proctor William Holbek, priest, that they have letters of William [Waynflete], the present bishop of Winchester, recording his grant of the appropriation of the parish church of Netherwallop otherwise Wallop *inferior*, in Hampshire and in diocese of Winchester, to the dean and chapter of the cathedral church of York for the augmentation of the income of the vicars choral and their successors, the grant being under the bishop's great seal, together with the common seal of the prior and chapter of the cathedral church of Winchester and the seal of mag. Vincent Clement, archdeacon of Winchester in red wax, and also the sign and subscription of mag. Thomas Lye, priest and apostolic notary (as **266**).

Worsley saw and examined the original grant presented by the proctor, and then ordered it to be written down by mag. William Westerdale, public notary.

In the cathedral church of York, 22 March 1464 [1464/5], and in the 1st year of the pontificate of Pope Paul II, in the presence of James Smeton and Robert Garnett, priests and parsons (*personis*) in the cathedral church of York, and of Robert Rudby, clerk and public notary of York diocese.

SOURCE: VC 3/4/NW/8 (413 mm. × 745 mm.)
ENDORSEMENT: *Instrumentum; bona evidencia rectorie de Wallope.*
SIGN: notarial sign of William Westerdale.
SEAL: remains of green wax hung on green cord.

268.   Notarial instrument of John Tullok, clerk of Exeter diocese and apostolic notary. On 22 October 1465, in the 2nd year of the pontificate of Pope Paul II, in the hall of the residence of mag. William Nessyngwyk, canon of the cathedral church of Salisbury, in the cathedral close there, William Fenton, rector of the parish church of Wallop *inferior*, in Winchester diocese, resigned and surrendered that church in the following words:

I, William Fenton, rector of the parish church of Wallop *inferior*, in Winchester diocese, wishing to be relieved of the burden of the cure and rule of the said church, and not having been coerced by force, nor induced by fraud or trick, but by my own spontaneous desire, resign the church into the hands of William [Waynflete], bishop of Winchester.

Done in the presence of Thomas Botton', chancellor, and Thomas Lyghtskyrte, chaplain of Salisbury and York dioceses.

SOURCE: Rehearsed in 269.

269.   Notarial instrument of Richard Horcyll, clerk of Coventry and Lichfield diocese and apostolic notary, made on 24 October 1465, in the 2nd year of the pontificate of Pope Paul II, in an upper room (*alta camera*) in the dwelling-house (*manerium*) of William [Waynflete], bishop of Winchester, at Waltham, rehearsing the resignation of William Fenton (as 268).

After the resignation was read out, the bishop received the resignation and surrender into his hands.

Done in the presence of mag. David Husband, doctor of canon law and chancellor of the bishop, and Guilleme (*Guillermo*) de Laguna, bachelor in decretals.

SOURCE: VC 3/4/NW/9 (384 mm. × 179 mm.)
ENDORSEMENT: none medieval.
SIGN: notarial sign of Richard Horcyll.

270.   Copy of a citation of the official of the court of Canterbury to Thomas Ryton, dean [of Christianity] of Winchester.

Mag. Thomas Paslew, doctor of decretals and advocate of the court of Canterbury, has informed (*extitit intimatum*) the official that although he was presented to the parish church of Nether Wallop, in Winchester diocese, vacant by the voluntary resignation of William Fenton, the last rector, and appeared personally before the diocesan and ordinary, William [Waynflete], bishop of Winchester, and showed his letters of presentation and petitioned the bishop to admit and institute him to the church and rectory; and that, although nothing stands in the way of his being admitted and instituted, nonetheless the bishop without reasonable cause expressly refused to do so.

Mag. Richard Andrew, dean, and the chapter of the cathedral church of St. Peter of York, unjustly opposes the presentation and contests its validity, claiming that the church is appropriated to them.

Wherefore, mag. Thomas has appealed to the apostolic see and for the protection of the court of Canterbury, with the result that the official has inhibited Bishop William and the dean and chapter, citing both parties to appear before him at the next feast of Corpus Christi [5 June 1466].

London, 7 Ides May [9 May] 1466.

[*Followed by a note*:] 4 Ides June [10 June] 1466 before the dean; Kent. It agrees with the original.

SOURCE: VC 3/4/NW/10 (287 mm. × 264 mm.)
ENDORSEMENT: none.

NOTE: In Paslew's petition to the pope he described himself as a priest of Norwich diocese: *Cal. Papal Letters*, xii. 568–9. For the context of the dispute, see Introduction: Appropriated Churches (Nether Wallop).

271.   Notarial instrument of Henry Aleyn, clerk of York diocese and apostolic and imperial notary, made on 7 June 1470 and in the 6th year of the pontificate of Pope Paul II, in a stone upper room or garret (*in quodam alta domo lapidea vel garit'*) commonly called the library (*libraria*), adjoining the cathedral and metropolitical church of blessed Peter of York, recording the protest of William Hoton', as follows:

I, William Hoton', priest, succentor of the vicars choral of the cathedral and metropolitical church of blessed Peter of York, as proctor of the dean and chapter of the cathedral church, appropriators of the parish church of Wallopp' *inferior*, in Winchester diocese, state and allege that it is lawful for the dean and chapter to hold the said church, having possessed it from its appropriation and having freely disposed of its income; fearing, however, that I, being in peaceful possession of the property, will be deprived as a result of threats made to the dean and chapter, I appeal directly to the holy apostolic see and the lord pope and for the protection of the court of Canterbury.

Done in the presence of mag. John Smertt, bachelor in laws and advocate of the court of York, and dom. John More, priest and vicar choral of the cathedral church [of York].

SOURCE: VC 3/4/NW/11 (334 mm. × 245 mm.)
ENDORSEMENT:
SIGN: notarial sign of Henry Aleyn.

272.   Letter of William Hoton, warden of the college of the vicars of the choir of the cathedral church of York, and all the vicars of the choir. The warden and vicars hold many benefices and common revenues (*communiones*) which mag. Richard Andrewe, dean of the cathedral church of York, has liberally given (*impendit*) them, and particularly the appropriation of the parish church of Nethir Walop', in Hampshire, and they especially remember with what constancy the dean resisted attempts to

cancel the appropriation and his gift of £50 for its confirmation. Wishing to return the favour (*regraciari*) in so far as they are able, the vicars hereby grant with the consent of the whole college and faithfully promise, a licence having been sought and obtained, that each year on the day of mag. Richard's death, if that is convenient or within 3 days before or after, they and their successors will celebrate, with note and [wearing] wearing silk copes in the choir of the cathedral church, solemn exequies, namely 'Placebo' and 'Dirige', together with Commendation of souls and requiem mass on the morrow, for mag. Richard's soul and for the souls of his father and mother and all his benefactors and all the faithful departed, along with the prayers 'Deus cum nunquam sine spe misericordie etc', 'Inclina domine', and 'Fidelium Deus devocius exequendas'. At each such celebration 8*d.* shall be given to each of the vicars present at the exequies and mass; 4*d.* to four senior vicars present at the mass; 2*d.* to each clerk of the vestibule; 12*d.* to the sacrists for tolling the bells for the exequies and mass; and 2*d.* to the city bell-ringer for tolling a bell throughout the city on the day preceding the obit, calling the people to pray devoutly for the said souls. The warden and vicars also grant that mag. Richard, his father and mother, and his benefactors shall share (*participes sunt*) in all the spiritual benefits of their college. If the vicars fail to celebrate the mass through malice or negligence, 10 marks [£6 13*s.* 4*d.*] shall be paid to the fabric fund of the cathedral church, and the dean and chapter may distrain all tenements and rents inside and outside the city until the warden of the fabric is satisfied. That part of the cirograph remaining with mag. Richard Andrewe is sealed with the vicars' common seal, and the other part remaining with the vicars with mag. Richard's seal.

York, 14 June 1471.

SOURCE: VC 3/4/NW/12 (372 mm. × 206 mm.). Indented at top.
ENDORSEMENT: *Obitus magistri Ricardi Andree quondam decani.*
SEAL: remains of red wax on tag.

NOTE: A copy of this obit foundation in L 2/2a, fo. 150 is followed by Dean Andrew's ordination of a chantry for himself in the Minster (fos. 150–51) and by the ordination of a further commemoration (273).

273. Notification by William Hoton, warden of the college of vicars of the cathedral church of York, and all the vicars of the choir, at the wish and with the consent of the chapter, that they have promised mag. Richard Andrew, doctor of laws and dean of York, in return for certain lands and tenements lately acquired by him from John Mowbray, esquire (*armigeri*), and given by him to the vicars, that they shall sing an antiphon of the blessed Virgin Mary before her image every day immediately after compline, except on major double feast days and except from the fourth weekday after Palm Sunday up to the octave of Easter, as has been the custom for many years; and moreover, that each Friday immediately after the antiphon they will sing, together with the choristers, another antiphon in honour of the name of Jesus before the crucifix (*coram ymagine crucifixi*) on the south side [of the cathedral] (*in quod solario ibidem posita*), in addition to the prayers customarily said there by the choristers (*adiunctis suffragiis iam per aliquos annos per eosdem choristas inibi tunc diei consuet'*); and moreover, immediately after both antiphons, the vicars and all the choristers will go down (*descendent*) in their habits to the dean's burial place, and standing there on both sides of it with their faces turned (*versisque eorum vultibus*) towards the crucifix, they shall distinctly and clearly say the psalm 'De profundis' with the customary prayers,

and in addition after the dean's death at the end of those prayers [they shall say] 'Fidelium Deus', 'Omnium Conditor et Redemptor' for his soul and the souls of all his benefactors and all the faithful departed. The choristers are to be paid one mark [13s. 4d.] a year, in equal portions at Martinmas and Pentecost. Moreover, each Friday when the antiphon is sung in honour of the name of Jesus the vicars shall find five candles to burn before the image of the blessed Virgin Mary in honour of the Five Sorrows (*in honore quinque grandiorum eius*), and also five candles to burn before the crucifix in honour of the Five Wounds (*vulnerium eius*). If the vicars fail to observe this ordinance, they may be censured by the dean and chapter.

York, 6 February 1471 [1471/2].

Ratification of the above by the dean and chapter in the chapter house on 7 February 1471 [1471/2].

SOURCE: L 2/2a, fo. 151.

NOTE: For the tenements which endowed the antiphons, see *Chs. Vicars Choral*, i, nos. 111–12 (where it was wrongly suggested that they supported Dean Andrew's chantry). The vicars began to receive an income from the property in 1474, and in the same year their chamberlain accounted for making a light before the cross; 4 lb. of wax was purchased in 1479–80 and 5 lb. in 1493–4 for a light before the statue of the Virgin Mary 'on the ruby chest' (*super sistam rubiam*): VC 6/2/64, 66, and 69. Both lights were still being maintained in 1539: VC 6/2/90.

274.   Notification by Angelus, bishop of Feltri (*Feltien'*), papal commissary in this matter, that the dean and chapter of the church of York were by apostolic authority obliged to pay 128 gold papal florins of the chamber for the annates or fruits, rents, and profits of the first year, of the parish church of Netherwalop, in Winchester diocese, on the occasion of the union of the church to the common fund (*mense*) of the chapter of the church of York. The money was paid this day to Bartholomew de Maraschis Mantua, receiver of the monies of the apostolic camera, by the hand of Thomas Hoppe, canon of York, and so Angelus absolves and frees the dean and chapter of the debt. Seal.

Rome at St. Peter, in the apostolic camera, 12 March 1471, 7th year of the pontificate of Pope Paul II [1471/2].

SOURCE: VC 3/4/NW/13 (284 mm. × 156 mm.)

ENDORSEMENT: none medieval.

SEAL: remains of vesica seal in red wax.

275.   Draft letter of N. bishop of Winchester. With the consent of N. de N., rector of Walope *inferior*, the bishop has ordained the endowment of a vicarage, as follows: vicarage house with curtilage in the said vill; herbage with all profits in the churchyard; oblations coming from the parish; tithes of all the wool of the whole parish; tithes of half the lambs of the whole parish; and lesser tithes, namely of mills, orchards, curtilages when they are cultivated by spade husbandry (*quando in pede fodiuntur*), calves, hemp, flax, apples, geese, piglets, doves, and eggs, and of legacies [i.e. for forgotten tithes] of all craftsmen (*ligacionum omnium artifficiorum*); and also of oblations pertaining to the church, except tithes of milk and cheese from which the vicar shall receive nothing.

The duties are these: the vicar and his successors are to serve the church in all divine offices, with the cure of souls of the whole parish [and] with two processions in the celebration of mass and at least two candles burning. He shall pay the taxation of the vicarage [being] 100s., and the pension of 26s. 8d. owed to the treasurer of the cathedral church of York. He shall celebrate on two week-days (*diebus ferialibus*) each week in the chapel of Demakok. He shall undertake the office of dean of the deanery of audience, when it is his turn. He shall appear at the visitations of archbishops, bishops, and archdeacons, and at general and special chapters, and at visitations of the clergy, whenever they are called.

SOURCE: VC 3/4/NW/14 (306 mm. × 131 mm.)
ENDORSEMENT: none.

276. Bond of Robert Dancourt clerk and Robert Salyce and William Benett, husbandmen, all of Walop, Hampshire, acknowledging that they are bound to the warden of the college of vicars of the choir of the cathedral church of York and the vicars in the sum of £30, payable next Christmas.
12 February 13 Edward IV [1473/4]
The condition of the obligation is that if Robert Dancourt observes and fulfils all the conditions contained in an indenture between the vicars and himself dated 12 February 1473 [1473/4], then the obligation shall be void.

SOURCE: VC 3/4/NW/16 (346 mm. × 102 mm.)
ENDORSEMENT: none.
SEALS: remains of red wax on three tags.

NOTE: Dancourt was the parochial vicar (**277**).

277. Letter of the succentor of the vicars in the choir of the cathedral church of York and his fellow vicars, as appropriators of the parish church of Nether Walop, in Winchester diocese, stating that they have received on the feast of St. Philip and St. James [1 May] 1478 from Robert Dancourt, vicar and farmer [i.e. lessee] of Walop church, the £24 owed for the rent of the church, and that he is quit. Seal.
1 May 1478.

SOURCE: VC 1/1, p. 83 (ink pagination).

278. Draft letter of the warden of the house of vicars of the cathedral church of blessed Peter of York and the vicars to Richard [Fox], bishop of Winchester, or his vicar general in spiritualities, presenting William Strete chaplain to the vicarage of the parish church of Wallope *Inferior*, vacant by the free resignation of Richard Slater. Seal.
York, in the Bedern chapel [*written over* in our said house: *struck through*] 31 March 1505.

SOURCE: VC 1/1, between pp. 34 and 25 (ink pagination).
ENDORSEMENT: *Presentacio vicarie de Walope Inferiori.*
SEAL: tag cut away.

279. Draft of bond of Peter Sympson, vicar of the cathedral church of blessed Peter of York and warden of the house of vicars choral, acknowledging that he is bound to pay William Strete, vicar of Walop *inferior*, Hampshire, £40 Easter.
6 November 22 Henry VII [1506]
The condition of the obligation is that if Peter and the vicars choral, as appropriators of the parish church of Walop, bind themselves to obey the award of John Dowman, Walter Stand, and Thomas Hede, doctors of laws, or any two of them, acting as arbitrators or reconcilers (*arbitratorum sive amicabilem compositorum*) in the dispute between the vicars and Strete over the rights and emoluments of the vicar of the parish church of Walop. If they fulfill the terms of the arbitrators' award before the feast of the invention of the Holy Cross next [3 May 1507], then the obligation shall be void.

SOURCE: VC 3/4/NW/17 (312 mm. × 214 mm.)
ENDORSEMENT: none.

280. Letter of John Chambr', clerk, succentor and warden of the college of vicars of the metropolitical church of blessed Peter of York, and the vicars appointing mag. William Hoilgill clerk, William Streitte, vicar of the parish church of Netherwalope, in Winchester diocese, and John Purdewe and Philip Purdewe, literate men (*literatos*) of the same diocese, as their proctors, to represent the vicars and their church of Netherwalope at the forthcoming royal visitation of the province of Canterbury.
Sealed with their common seal.
4 May 1538, 30 [Henry VIII].

SOURCE: VC 1/1, pp. 122–3 (ink pagination).

Index of Persons and Places

Arabic numerals indicate the continuous series of charters and other documents; Roman numerals refer to pages in the Introduction. The letter 'w' before an Arabic numeral indicates the occurrence of a name in a witness list, or that a person was present at a transaction; 'address' and 'dated at' as sub-headings indicate, respectively, that a place is mentioned as a person's residence and that a document was dated at a place. People whose names are patronymics are indexed under the name of the father (or mother), and where there are several entries under a single name, those identified by occupation or by-name precede patronymics.

Place names, where identifications have been suggested, are given in their modern form with original variations following in brackets; places in Yorkshire are preferred to those in other counties and are assigned to their ancient parishes and ridings; and counties are given according to their pre-1974 areas.

The following abbreviations, besides those normal for Christian names, are used: bp. for bishop, bro. for brother, c. for century, cath. for cathedral, ch. for church, coll. for collegiate, ct. for court, dau. for daughter, mag. for magister, par. for parish, s. for son, and w. for wife or widow.

Amfrey, Stephen s. of, 130
Ampleforth (Ampleford; NR), Wm. de,
    chaplain, w 193
Andrew (Andrewe), mag. Ric., doctor of
    laws, dean of York, xxi, 263, 265, 270,
    272
    antiphon for, 273
    chantry for, 272 note
    obit for, 272
    tomb, 273
Angelus, bishop of Feltri, papal commissary,
    274
Anglicus, Ric., 69, w 137
Anketil (Anketin) of the chapel, servant of
    Hamo, treasurer of York, w 38–9
Anlaby, John, w 86
Anne, consort of Richard II, antiphon and
    obit for, xx, 241, 254
Appilton, Rob., chaplain, vicar choral, 5, 226
Appleby (Apelbi, Apelby, Appelby;
    Westmorland), rural dean of, see
    Murdac
    Wm. de, of York, clerk, w 42–4, w 74, w
    234
Apulia (Italy), Simon de, dean of York, w 39
Aquila, Ric. de, clerk, w 28–9
Aresom (Areshom, Ayrisom, Ayrsam),
    Walter, vicar of ch. of Huntington,
    226–8
    chantry chaplain in St. Sampson's ch.,
    York, 257–8
Armthorpe (Armtorp; WR), Jocelin de, w
    111
Arnold (Arnale, Arne'hale; par. Swine, ER),
    Henry de, w 40
    Peter de, w 42–3
    Nic. de, w 41–3
Arundel, chaplain, w 37
Arundel (Darundell'), Reynold, canon of
    York, w 137
    Thos., archbp. of York, xix, 138, 244, 246
    letter of, 243
    Wm., clerk, w 110, w 113
Asby (Askebi, Askeby; Westmorland), 137
Askham (WR), rector of ch. of, see, Langton,
    Walter de
    Thos. de, 236
    Walter de, 118, 123
Aslackby (Aslakby; Lincs.), Ric. de, vicar
    choral, 76–81, 83
Astin, w 38
Attewater (ad aquam, atte Water, atte Watre,
    Attewatt'), Henry, of Earswick, w
    24–5
    Hugh, w 46–9

Hugh (probably same man), of Earswick, 214
    Rob., w 172
d'Aunay, Ralph, archdeacon of York, w 137
Aughton (Acton, Aukton; ER), 15
    address, w 18, w 142
Aurelianis, see Orléans
Awger, John, husbandman, 51, w 51 (? same
    as John Algar q.v.)
Ayrisom, Ayrsam, see Aresom

Bacheler, Walter, w 141
Bacile (Bacil, Bathele), Roger de, of
    Skirpenbeck, w 98–9, w 101–2
Bacoun, Bartholomew, w 42, 43, w 43
Bagby (Baggeby; par. Kirby Knowle, NR),
    John de, w 122
Bageby, Wm., of Thirsk, w 127
Baker, John le, w 117
Balkholme (Balcolm'; par. Howden, ER),
    drainage channel, 96
    Thos. s. of Peter de, w 96
Bamburgh, Rob., of Scarborough, 58
Bampton (Bamt'; Westmorland), Rob. de, w
    137
Banners, Wm., royal justice, 56
Barker, John, 119
    Roger, 138
Barley, Wm., citizen and mercer of York, 259
Barnby-upon-Don (Barneby on Done; WR),
    John de, notary public, w 182
    John Thomas de (? another), apostolic and
    imperial notary, 184
Barningham (Berningham; probably NR),
    rector of ch. of, see Milford, Henry de
    and see Bernyngham
Barthorpe (Berthetorp; par. Acklam, ER),
    Orm de, w 27
Barton (NR), 6–8
    St. Mary's chapel, 6
    Patrick de, w 43
    Ralph s. of Thos. de, 8
    Ric. de (1279), w 64–5
    Ric. de (1321), 43, 47–8 (otherwise Ric.
    Dunpole of Barton)
        Alice, his w. (dau. of Rob. s. of Simon
        de Huntington), 43
    Roger de, w 7
Basset (Basseth), Fulk, dean of York, w 114–
    15
    Wm., royal justice, 118–20, 124–5, 236
Basy, Roger (1260s), bailiff of York, w 26
    Roger (1316), w 234
Bataille (Batail'), James, w 141–2
    Peter, w 141
Batayl, Adam, 10

Cockerington (Cokeryngton; Lincs.), Gilbert
    de, w 142
Cocus, Cok, *see* Cook
Coi'gneres, *see* Conyers
Coke, John, of Scarborough, his w. Maud, *see*
    Cowper, Ric.
  Ric., *see* Mar', Ric. de
Colburn (Coleburn'; par. Catterick, NR),
    Geof. de, w 6
Coleville (Colevile), Philip de, w 108
Colman, Wm. s. of Rob. s. of, 137
Cologne (Colonia; Germany), Nic. de, bailiff
    of York, w 234
Colwall (Collewell; Herefs.), rector of ch. of,
    see Horworth, Wm. de
Conisbrough (Conyngesburgh; WR), John
    de, clerk, vicars' janitor, 168
Conquest, Henry, of Chefierton, 138
Conyers (Coi'gneres), Geof. de, w 107
Cook (*Cocus*, Cok), Henry s. of Walter, of
    Thirsk, clerk, 116
  Wm., of Thirsk, 117, 119
Copgrove (Coppegrave; WR), John de, w
    203
Cop'll'a, Philip de, w 39
Copmanthorpe (Coupemanthorp,
    Coupmanthorp; detached part of par.
    St. Mary Bishophill Junior, WR),
    Geo. de, w 46
  Henry de, w 47
  Henry s. of Peter de, w 2–4
  John de, 236
Corbridge (Corebryg'; Northumb.), mag.
    Thos. de, chancellor of York, w 35
Corder, Geof. s. of Ric. le, 87
Cornburgh, *see* Thornborough
Cothurstoke, Wm., 138
Cottingham (Cotingham, Cotyngham; ER),
    church of, xv–xvi, xxviii, 143
  advowson, 143
  appropriation, 143, 145
  vicarage, ordination of, 145
  poor parishioners, 144
  John de, rector of ch. of Huntington, 220,
    225
    obit for, 223
    pension, 223
  Wm. de, chaplain, 159, w 193
  Wm. de (? *same man*), vicar choral, 193
Cottingwith (Cotingwit; ER), Adam s. of
    Benet de, 16
  Maud, his w., *see* Bubwith, Maud dau.
    of Wm. s. of Alice de,
  Thos. de, 10
    Alice, his w., 10

Couper, Ric., chaplain, vicar of ch. of
    Huntington, 227–9
Coventry (Coventre; Warws.), dated at, 264
Coventry and Lichfield diocese, chaplain of,
    145
  clerk of, 145, w 266, 269
  priest of, 266
Cowper, Ric., of Scarborough, 84
  Maud, his w. (widow of John Coke),
    84
Crakehall (Crakall'; par. Bedale, NR), Wm.
    de, of Towthorpe, w 25
Cranswick (Crancewiht; par. Hutton
    Cranswick, ER), Alexander de, of
    Bubwith, carpenter, 13–14, 16
Cras (Crase, Gras), mag. John le, canon of
    York, 27 note, 131–5
  obit for, 131 note, 133
Craven (several in WR), Wm. de, servant of
    Henry le Vavasour, 152, 172
Crayke (Crayk; NR), Rob. de, of Shipton in
    Galtres, w 95
Crigglestone (Crigelston; par. Sandal Magna,
    WR), Rob. de, w 96
Crisping, Wm., of Scagglethorpe, w 31
Croft (*probably* NR), rector of ch. of, *see*
    Langton, Wm. de
Cropton (par. Middleton; NR), John de, 76
Crosby (Crosseby; *possibly* par. Leake, NR),
    Nic. de, w 64–5
Cross (*ad Crucem*), Roger at the, w 70–1, 76–
    9, 81, 83–6
Crowcombe (Craucombe; Somerset), mag.
    John de, commissary of archdeacon of
    Richmond, 236–7
Curtays, Rob., w 102
Cutt', Wm., of Scarborough, w 74
Cutteller, Rob., of Ferrybridge, 196

Dalby, mag. Thos., canon of York,
    archdeacon of Richmond, 252
Dalton (three in NR), address, w 116, w 122
  John, chaplain, 197
Damiet, Henry de, w 64–5
Dancourt, Rob., clerk, vicar of Nether
    Wallop, 276
Daniel, Rob., w 32
Darel (Darell'), Wm. (1260s), w 26
  Wm. (1415), of Huntington, 226
  Wm. (1431), w 58
Darlington (Derlington; co. Durham), John
    de, 119
  Tessanta, his dau., 118–21
  Walter de, vicar choral, 121–2, 176, 181–2,
    184, 187, 190

Index of Subjects

Entries have been grouped under the following headings: buildings; documents; grantors; occupations (clerical); occupations (secular); parishes; religious services; rents; social status; miscelleanous.

BUILDINGS
barn, 50, 59–61
kiln, 36
mill, 190
   water, 137
   wind, 19
tileworks (in York), 22

DOCUMENTS
cirographs, 4, 12–15, 41, 44–5, 98–99, 101, 114–15, 135, 170, 200
final concord, 53–4, 56
grants, motives for:
   as marriage portions, 17, 41, 108–9, 119 (ref. to); *and see* land held as dowry, 40
   in free or pure alms, 6–7, 19, 23, 26–7, 33–5, 63, 67–9, 97–9, 108, 130, 137, 143, 146, 170
   for salvation of souls, 6–7, 23, 27, 34, 68–9, 104, 108, 130, 133
   to endow obits, 11, 979, 133
   to raise money, 96–7, 136
      for support of grantor and family, 12, 16–18, 33, 40
lease:
   for 3 years, 57, 259
   for 10 years, 21–2
   for 12 years, 13, 127, 195
   for 15 years, 129
   for 16 years, 260
   for 20 years, 12, 15, 36, 61, 84–5
   for 24 years, 14
   for 30 years, 59–60
   for 39 years, 128
   for 200 years, 58
   for life, 36, 41, 43, 86
notarial instruments, 145, 154 note, 172, 182, 184, 193, 203, 221, 226, 229, 246, 266–9, 271
will, 76
writ, 30, 35, 75, 82

GRANTORS
man with wife, 1, 3, 10, 25, 59, 70–1, 96
wife a bastard, 10
widow, 9, 17, 40, 48, 67, 108
wife (in absence of husband), 12–15

OCCUPATIONS (clerical)
chaplain, *see* Alexander the succentor; Alkborough, John de; Alynson, Wm.; Ampleforth, Wm. de; Appilton, Rob.; Aresom, Walter; Arundel; Blakewell, John de; Brampton, Roger; Brotherton, John de; Cottingham, Wm. de; Couper, Ric.; Dalton, John; Easingwold, Roger de; Fenton, Rob. de; Folkton, Rob. de; Forest, Wm.; Forster, Ric.; Fryston, Roger de; Fulford, John de; Garforth, Adam de; Gowcell, Henry; Harpham, Thos.; Herryson, Laurence; Hert, John; Hillary, Thos.; Horneby, Ric.; Houk, John; Huntington, Wm. de; James; Lyghtskyrte, Thos.; Martyn, Thos.; Morel, Wm.; Nicholas; Nosterfeld, John; Orléans, Wm. de; Otley, Wm. de; Peter; St. Salvator, Rob. de; Scrayingham, Ric. de; Serlo; Skirpenbeck, Peter de; Stowe, John de; Strensall, Ric. de; Strete, Wm.; Symson, Peter; Thomas (*bis*); Thomson, Roger; Towthorpe, Wm.; Ussher, John; Uttersall', Thos.; Walter; Wawne, Rob. de; Wayder, Wm. le; Weaverthorpe, Wm. de; Welton, Wm. de; Welwick, Wm.; Wodeward, John
clerk, *see* Adam, John s. of; Ainderby, Wm. de; Alan; Aleyn, Henry; Appleby, Wm. de; Aquila, Ric. de; Arundel, Wm.; Barnby, John de; Bootham, Wm. de; Brantyngham, John; Burgh, Ric. de; Burton, Nic. de; Carlton, Geof. de and Wm. de (*bis*); Chambr', John; Cleveland, Wm.; Conisbrough, John de; Cook, Henry s. of Walter; Dancourt, Rob.; Deyce, John;

THE YORKSHIRE
ARCHAEOLOGICAL SOCIETY

Enquiries about subscriptions to the YAS Record Series should be addressed to:
The Yorkshire Archaeological Society, Claremont, 23 Clarendon Road,
Leeds LS2 9NZ

The Editor welcomes suggestions for possible future publications, which should be
addressed to:
YASRS Editor, Borthwick Institute of Historical Research, University of York,
St Anthony's Hall, Peasholme Green, York YO1 7PW

Record Series volumes can be purchased from the publisher:
Boydell & Brewer Ltd, PO Box 9, Woodbridge, Suffolk IP12 3DF
or via the Boydell & Brewer website:
www.boydell.co.uk